Soar

Soar

A MEMOIR

Gail Campbell Woolley

(1957–2015)

BOLDEN

AN **AGATE** IMPRINT

CHICAGO

Printed in the United States of America

Library of Congress Cataloging-in-Publication Data

Names: Woolley, Gail Campbell, 1957-2015, author.
Title: Soar / Gail Campbell Woolley (1957-2015).
Description: Chicago : Bolden, an Agate imprint, [2017]
Identifiers: LCCN 2017041476 (print) | LCCN 2017048653 (ebook) | ISBN 9781572848115 (e-book) | ISBN 1572848111 (e-book) | ISBN 9781572842380 (paperback) | ISBN 9781572842380 (paperback) | ISBN 1572842385 (paperback) | ISBN 9781572848115 (ebook) | ISBN 1572848111 (ebook)
Subjects: LCSH: Woolley, Gail Campbell, 1957-2015--Health. | Sickle cell anemia--Patients--United States--Biography. | African American journalists--United States--Biography.
Classification: LCC RC641.7.S5 (ebook) | LCC RC641.7.S5 W66 2017 (print) | DDC 616.1/5270092 [B] --dc23
LC record available at https://lccn.loc.gov/2017041476

10 9 8 7 6 5 4 3 2 1   17 18 19 20 21

Bolden Books is an imprint of Agate Publishing. Agate books are available in bulk at discount prices. Learn more at agatepublishing.com.

This book is dedicated to my late brother, Tim, and to the millions afflicted with sickle cell anemia around the world. We have suffered in silence long enough.

It is also dedicated to the love of my life—my husband, Howard. Without you, I could never have survived this painful yet surprisingly fulfilling existence. You have made me so happy. Loving me exactly as I am is your greatest gift to me. Your strong, unwavering support gave me the strength I needed to fight this illness until my last breath and the bravery to at last shine some light on this disease, hoping it helps to inspire others.

TABLE OF CONTENTS

AUTHOR'S NOTE

*I*T'S NOT A BAD THING TO HAVE A HEALTHY SELF-ESTEEM. But it is imperative if you happen to be born black, female, and with a ticking time bomb ingrained in every cell in your body—each one about to implode without notice.

My healthy self-esteem helps me drown out the ticking and believe I can do anything I choose as long as I try hard enough.

When R. Kelly released his song "I Believe I Can Fly" in 1996, I took his lyrics to heart—I have always believed I can fly. But even in my most pragmatic moments, when I know my wings are broken, I still believe I can *soar*!

—*G.C.W.*

PREFACE

EATH HAUNTS THE LIVING FROM THE VERY FIRST moment that we learn of its inevitability. Children cower from the world when they discover that one day they—and everyone they love—will leave it. They become dreadfully afraid, searching for comfort, reassurance.

Though we get older and force ourselves to no longer shrink from the world, we never really reconcile ourselves to death's certainty. Most of us spend our days doing whatever we can to avoid even the vaguest intimation that the end will come, for us and our loved ones. The thought is too much to bear.

But what if you are told at a precious young age that death will soon come knocking, depriving you of the normal lifespan we all expect? How can you bear knowing? Such is the remarkable story of Gail Campbell Woolley.

When she was seven, a well-meaning pediatrician told her mother that Gail and her younger brother Tim suffered from sickle cell anemia. He said they would be dead by age thirty-five.

Those two sentences from the doctor's mouth profoundly shaped the lives of every member of Gail's family. But of course, the two people most severely affected were Gail and her brother.

Tim descended into a fog of pain, self-pity, and self-destruction. Horribly, he turned the doctor's dark prediction into fact and died at exactly age thirty-five.

But Gail went in the opposite direction. She acknowledged the Grim Reaper's presence, as a matter of fact, but did not let him slow her down. She decided to live an improbably eventful and exciting life, traveling to the ends of the Earth, diving lustily into an impressive journalism and public relations career, leaving her unmistakable stamp on every person who came into contact with her. Gail was clear-eyed and straightforward about confronting death. During her time at Syracuse, she even endeavored to study death from a sociological perspective.

As you will discover in these pages, she is direct and honest about describing the pain she endured. Always a journalist, she wanted to pass along to the reader all the information she had at her disposal— as disturbing as some of it may be to read. She wanted you to have the whole truth and nothing but the truth.

When she finally succumbed to death at fifty-eight, she had reduced that pediatrician's words into meaningless drivel.

I was introduced to Gail after she was already gone. I was asked to help finish this book, which was already 90 percent complete when it was first sent to me by her loving husband, Howard Woolley. As I went through it, I could feel the devotion that Gail poured onto every page. She was nearly blind as she labored through the final chapters, but she wouldn't stop. For most of the last two years of her life, she worked on the manuscript for four or five hours a day, despite the physical difficulties. Completing this manuscript and getting it out into the world was the last item on Gail's impressive bucket list. After she passed, Howard pushed himself through the grieving process to make sure that happened.

In many long, deeply pleasurable conversations, Howard entertained me with delightful tales of his wife and her stubborn, strong-willed ways. It was clear that when Gail put her mind to something, the rest of us mere mortals were wise to step aside and avoid getting in her way.

Even though I never met her, I came to love her through the words on these pages. Her fervent embracing of life and fierce commitment to squeezing the joy out of every moment are principles that have served me well in thinking about my days and my own mortality.

Is it necessary for death to hang over our heads for us to attack living with a jubilant gusto? Surely not. I know not to waste the time I have, when so many others, people like Gail Campbell Woolley, would have treasured every one of my moments.

Time is not to be wasted, even by those who assume they have been blessed with abundance. Perhaps the most shocking and painful lesson that time in this blessed realm has granted us is that it all can end so quickly, so unexpectedly.

Do yourself a favor and hold on to the words and the thoughts that Gail unfurls so passionately within these pages. Let them wash over you; try to keep them in your grasp long after her story has faded from your memory. Even if you don't forever retain the details of the life of Gail Campbell Woolley, you must remember the sentiment contained herein: every moment of every day is a gift too precious to waste.

—*Nick Chiles*

INTRODUCTION

I CONFESS THERE ARE MANY TEARS ON THESE PAGES. It has always been too painful for me to talk—much less write—about my life with sickle cell anemia. I even started this book as a novel, mistakenly thinking that fictionalizing it would give me the distance I needed to remain objective. But then I decided: to hell with it. No guts, no glory. Tell your own story. There is no shame in truth.

I accepted it was my destiny to suffer excruciating physical pain a long time ago, but I only recently discovered I was put on this Earth to learn something from it. Somewhere deep within me, I've had the ability to overcome my demons long enough to live a satisfying, productive life. To help others do the same, I must be brave enough to divulge the details of my own personal darkness.

Most people see the smiling face I present in public to make them believe I am a confident, professional woman without a care in the world. The truth is, I am one of millions of people who must navigate the unpredictability of a genetic nightmare. Mine is sickle cell anemia, a particularly cruel and rare inherited blood disorder, which, like the sword of Damocles, hangs over my head, waiting to drop me where I stand without warning.

1

Very few people know much about my disease. Some of my red blood cells are malformed—they are an inflexible crescent shape instead of a flexible round one. Red blood cells carry oxygen to all parts of the body, but the stiff, misshapen ones cannot do this well. They can cause blockages in blood vessels, which slows or stops the flow of oxygen. This lack of oxygen causes periods of sudden, intense pain—a sickle cell crisis.

There is no readily available cure for the disease, and not enough research is being done to find one. In 1973, when I was already a teenager, the average lifespan of someone with sickle cell anemia was only fourteen years. But sickle cell anemia is not contagious. You can only inherit it from a certain combination of recessive genes passed down from your parents, who are usually—but not always—of African descent.

I hear a lot of relieved "Whews!" out there. I don't blame you. If I could be healthy, I would be—and that's saying something because I like the person I have become in spite of it.

The most frustrating part of living with my illness is the widespread ignorance surrounding it. Most people never hear the term *sickle cell anemia* (also called *sickle cell disease*) unless a researcher accidentally stumbles over a treatment that might help, and it gets a small mention in their local news. But it's hard to stumble over anything when the research dollars spent on finding a cure for sickle cell disease are only a small fraction of the amount spent on similar maladies with far fewer victims.

Since treatments are not cures, I have tried to survive my fate with as much dignity and fortitude as I can muster. I made up my mind early to live the best possible life, no matter how long it lasts. As a result, I will have no regrets about the things I did not do.

As you will see, I can be pretty blunt. I am direct because I cannot stand to waste time I do not have. I would rather spend time doing what I love—laughing raucously and with wild abandon as I see the world with Howard, my beloved husband—because it makes me feel better and keeps me from bemoaning the things I cannot change.

The best advice I've ever received was from a boss I did not particularly like. He told me, "It is not *what* happens to you in life that matters. It is how you *react* to it that counts."

There is so much truth in that. It's probably why I instinctively reacted to my illness by living intensely. When my fate was unveiled at a tender age, I knew I had two choices: I could be negative, whine, and bemoan my bad luck, accomplishing nothing with my life, or I could be positive, educate myself about my illness, and get on with living like every single *second* matters.

I always seem to hear that famous *60 Minutes* clock ticking in the back of my mind. Those ticking seconds are like bullets shooting at my feet. As a young woman, they compelled me to accomplish as much as I could, eschew procrastination, and prepare myself for all the thrilling moments a career as a reporter and public relations professional can bring.

For as long as I can remember, I've wanted to live as grandly, as thoroughly, as fully, as I possibly could—as much as my mind and body would allow. Because I have no specific idea of an end date—just that it is finite and probably closer than I want—living fully means segmenting time into small blocks. Each block has to be maximized, stretched to its limit. None are to be wasted. A block could be a minute or an hour or a day; none of these are too small to cherish. It could be time spent alone or amidst a stadium of other people. But each block has to be parsed, dissected, sliced open, and inspected like a specimen in a Petri dish under a microscope. Am I wrenching every fiber of life contained therein? Am I leaving anything, any stray moments, on the table? Maximization is always my goal, the lighthouse that guides my steps. Squeezing everything out of those damn blocks.

Howard has been my ideal partner because, early on, I saw that he immediately understood my need to squeeze, to maximize. He knew that at times, my conversations, my interactions, could be easily misunderstood. Sometimes it looked more like disinterest, when in fact, it was more like impatience. I saw the time block slipping away, sliding between my fingers. Wasted. I found this to be a personal affront, a disregard for my carefully tended segments. But Howard gets it. He maximizes my maximization. He keeps the blocks dripping with promise, filled with excitement. He makes sure I get the chance to wrench every ounce of life out of every moment of every day. And he keeps me laughing every step of the way.

I often ended up in hospitals when the pain of my disease got the best of me.

A lifetime in and out of hospitals has made me, admittedly, less than a model patient. I sometimes grill doctors, probing for more knowledge about my condition. It's the only way I know to better manage my health. In this book, I have not hidden the fact that I always speak up when something doesn't seem right, particularly when medical staffs treat me indifferently or carelessly, which has happened too often. That's why I routinely keep my doctors on their toes, asking questions throughout any examination. A renowned specialist once looked up from his stethoscope and said to my husband, "You must never get bored around *her*."

Sitting close to me, anxiously awaiting the specialist's opinion about my latest health wrinkle, my husband replied, "No, I never have."

For thirty-four years, Howard has been my rock, my joy, my *everything*. I think our love story is as rare and special as any I ever read about in a romance novel. We live our lives like a speeding train, always afraid of running out of time before I can do everything I most desire.

Howard says I am as driven and focused now as the day he met me on the campus of Syracuse University. With him, I have realized most of my dreams. My husband has selflessly helped me live the adventurous life I craved, systematically checking off every item on my bucket list. Seeing the world was the first item on my bucket list. That's a tall order for anyone, but Howard and I have done it together, traveling to every continent except Antarctica—Antarctica is way too cold for someone with my health.

Another item on my bucket list was to own a house by the sea. Many years ago, when it came time to custom build our seaside dream house in the Outer Banks of North Carolina, I know I ran my contractor a little crazy, asking about every little detail and insisting on the highest-quality materials. I found it intensely gratifying to wake up in a place whose angles, planes, and crevices all sprang from my imagination. It was like stepping into a piece of my own artwork, a canvas of wood and glass that I had conjured in many flights of fancy.

We named our house Dreamcastle, after a line I adore from *Walden* by Henry David Thoreau: "If you have built castles in the air, your work need not be lost; that is where they should be. Now put the foundations under them." I first read it in my high school English class, where it resonated with my goals and became the blueprint for my life—build the foundations under your dreams to make them come true.

For me, that means do the things that help me live a rich life—attain a good education, find progressively more advanced and well-paying jobs, save enough money and keep building enough wealth to enable me to step away from the world of work. They call it retirement, but I have no intent to slow down. My plan is to have plenty of fun, plenty of experiences, plenty of moments to take my breath away.

I turned fifty-five in March of 2012. On my birthday, Howard kissed me awake and whispered, "Fifty-five and still alive." He grinned, pleased.

Every year I have lived beyond the age of thirty-five is a triumph for us. The pediatrician told my mother when I was seven that I wouldn't live past thirty-five—that I would die from sickle cell anemia—but I have proven that pediatrician wrong, very wrong. For my husband and me, that counts as an astounding victory. He loves me so deeply, it shows in everything he does—every glance and every touch. Even in a rare burst of anger, he is helpless to show me anything but infinite love.

We met another couple for dinner at a New York restaurant once, and the wife watched Howard help me into my chair and turn to me to see if there was anything else I needed before he sat down himself.

"I wish you would take such wonderful care of *me*," the woman said to her husband. He looked surprised, then responded with a weak rejoinder that made her sniff with irritation and roll her eyes. But Howard and I long ago formed a partnership; we are a team of explorers intent on leaving no adventure unexamined. It's hard to compete with that.

A couple of our beach friends who live near Dreamcastle marvel at us. Married four or five times, the wife says she finally got it right in her sixties. Her current husband loves her in a similar way.

"Gail, it's written all over both your faces," she once said to me. "You adore each other. You can't even look at each other without showing everybody how you feel."

"You say that like it's a bad thing!" I responded.

"I didn't say it was bad, Miss Thing," she replied. "I just said it was obvious to anyone who sees the two of you together. It took me a very long time to find the right one for me. You have been lucky at love."

Howard has taught me to trust there will always be an "us," not just an "I" or a "him."

He says everything that hurts me hurts him, too. After decades of watching him support me through everything that's happened to me, I have to believe him. He has never made a decision since we've been together that doesn't include me. There is security in knowing that. There is comfort. There is infinite trust. That's why I trust him to do the right thing when the time comes. I signed all the legal papers that give him the right to turn off any lifesaving machine that simply breathes for my body when my mind has long gone.

I tell Howard if I don't have my mind, I am no longer me; there is no need to hold on to a body that is a ravaged, wasted thing. It will be merciful to let it die.

My intent with this book is not to overwhelm you with a mind-numbing litany of my medical challenges. That would be a depressing journey for you, with little upside. What I hope to do with my words—my truth—is to explain how my medical challenges created in me a particular mindset, a driven and fearless approach to living my life, that I believe might serve to inspire you to follow suit—even if you don't have a killer disease brooding inside of you.

This book is the last item on my bucket list. It is the reason I have survived long enough to tell you my story. It is my *raison d'etre*, my reason for being. If it becomes necessary, I've asked my husband to put it on the internet for free after I die. I hope it helps you face your own tremendous challenges and be brave enough to soar over obstacles whenever *your* wings are broken.

PART I

Grounded

CHAPTER I

Sentenced to Death

WASHINGTON, DC, 1964

I WAS SENTENCED TO DEATH AT SEVEN YEARS OLD, THOUGH I never committed a crime. With my hair braided into one long ponytail on top of my head and two others hanging down my back—my mother's favorite way to style my hair—I could not have looked more innocent. Barely four feet tall, wearing a dress that swirled around my knees just above my patent leather shoes and frilly white socks, I smiled a lot, even though I was missing my front teeth. My worst offense was being reluctant to eat wilted green vegetables and yucky liver, no matter how many onions my mother smothered it in. My two younger brothers, Tim and Kenneth, nicknamed me Goody Two-Shoes because I refused to do anything naughty enough to entertain them. I took the role of being the oldest child very seriously. As a latchkey kid, I spent much of my time keeping *them* out of trouble. Felonious behavior, this was not.

My only transgression—if you can call it that—was being born with a defective gene that will one day kill me. Before it grants me that mercy, however, that one tiny aberration in my DNA will torture me for decades with excruciating pain, and weaken my immune system so that I am plagued by predatory infections all my life.

How did I get so unlucky? If I believed in past lives, I would say

11

that in some earlier incarnation, I must have been an evil dictator who tortured and killed thousands of innocent people to have earned karma this bad. But I don't believe in reincarnation. So I choose to go with the randomness of the universe theory—that there's no reason or predictability behind the things that happen to us. It's as good as any other. Besides, there's never a good answer for the question, "Why?"

I would not have learned I had sickle cell disease when I did if my mother had not begun to work for the federal government in the early 1960s. Although she trained to be a teacher, Washington authorities insisted she get more teaching credentials before she could begin her career as an elementary school teacher. She needed a job in the meantime and applied for a clerical one with the federal government. To qualify for the job, she had to undergo a pre-employment physical. She had a thorough blood test, the first of her life. Growing up poor in rural South Carolina, doctor visits were reserved only for the mortally ill in her large family. The test detected an abnormality in her blood. The result alarmed the government physician, who called her into his office to explain his findings and recommended she have our whole family tested to determine our blood types. He said my mother's abnormal hemoglobin SC indicated her children likely had similar abnormalities.

So, on a sunny afternoon in 1964, I accompanied my mother and two younger brothers to visit our pediatrician, Dr. Brunschweiler. We really liked him because he had a waiting room full of games and play areas. The doctor must have had a lot of children himself because he seemed to love kids. He had pictures of them all over his desk and on every wall in his office. He used to make us smile even while administering painful vaccination shots, and he rewarded us with brightly colored lollipops.

My brothers and I were playing games and jostling each other in his outer office when Dr. Brunschweiler asked to speak to our mother alone. They stepped inside his private office, and he closed the door. Through the glass walls that enclosed the office, they could watch us playing, but we could not hear them. I saw him motion to my mother to sit down.

Something was wrong. He had never pulled her away from us before.

His craggy face grew serious as he leaned in to speak to my mother. She gasped—I could see her mouth drop open and her eyes shine with tears—and blanched, which is hard to do when you have brown skin. She was clearly shocked; her eyes widened so much her eyebrows arched upwards, crinkling her forehead.

In a brisk, no-nonsense fashion, she was told that her two oldest children had sickle cell anemia. Her youngest, Kenneth, had the trait and probably wouldn't notice it, but Tim and I likely wouldn't live past thirty-five years old.

If our pediatrician had been a character in one of our favorite Charlie Brown cartoons, the rest of what he said to her would have faded to a *wonk, wonk, wonk* sound. His lips were moving, but nothing he said sank in as my mother sat there reeling, our death sentence echoing in her head. As I watched her through the glass window of the doctor's office, she looked down, fumbling in her purse for tissues. Tears flooded her eyes and dripped down her cheeks. She shook her head, saying, "No," over and over again.

Just like that, Tim and I were sentenced to a premature death. We would remain imprisoned in our bodies, never to be free from the excruciating pain and horrific side effects of sickle cell anemia. Many years later, when I was old enough to understand, my mother told me her mind was racing as that doctor droned on. Her head was full of questions:

"How can two of my precious children be stricken with such a deadly disease?"

"They will never grow old?"

"They will suffer horrible pain all their lives?"

"How could this happen?"

"How?"

Shock does that to you. Such unbelievable words get wrapped up in a mental cotton wool until your mind is ready to accept them. My mother was so shocked, her ears shut down to protect her from the horror. She simply could not hear him anymore. Regardless of what the doctor actually *said*, all she heard was that something inside of her and something inside of our father had caused this. Was it *their* fault their children were going to die young after a very painful life? How could it be their fault if they didn't know?

When she finally stumbled out of our doctor's office, my mother said little as she gathered us together and left the HMO building on Pennsylvania Avenue NW. My brothers and I sat wide-eyed with tension during the ride home. We watched our mother's sad, red eyes and tight lips. She remained silent despite our queries about what was wrong. Her silence frightened us because we did not yet know what to fear—it was so unlike her normal vivacious chatter.

My mother knew she had to break the bad news to our father first. With his lightning-quick temper, she knew she had to tread carefully when explaining it to him. More importantly, she had to figure out a way to explain it to *us* so we would not be terrified of our own future. She knew it was important for us to understand the effects this disease would have as we matured, but she did not want to rob us completely of a joyful childhood. She took the time she needed to find the perfect balance.

We were fortunate that she understood young children so well. It was going to be her profession, after all. She was training to be an elementary school teacher at the time; she ended up teaching in Washington and suburban Maryland for more than forty years. She eventually earned both a bachelor's and a master's degree in early childhood education, so she was learning how to break bad news to little kids. She was gentle and used simple words that empathized with our fear. We asked bewildered questions and, for most of them, she answered, "I don't know." I suppose she thought it best not to scare us.

"Will we die soon?" I asked. As the eldest, I was bold—even though I was shaking inside and my eyes glistened with tears.

"I hope not," she said, and hugged Tim and me to her chest. "It'll be all right. You'll see." She rubbed our backs to soothe us, like she always did, and pulled Kenneth into her arms, ran her fingers through his profusion of curly hair. Poor Kenneth was the most bewildered of all. At four years old, he didn't really understand what was happening. He was as scared as Tim and me. He thought he was sick, too.

Some of the details of my hundreds of pain episodes in and out of hospitals have blurred in my memory, probably due to all the narcotics I've received. That's probably for the best. But the refrain "may not live past thirty-five" has replayed in my head like a broken record for decades. Although my diagnosis frightened me at first, I stopped crying pretty quickly. Having the simplistic mind of a child actually helped. I used my second-grade logic to make myself feel better.

"I'm only seven years old," I told myself. "There's still plenty of time to have fun."

Fun was my main pursuit as a second grader at LaSalle Elementary School in Northeast Washington. I loved playing with my Barbie, Ken, and Francie dolls and jumping rope. I particularly liked my favorite game, double Dutch—where I jumped over two ropes swinging in opposite directions—on the sidewalk outside my house.

I did not let my disease stop me from running around and jumping out of low-hanging tree limbs. I wore a sheet as a cape on my back, like Superman. "Thirty-five is a long way away," I thought, with the naïveté of youth, then forgot all about it. My friends never knew anything was wrong with me as we giggled with abandon and chased each other along the city blocks of my Northeast neighborhood. I was always home by the time the streetlights came on at dusk, the only rule my mother imposed on our daily playtime.

Growing up with only brothers, I was a bit of a tomboy myself, and a very stubborn one at that. One day, all the boys in our small community had gathered to play softball at my neighbor's house. I saw no reason not to join them.

It was a summer day in the early 1960s, and my three braids were secured tightly as I stood at home base insisting it was my turn up at bat.

"You can't play because you're a girl!" my devilish neighbor said. He grabbed the bat from me and pushed me out of his way to take his turn. Arms crossed, I refused to move from home base. He told his friend to go ahead and pitch, and as he swung the bat, he hit me in the head so hard that I fell down, unconscious.

I was told that the boys, wide-eyed, scurried around in a panic as copious amounts of blood ran down my face and into my braids as I lay in the dirt behind home base. My shorts and sneakers were covered in dust. I was unresponsive when they yelled my name; fear made their voices shrill.

One of the boys, probably one of my brothers, ran next door to tell my mother. An emergency room visit swiftly followed. The doctor told my mother I was lucky I did not lose my left eye. It took several stitches to repair the deep cut on my left eyelid, but the wounds in my scalp were not as deep. The bat had hit the bony area of my skull just above the eye socket. I still bear a scar over that eye more than fifty years later, a reminder of my younger self.

When I returned home with a bandaged head and eye, I was unrepentant about trying to play softball with the boys. Forced to stay inside for several days, I cooled my heels. I never retaliated against that boy who hit me with the bat, as much as I wanted to. He said it was an accident; he hadn't meant to knock me out or hurt my eye. Before long I was outside again, laughing, playing, and running around with my friends. Kenneth once asked me, "How did you get like that?" I'm not even sure.

CHAPTER 2

A Question of Faith

I HAVE OFTEN BEEN TOLD I HAVE A "STRONG PERSONALITY." Depending on who says it, they mean I can be loud, frank, and/or unpredictable. Some people do not like this about me, but there's not much I can do about it. I was predisposed to a certain amount of stubbornness, but I think my disease put its hands on my personality, forging my idiosyncrasies like a blacksmith shaping steel. With time at a premium, I became a miser to those who would waste it, bereft of patience with anything or anyone that squandered this precious resource. At times it may have verged into obnoxiousness in the eyes of some. I found myself unable to muster the will to do anything of little significance, particularly small talk, which became a poison that I was desperate to avoid. Blunt, plainspoken, and at times, painfully honest was the only way I knew how to be. In essence it was a protective device, like a puffer fish's. My impatience was my poisonous and prickly outer shell that kept away the time wasters.

My husband says I will leave this world with nothing left unsaid. There will be no brooding about anything because I will have gotten everything off my chest. He says I rarely remember anything I say to people, but their hurt feelings linger for years.

I can only shrug and try to guard my tongue a little better the next time. The good thing about middle age is that I have accepted myself and all my flaws. I am who I am. Whatever clay mold I came out of has hardened into a permanent shape. I am the woman my mother raised me to be.

The stubbornness that others attach to me has definitely affected my relationship with my mother, especially when it comes to religion. My mother has clung to her faith to get her through the most trying times in her life. She worries about me and fears for my salvation, so she nags me to go to church. It does little good since I haven't gone regularly since I left for college—my mother's single greatest disappointment in me.

My mother is a preacher's daughter; her devotion to the Lord is genuine and her faith is as real to her as a part of her body. She took us to church on Sundays from the time my feet still dangled over the edge of the pews until I was in high school. She did everything she could to make sure I believed in "the Lord." My lack of faith is not her fault.

As I grew more cynical with age and more tortured by sickle cell, my faith withered. I could not understand a God that would let children suffer from such a painful disease their entire lives, only to kill them in their prime. My skepticism was compounded as I studied Marxism and other philosophies during college. Something about "opiate of the masses" resonated with me. I also learned about holy wars launched by opportunists bent on power. I took a class on witchcraft just to be arbitrary when my college insisted I meet a religion requirement. It was preferable to my philosophy class, where the professor asked ridiculous questions like, "If a tree falls in the woods and no one is there to hear it, did it happen?" I dropped that class after a week. I liked the witch the professor brought in from Watertown. She told us about her coven's Earth mother practices; it was nothing like the witchcraft I had seen on television. But I no longer stepped inside a church, unless I was dragged there by a friend trying to save my soul.

At the age of four, still small enough to wear patent leather shoes and ribbons in my hair, I never understood why the preacher yelled at us and called us sinners, spraying spittle on those of us unlucky enough to be sitting in the front pews. I could not think of a single sin I had committed. Nevertheless, I sat there, numb with boredom as he droned on, dutifully placing the change my mother pressed into my hand into the offering basket as it was passed around. I went through the motions, going to Bible school and church functions. I did what was expected of the child of a preacher's child. But when I was fifteen, my grandfather Reverend Stewart looked into my eyes and asked me if I believed in God. I was as honest then as I always have been.

"I'm not sure that I do," I said, looking back into his eyes, which were slightly cloudy and gray from cataracts. He took my hand and studied the lines in it. I had no idea what he was looking for. I knew my lifeline was especially short compared to all my friends, but I waited quietly until he was finished.

"You will believe when you are ready," he said solemnly. He let go of my hand, then closed his eyes to take one of the naps he favored in old age. At the time, I thought my grandfather was trying to comfort himself. It seemed highly unlikely that I would ever change my mind.

A few years later when I was in college, two of my best friends were Catholic girls from large families. My roommate Linda was one of twelve children; my other roommate Maura was one of nine. They dragged me to Mass, mistaking the AME Zion church I grew up in as the root of my faith problem. I sat in Mass a couple of times, jumping up, kneeling, genuflecting, and sitting down when they did. After a lot of getting up and down, the priest began to talk about "the body and blood of Christ" and urged everyone to come up for Communion. People formed a line to receive a wafer on their tongues and a sip of cheap red wine. I refused to join them at the altar. I know my revulsion was illogical, but I later confessed: it was just gross!

"Why would you want to eat Christ and drink his blood? That's cannibalism!" I said.

Of course, they just rolled their eyes at me, called me hopeless, and suggested I read the passage in the Bible that gave rise to the 2,000-year-old ritual. But I already knew that the rituals of most churches I visited would never move me. I never got "the Spirit" the way my closest friends and family hoped I would. I've sat through Baptist preachers yelling their sermons with veins standing out on their foreheads. I've sat through Episcopalian priests intoning Latin prayers in a soft voice. I've sat through several Catholic priests giving full sermons during weddings as, one after the other, my roommates got married.

As I grew older, friends continued to drag me to "their" churches, hoping for a different reaction. My friends were so concerned for my eternal soul that they had deep, philosophical discussions with me about why I would not, or could not, believe in God. Once or twice, our discussions grew so heated we started raising our voices. I was as stubborn about my position as they were. I told one of my best friends it was unfair that while I respected her right to believe whatever she wanted, she did not respect my right *not* to believe what she did.

"But aren't you afraid of what will happen to your soul when you die?" she asked.

"I will likely become fertilizer and continue the cycle of life on Earth," I said. "That's if I am buried. I will likely be cremated, so I will just be dust."

I could not see anything else beyond that, although I could tell she was worried for me. She knew my hold on life was tenuous with this disease, and she worried about my afterlife. Whenever I pondered an afterlife, I only saw an end to my pain; I would not feel or care about anything.

Then, a few years ago, I had what you might call an epiphany.

By the time I was in my early fifties, I had already had three lives' worth of hospitalizations, but in my mid-fifties, my health began deteriorating quickly. While I was hospitalized for a difficult-to-treat infection, I had a sudden ileus (an obstruction in my intestines) and compacted bowels from lying in bed with a waist-high cast for six months. In the emergency room, doctors forced a nasogastric tube down my throat, which gagged me for nearly a month. They rushed me into surgery and operated on my intestines twice in three days without success. Week after week, I kept failing. The bile piled up in a container behind me, with no way for it to exit out of my intestines. My surgeon was puzzled. He was clearly worried that I could expire any day. I lay listlessly in my hospital bed, so miserable I wondered why in the world I was still alive.

Then something—I'm not sure what—came to me. It was almost like my subconscious took over so it could whisper to my conscious mind:

> Gail, you are still alive because you have not yet done what I sent you to do. I gave you a painful life for a reason, but I also gave you the grit and the will to endure it. You filled your own life with love and adventure. I have allowed you to realize so many possibilities so you can use what you have learned to help others. Go and write that book I have been pushing you to write since you were eleven years old. You only think you were procrastinating all these years, but you were not ready yet. You had not lived long enough to learn the right lessons. Now you have.

I don't know if it was a dream or a daydream, but shortly after that internal communication, I started feeling better. The bile started moving through my intestines again. The doctors were astonished and relieved by what they called my "miraculous rebound." None of them understood why my ileus suddenly cleared up and my bowels began to function again. I was released from the hospital after a month— thirty pounds thinner and weak as a newborn kitten.

I did not take my reprieve lightly. Shortly after my recovery, I sat down to write the story of my life. As I sat at my computer the first day, it was like a dam had burst. The story simply flowed out of me. I had previously attempted to tell my story through fiction, but every attempt had failed. They were meant to fail. I was not using my authentic voice in those stories. *This* is my true voice.

Everyone says to write what you know. I am trying. Nobody knows the depth of my misery or the abundance of my gratitude to be able to take another breath each day. After half a century of suffering and wondering what was the point of it all, I had finally gotten the message: I was born to use my difficult, wonderful life as an example to inspire others, to help other people struggling to overcome what seems impossible. No matter how much I have to sacrifice my own privacy, I need to let others know you can live a good, rich life if you never give up on your dreams, no matter what lousy hand life deals you.

When I told my mother about the sudden understanding of my purpose, she was elated. "That was God speaking to you," she said. All my life, my mother had hoped I would communicate with God. Maybe now she was right. Maybe God had spoken to me, whispering inside my head as I lay almost dying, "I am only saving you because you have not yet done what I sent you there to do." Maybe I was finally ready, as my grandfather predicted all those years ago.

I had to live long enough to finish this book. It is the only way I know to help the world understand what is happening to people suffering from sickle cell disease. And, more importantly, what is still *not* happening. What has God got to do with it? Pretty much everything, it turns out. He speaks to even a faithless sap like me.

CHAPTER 3

It's All in the Blood

MY BROTHER TIM AND I SET OUT TOGETHER ON OUR predestined journey of misery. As children, we supported each other through minor sickle cell crises. My mother boiled water, filled hot-water bottles, wrapped them in towels, and placed them on our aching joints. She gave us analgesics to ease our pain. When all else failed, she rubbed our joints with her hands, hoping to soothe us to sleep. Tim and I understood what the other was going through better than anyone else in our household, except perhaps our mother, who occasionally had pain knifing through her veins and no one to soothe her through it.

However, Tim and I reached a fork in the road when we hit adolescence. When our pain grew more intense after puberty, I chose to follow a path of hope, while Tim raced along a path of despair. I stuck to my Goody Two-Shoes ways: I studied hard, ate well, never smoked, drank, or did illegal drugs. My poor brother chose to do the opposite.

Sickle cell disease rode Tim hard all of his short life. Hope became an ever more elusive palliative for him. Decade after decade, our treatments during a crisis never changed—oxygen, intravenous fluids, and narcotics to ease the pain. Nobody seemed to be doing anything to address the underlying cause of our symptoms. Tim could never see beyond the sameness of his misery.

As a teenager, he grew rebellious. He hung out late with his high school dropout friends, drank, smoked, and did drugs. He was trying to get our parents' attention, but all he got was their fury. No matter his behavior, whether getting arrested while smoking pot with his friends or twisting my mother's brand-new Pontiac Firebird around a tree late one night, he shrugged off their anger and pursued a pattern of self-destruction. We never understood why he kept hurting himself this way. It only made his sickle cell crises more painful.

Much later in his life, Tim disappeared. We did not hear from him for years. I have a picture of just the four of us—my mother, my father, Kenneth, and me—posed together at my thirtieth birthday party. Tim is not in the picture; there is an underlying sadness in my mother's eyes because he had been missing for so long. We never heard a word from him.

I shudder to think of the pit of desolation he fell into during those missing years. Evidently, they were a blur of illegal drugs and endless fights he was too weak to win. He was rail thin when I finally spied him in a crowd at an outdoor concert in Northern Virginia. I gasped. Tears blurred my vision as I ran to him and shouted his name. When I got close, I grabbed him around the middle and hugged him tightly.

"Tim, where have you *been?*" I asked, my voice muffled in his chest. He was six feet tall by then; I reached the middle of his chest. He was evasive and did not answer me directly. Instead, he awkwardly patted my back. We had never been a particularly demonstrative family, so I am sure my hug overwhelmed him. He looked worn out. He told me he was only eating once a day because it was all he could afford. My eyes filled with tears again, and I pleaded with him for a phone number, address, anything so I could stay in touch with him. Eventually, he scribbled a telephone number on the back of one of my business cards and said he had to go because he was staying "with some people."

That evening, I called my mother to give her his telephone number and tell her about our encounter. She broke down on the phone. I could tell from her tears the depth of her relief. I think she had believed Tim was lost to her forever. She called him, and Tim eventually moved back in with our parents. He also reconnected with his school-age daughter, Alicia. He had divorced her mother many years before.

I will never forget our last vacation together on the Outer Banks, a bittersweet memory. Tim could be charming. One night he prepared a delicious seafood meal that my husband still raves about. Alicia was with him that week, and they were able to bond again. This was both good and bad because not long after Tim returned to our lives, he left us again—this time, forever. In 1993, he died suddenly after a sickle cell crisis. He was thirty-five. His daughter was only eleven. She felt lost for quite a while afterward.

As I wrestled with my own grief, it galled me to think our pediatrician had been right. But I also had to wonder, was Tim's behavior a factor in fulfilling the prophecy of his life expectancy? My favorite primary care physician, an African American man himself, once explained to me that males have a much harder time accepting the inherent frailties of our disease.

"Many of my male patients seem to be self-destructive," he admitted once. "It is harder for them as men to be perceived as weak." Subconsciously, some male sickle cell patients resort to suicide to avoid more years of suffering.

I thought about this for years. It explained so much. Tim lost hope. He saw nothing that could improve his condition. Living for years in intermittent—often excruciating—pain had affected his mind and bruised his psyche. He could not join the military like his friends, or play sports like our baby brother, because he could never pass a physical examination for either one. Underneath all his rebellion, I am sure he was deeply depressed.

I can relate. It takes a strong will not to succumb to depression when you have this disease. Sometimes, the pain of a crisis is so intense, it leaves you gasping for breath like the late stages of cancer, and the narcotics used to treat it are identical.

Since blood is so ubiquitous in the human body, the potential for internal damage is immense. No part of you is safe because crescent-shaped cells can clog capillaries anywhere—and capillaries are everywhere. The cells emit a sticky substance that causes clots that block normal blood flow, and eventually, the body's tissues, organs, and bones die. This pattern causes anemia because the fragile sickle cells break down in ten to twenty days, compared to normal hemoglobin cells, which last four months. The constant anemia makes us feel weak, tire more easily, and appear run-down or jaundiced.

The doctor who delivered me at Freedmen's Hospital in Washington believed I had jaundice at birth. My skin appeared so sallow, he kept me in the hospital for several extra days. Never once did he suspect the true reason. My jaundice was caused by the high rate of red blood cell breakdown in my liver. It gave my skin and the whites of my eyes a yellowish tint. I think it is probably the reason my father said I looked like a bald Asian man when I was first born. On overseas trips I am often thought by others to be Polynesian because of my features.

I spent my entire life never knowing when a crisis would occur. I would go months living normally, then feel a sudden heaviness in my limbs, followed by sharp, fiery pains erupting in my arms, elbows, knees, shins, ankles, hips, wrists, and shoulders. It usually made me too weak to walk or get to help. I often had to whisper to a classmate or work colleague nearby that I was feeling ill and needed medical help. I felt embarrassed while ambulance personnel loaded me onto a stretcher and carried me past dozens of people staring at me with shocked expressions before the crew could rush me to the hospital.

As the crisis raged on, I got inflammation and swelling in the affected areas. Those puffy, swollen areas usually felt warm to the touch, as if the joints had a fever, and were so painful I could not stand to be touched.

Every crisis causes some internal damage. As I aged, my ophthalmologist found scarring caused by burst blood vessels in the backs of my eyes. This kind of optical damage has caused me serious vision problems, including partial blindness, retinal detachments, cataracts, and distorting floaters as an older adult.

All of this because of one little amino acid substitution in my chromosomes and some bad luck. Normal adult hemoglobin is called hemoglobin A. Sickle cell disease is caused by a hemoglobin mutation called hemoglobin S. In order to have sickle cell disease, you need to inherit hemoglobin S from both parents. If you only inherit it from one parent, you have the sickle cell trait, hemoglobin genotype AS, but likely won't experience symptoms.

A geneticist would typically predict that two parents with the sickle cell trait would have just a one in four chance of having a child with sickle cell disease. But my family's bloodline skewed those statistics, giving two out of three of us the deadly disease and one of us the sickle cell trait.

My mother has a rare blood disorder—a version of sickle cell disease—called hemoglobin SC, which may be the reason our odds were skewed. This blood disorder causes milder symptoms than sickle cell disease, but it has given her pain, bone, and eye problems most of her life. She received hemoglobin S from one parent and hemoglobin C, another type of mutation, from the other. My father and brother Kenneth were both born with just a sickle cell trait, so neither one has ever experienced symptoms.

Both sets of my grandparents are dead, so we cannot be certain which type of hemoglobin my grandparents carried. We do know my maternal grandmother, Gladys Aldridge Stewart, who was born in Great Falls, South Carolina, in 1903, died when my mother was just ten years old. Given her youthful demise, I think we can assume my maternal grandmother carried hemoglobin S. She passed that, and the name Gladys, on to my mother.

My maternal grandfather, George Washington Stewart, born in

Columbia, South Carolina, in 1886, lived into his mid-nineties. He was a Methodist AME Zion minister with dark-chocolate skin and arresting hazel eyes that stood out from a proud, carved face. He passed his high cheekbones, hazel eyes, and, we suspect, the rare hemoglobin C gene to my mother.

My brothers and I did not inherit my mother's beautiful eyes, but I did inherit their distinctive almond shape. My brothers got my father's long eyelashes, however, a fact I still find a total waste. All of us somewhat favor our paternal side, with dark brown eyes and thick, curly hair. But in some instances, we also resemble our maternal cousins even more strongly than we resemble each other.

While she was growing up poor in the South during the Great Depression, my mother felt something was wrong with her. Occasionally, she screamed in pain when her limbs ached, but she'd get whipped by my grandfather, who believed she was faking illness to get out of chores like picking her share of the cotton that helped supplement the family's meager parish income. In the early 1950s, when she was a student at Livingstone College, a historically black college in Salisbury, North Carolina, she complained of sudden pains in her body. The school doctor dismissed her symptoms as "growing pains."

"I would go back to my dormitory room and hurt so bad, I would start hallucinating," my mother once told me. She had nothing more to take for the pain than a powdered over-the-counter analgesic. Eventually her crises subsided.

My paternal health history is even more of a mystery. My great-grandfather John Campbell, born in 1862, was a farmer married to Millie Davis, a former slave who was also born in 1862. Farmers all their lives, they had a large brood to help them—including my paternal grandfather, Ed Campbell, Sr., whom we called Granddaddy—and his siblings Robert, Bert, Walter, Francis (Missy), Herbert, and Willie.

With only a third-grade education, Granddaddy worked as a farm laborer his entire life. He was a very dark-skinned man and was already elderly when I was a small child. He most likely carried at least the sickle cell trait for my father to have inherited it, although he probably never knew it. He physically toiled for decades, scratching out a living on his tiny farm, and had no reason to suspect he carried an illness. Like thousands of other trait carriers, he lived his entire life not knowing he carried a potential genetic bomb.

Granddaddy smoked unfiltered Camel cigarettes and squinted like Popeye when he talked to my brothers and me. We spent summers on their tiny farm in Chesterfield, South Carolina, playing in the sandy soil under the pecan trees. My parents needed to save money on childcare while they worked back home in Washington, so they dutifully carted us down to spend the summer with our grandparents and learn about our roots.

Granddaddy was a soldier in World War I. My father inherited his old brown Army uniform, which he kept in a cluttered bedroom closet and pulled out when he was feeling sentimental. Somewhere in my father's collection of old family photos is one of Granddaddy wearing the uniform. He served at a time when soldiers of color were segregated from white soldiers and given the most demeaning jobs, like digging latrines, by the US Army. But Granddaddy did his duty with pride and was honorably discharged. When you are the child of a former slave, you take your pride wherever you can get it, so his chest was properly inflated when he returned home as a veteran looking for work.

With his very dark skin and the yellow-brown whites of his eyes, I suspect Granddaddy was descended from slaves on his mother's side who were born in West or Central Africa, where the sickle cell gene is most dominant.

When Granddaddy returned to South Carolina after the war, he married Pearlie Little. Ten years his junior, she was a beautiful light-skinned woman who had long, silky black hair. The 1920 census agent who visited her mother's household described Pearlie as *mulatto*, an outdated term—still used a half century after slavery ended—for someone with both black and white ancestry. My grandmother Pearlie never knew her white father, but she grew up in a houseful of siblings: Julia, Harriet, Essie, Rillie, Floyd, Mason, Thelma, and Georgiana.

If the census agent had been a stickler for facts, he would have described my grandmother as a *quadroon*, since only one of her grandparents was African American. Her mother, Sallie Little, was the biracial daughter of a Scottish woman and Aron Little, a workman at the woman's home. Sallie's mother never acknowledged the liaison, and before she went to live with her biological father, the time Sallie spent in her mother's household was a painful one.

After Pearlie married Granddaddy, they settled down on a small parcel of land he bought and had six children, including my father, Legrant, and his siblings Juanita, Eddie, Evelyn, Carolyn, and Charles Rae. Two of Pearlie and Granddaddy's children did not survive. Evelyn died as a teenager during childbirth. My grandparents raised her daughter, also named Evelyn, whom our relatives call either Missy or Sweetbaby, depending on the intensity of their Southern twang. My grandmother, whom our family called Miss Pearlie or Mama Campbell, did not have any sign of the disease.

Juanita, my father's oldest sister, most resembles Mama Campbell. As a young woman, Juanita married Burly Page, who later became one of the famous Tuskegee Airmen. Uncle Burly was the first African American man to obtain a pilot's license in Durham County, North Carolina. Uncle Eddie and his late wife, Dorothea, were both mayors of Willingboro, New Jersey. When Aunt Dorothea died, she had an impressive funeral, lying in state with an honor guard and New Jersey politicians flocking inside to sing her praises at the service.

Granddaddy died in his sixties when I was a teenager. Mama Campbell lived well into her nineties, but her longevity is not the only reason I believe she passed on the normal hemoglobin A gene to my father. She was only a quarter African American, which significantly decreased her chances of having the trait.

Growing up in the tiny rural town of Chesterfield, South Carolina, during the late nineteenth and early twentieth centuries, neither Mama Campbell nor her mother discussed their origins. The segregated town was still caught up in the old ways of the South, and the miscegenation that brought them into the world caused them decades of shame that rode them hard and sealed their lips so tightly we have completely lost the history of the white side of our family.

I once had to complete a family tree for a training assignment at work and asked Mama Campbell to tell me more about her white father. She refused to utter his name. "I don't know who he is!" she finally snapped, refusing to say another word.

My great-grandmother Sallie never talked about her Scottish mother either. Uncle Eddie told me he remembers his grandmother Sallie a little bit. Being Scottish in South Carolina was not unusual—it was a region settled by Highland Scots, after all, many of whom landed in the New World after the failed Jacobite uprising of 1745. Those Highland Scots supported the Catholic Stuarts in their fight for the British throne, but they backed the wrong horse in Prince Charles Edward Stuart, who saved his own neck by fleeing to France. Many of his followers, lucky enough to escape being slaughtered at the Battle of Culloden, sailed to the New World and settled in the Carolina mountains that so reminded them of home.

My father's family name, Campbell, was likely inherited from yet another Scottish family who held my ancestors as slaves. There was even once a governor of South Carolina who bore that name.

Other than her heritage, all my father can remember about his grandmother Sallie is that she was not treated very well because her skin was just slightly darker than her white siblings' skin. We can only guess how much anguish being shunned by her own family caused her.

Every day Mama Campbell and my great-grandmother Sallie looked into a mirror, they must have been reminded of their painful pasts. Both were very fair-skinned women with long, straight hair that had only a hint of curl. Living in a small segregated town like Chesterfield meant neither woman ever thought themselves anything but "negro" or "colored," depending on the era. The stubborn legacy of slavery meant the one drop rule was firmly fixed in the minds of their neighbors—to them, only one drop of black blood meant you were black. Everybody put my ancestors firmly in that box. It was rare to publicly acknowledge mixed-race people in Southern towns like theirs. Everybody gossiped, of course, and many suspected that the white men in town occasionally grabbed a good-looking colored gal (willing or not) and had their way with her. White women crossed the color line too, but probably less often and with more dire results.

Still, it doesn't really matter how the sickle cell gene hopped from generation to generation in our family. What matters is that it wreaked havoc on our lives, affecting us all in different ways. I think only Kenneth was spared some of the emotional anguish, as he was too young to understand what was going on when we were first diagnosed. He had a sweet innocence about him as a child. Scratching his curly hair, he watched Tim and me suffering and felt helpless to do anything about it.

My mother was most affected. On top of dealing with the news of her children's early demise, she finally learned—at age thirty—what had been wrong with her all her life, a small silver lining. The results of that routine pre-employment physical were a vindication for her. She had proof she had not been faking pain as a child, and that her intermittent crises were not simply "growing pains." Her condition had a name and a cause—finally—but she had unknowingly passed along the genetic defect to her own family.

My father never knew he had the sickle cell trait before our diagnosis in 1964, and his knee-jerk response was denial. "I was a Marine!" he often yelled, inebriated, throughout my childhood, adolescence, and young adult years. His constant drinking made our already difficult situation much worse. He lived in a world of denial—about our illness and his alcoholism—for most of my life.

"I'm healthy," he declared, slurring his words. "I swam for miles and played sports. I was in top physical shape when I was at Camp Lejeune. How could I have had anything to do with this? It's all *your* fault." He sneered, pointing at my mother. "You gave me sick kids!"

As hurtful as that was to hear when I was growing up, I can see now, with the crisp hindsight of maturity, that he was as ignorant about sickle cell disease as everyone else. Since he felt no symptoms himself, it was easy to wrap himself in the fantasy that his genes had no impact on our poor health.

I realize now he only had a high school education from a second-rate segregated school in the South, so he had little understanding of genetics. He wasn't with us at Dr. Brunschweiler's office when the doctor explained it all to my mother. But whether he admitted it or not, he passed along half of the defective genes that were destroying our lives.

Still, I hated his drunken rages. It was like tiptoeing around a wild tiger when my father was drunk. It took so little to send him into a blind, destructive rage that usually lasted until he passed out. We braced ourselves when he came home from his federal government job, weaving unsteadily on his feet. We knew the slightest look or word from any of us would set him off on an angry, irrational rant that might last for hours. Having a family dinner and doing homework were very difficult as he stalked about the house, yelling about slight or imagined offenses. He broke things we could not afford to replace out of spite and just plain meanness. My poor mother took the brunt of it. He was physically violent on occasion and always took it out on her. I hated him most for that. Like all bullies, he jumped on the weakest person in sight.

A lot of what he said during his drunken binges has lingered with me for years. People say a person's true beliefs come out when they drink. "In vino, veritas," the Latin saying goes. If he really believed some of the hurtful things he said and did over the years, I am not sure I can ever forgive him. I hope I can one day. I know forgiveness will help me let go of my painful past and diminish any lingering anger at him.

Tim cringed whenever my father verbally abused us about our poor health, which was agitated by the stress of living in that tense household. Tim later grew a hard outer shell to deflect some of the hurt. I did too, but not as quickly, or as well. It didn't help us feel better to know my parents were not handling the fallout from our disease very well. We felt guilty when we got sick and had to go to the hospital. We knew our family could not afford the mountains of medical bills. For decades, our insurance company, that scourge of modern medicine, used its favorite term, *preexisting condition*, like a club to beat us over the head, trying to get out of paying as many of our medical bills as possible.

The only way our sickle cell disease would not have been a preexisting condition is if we were never born at all. Since they were part of an HMO, my parents won more battles than they lost, but it still fatigued my mother to have to fight for what was right all the time. Meanwhile, life insurance companies ran for the hills, refusing to insure both Tim and me, believing we would die young and they would have to pay a claim.

While our father handled the family crisis by drowning himself in a liquor bottle, my mother was there with us every step of the way. When Tim and I succumbed to minor crises in our limbs, she tried treating them at home first with over-the-counter analgesics. She pushed endless glasses of water or juice on us to thin out our clotted blood, as the doctors instructed her to do. Sometimes her remedies worked and the crises eased after a few hours. But most of the time, they were too bad to be treated at home, and my parents had to carry one of us to a hospital emergency room for treatment. Often, they would have to leave us there to be admitted into the hospital, and hurry home to the two of us left behind.

During our elementary school years, Tim was admitted more often than I was, but I had my fair share of middle-of-the-night emergency room drama. As we grew older and our disease grew worse, we were admitted to the hospital more often than we were sent home. Luckily, Tim and I rarely had a sickle cell crisis at the same time.

Though our ailment was a direct result of the conjoining of my parents' genetic makeup, there was only hope in the air when they joined together in holy matrimony in 1955.

CHAPTER 4

Growing Up with a Secret

WASHINGTON, DC, 1963–1975

I AM SURE MY MOTHER WAS OPTIMISTIC WHEN SHE ELOPED with my father, a US Marine, in May of 1955, while she was still a senior in college. My father then returned to Camp Lejeune until he was honorably discharged. My mother returned to Livingstone College until her graduation. They reunited to join the millions of Negroes (as African Americans were commonly referred to during that period of history) migrating north to seek better job opportunities. They moved in with my mother's older sister, Comila, who lived in a Federalist-era row house in Northwest Washington, and began looking for work.

Two years later, when my parents were settled into a Southwest Washington apartment awaiting my birth, my mother ran headfirst into the fact that, at the time, Washington was still a segregated city. She wanted to deliver me at Providence Hospital, but the nuns there discouraged her, which led my parents to believe the hospital may have been de facto whites only. Instead, she and my father were forced to take a very long taxi ride that cold night to Freedmen's Hospital in Northwest Washington while she was in labor. I was born at 10:40 p.m. on March 7, 1957.

As its name implies, Freedmen's Hospital was created for the freed black slaves who poured into the nation's capital after the Civil War.

It has always been situated on federal land. The city's new residents of color were denied medical care at every hospital in Washington, so President Abraham Lincoln had to donate an old army installation to create a hospital for them. President John F. Kennedy combined Freedmen's Hospital with Howard University in 1961; it is now known as Howard University Hospital. Almost 100 years after the Emancipation Proclamation was issued in 1863 and the Thirteenth Amendment to the US Constitution narrowly passed in Congress, freeing American slaves forever, Freedmen's Hospital was still one of very few places babies of color like me and my brothers could be born in our nation's capital.

The reality of raising children with sickle cell disease rocked my parents' foundation. Our home life disintegrated into years of tears, denial, recrimination, and blame. We were lower middle class at best. My father worked in a lower management job for the US Department of Defense, and my mother was an elementary school teacher in Southeast Washington. Their salaries were slight and further drained by my father's drinking and financial irresponsibility. The bills were never paid on time, and bill collectors hounded us weekly—which caused my parents to fight frequently.

My mother prayed a lot. It was her salvation in the midst of so much misery. She rarely talked about our illness or my father's drinking to anyone outside the family. She gave us the impression that our dysfunctional family life should remain secret. As a child of the Great Depression, she learned you did not air your dirty laundry in public. It didn't matter that everyone else had dirty laundry too. You just never aired *yours*.

As children, we were frightened when our father went into one of his rages, often a by-product of his drinking. We always hoped he would pass out quickly so we could have some peace and quiet to focus on our homework or a favorite television show. It was not easy walking around on eggshells every day, trying not to incite his fury. My father often drank until he passed out. He never seemed to remember the terror he caused during his drunken rages, and never apologized for the destruction left in his wake. Once sober, it was as if it never happened.

What he could not ignore was that his paycheck seemed to slip between his fingers, lost at the liquor store or on adult entertainment that reminded him of his single days, instead of his real life as a married father of three kids. He never said and we will never know what really happened. What I do remember is he never had the money for simple things we needed, like school supplies, class pictures or trips, and regular dental checkups.

Back then, it was still legal for bill collectors to terrorize us on the telephone about overdue bills. My mother often put me on the telephone to say, "My parents are not home right now," but that just infuriated them even more. All those mean people calling all the time only added to the tension in our house.

Of course, we also had some lighter moments. We were still quite young when my brothers almost burned down our rented house on Madison Street NE. Tim was the mastermind of mischief. Both my brothers loved their Hot Wheels cars and their plastic track. One day, when our elderly babysitter was asleep downstairs, they erected their Hot Wheels track in my parents' bedroom. Then they stretched their track from the end of my parents' bed to the closest electrical outlet on the wall. Tim had seen race cars jumping through a fiery wheel on television, and he wanted the same effect for his toy cars. Somehow, he managed to ignite the track, and when I walked in both my brothers were rolling their Hot Wheels cars through a fiery circle on the floor. When the plastic track began to melt, the fire spread to the footboard of my parents' bed.

I ran downstairs to wake our babysitter, screaming, "The house is on fire!" She ran upstairs to see the mess my parents' bedroom had become and did her best to douse the flames. The bed was barely salvageable. The white wooden footboard was burned black, as was the wood floor between their bed and the wall outlet that had provided the magnificent sparks that ignited the track.

My brothers were punished, of course, but it did not stop Tim from figuring out new ways to get into mischief. Once, our cousin Erickson, the son of my mother's youngest sister, Daisy, came to visit for a while. With three boys under ten years old in the house, there was total mayhem. Tim loved war games, so he decided that he needed a flamethrower to stop "the enemy," which on that day was Erickson.

Tim went downstairs and rummaged through the bottom of the kitchen sink, where our mother kept household cleaning products. He was looking for any product that said *flammable*. Gleeful, Tim took a can of Lysol spray and ran back upstairs to continue the game. At one point, Tim lit a match and sprayed the Lysol on it. Flames shot out at least three feet in front of him and up Erickson's arm, singeing his arm hair. Erickson yelped in pain and waved his arm around.

After that episode, my mother made Tim go out to our yard and pick his own switch from the bushes to use for his whipping. She always warned us not to bring back a stick that was too thin or she would go out and pick one herself, implying that it would be thicker and hurt more if she had to pick it. When a sullen Tim returned from the yard with his switch, she used it to hit him around the legs. Erickson, Kenneth, and I watched Tim dance and jump around to avoid the switch. No matter how often my mother punished him, though, she could never subdue Tim's devilish streak.

There was one occasion when we'd be sure to see joy in my father's eyes: Christmas. In his better moments, my father got just as excited about Christmas as we did. He spray-painted our living room windows with fake snow even though some of our Christmases had 60°F or 70°F temperatures. He put lights on the house and around the yard to make it as festive as possible. We believed in Santa Claus a lot longer than most kids in our neighborhood—until the day my brother Tim brought that myth to a screeching halt. Always curious, he found our toys hidden in a linen closet one afternoon and gleefully shouted, "See, I *told* you there was no Santa Claus!"

Kenneth and I were crestfallen. We had spent hours watching the night sky, trying to catch a glimpse of reindeer pulling a fat man in a sleigh. I used to watch the moon in particular, because I believed I would catch their silhouette crossing its bright surface before once again being cloaked by an inky sky. Once I even asked my mother how Santa could get into our brick row house because we did not have a chimney or fireplace. "We let him in the front door," she replied, as if that explained everything.

After Tim ruined the magic of Christmas for us, my parents became pragmatic and started giving us an allowance each Christmas. They explained we could only buy the toys our allowance afforded us. Occasionally, my mother would sneak an extra present or two under the tree, but the day was never again as much fun as before Tim's revelation.

Our lives were like that. Good one day, not so good the next. My father was the unpredictable element. Without his violent outbursts when drunk, we would have had a more harmonious existence. Somehow, mostly because of my mother's endless patience, our family managed to stay together. Maybe it was because she was a preacher's kid and believed everything would eventually get better if she prayed hard enough.

Washington life was restrictive. My family could not live, work, shop, or go to a movie theater anywhere we chose in the 1950s or early 1960s. But more freedom was coming soon in the wake of brave Negro students who staged sit-ins at whites-only soda shops down South. They were following the nonviolence credo of an extraordinary preacher whose oration on the steps of the Lincoln Memorial in August of 1963 sparked a peaceful revolution that led to more equality for us.

That summer, we were in the crowd of hundreds of thousands who marched on Washington seeking better treatment for Negroes in America. We sat with our feet cooling in the Lincoln Memorial Reflecting Pool, that famous stretch of water between the Washington Monument and the Lincoln Memorial. It was a hot day in August and we let history flow through us. My father was lost somewhere in the crowd. He left earlier than we did, eager to walk the entire march route with the other protesters. There were people of many different colors there, lending their voices to the ideals of freedom for *everyone*. It was thrilling to see so many people united for a common cause. However, the crowd was too thick for my mother to navigate with three kids, so we sat by the pool to listen to the speeches of famous civil rights leaders—including Dr. Martin Luther King, Jr.'s famous "I Have a Dream" speech.

While we sat, Tim, who was four at the time, tried to touch one of the huge goldfish that swam by his bare feet. Instead, he tumbled headfirst into the water and came up sputtering but grinning like a fool as dozens of adult hands reached to pull him out. For the rest of the afternoon, he had to sit on the edge of the pool with his wet clothes clinging to him as the hot sun dried them right on his body.

Growing up in Washington was like that. You were never too far from historic events. I remember the day, later that fall, when my teacher sent us home early. It was November 22, 1963, and President Kennedy had been shot in Dallas. My mother cried for days. He was the only president to whom she wrote a letter, telling him about our difficult life and asking him to help people like us. She admired the young president and his glamorous wife, Jackie, so much that she made me Barbie doll clothes that resembled the stylish wardrobe the First Lady favored. My Barbie was the best-dressed doll on my block. I preened when I showed all my friends.

We stood in line all day long to file past President Kennedy's coffin lying at the United States Capitol. After several hours of standing, I got tired and my uncle James, my mother's younger brother, carried me on his shoulders. A few days later, I watched little John-John salute his father's caisson on television and saw Caroline wearing a winter coat very much like my own. Kenneth and I were the same ages as John-John and Caroline. I felt their pain all the more because I could identify with them. It felt as though one of our own relatives had died. It took me a long time to get over it.

Five years later, tear gas stung our eyes as we rode in the back seat of our car to John Wesley AME Zion church in Northwest Washington. It was Easter Sunday, just a few days after Dr. King was assassinated in April 1968. Our parents told us to roll up our windows as we drove through neighborhoods ravaged by fires set during the riots that broke out after Dr. King's death. The city's African American residents erupted when they heard the news. Thousands of shocked people took to the streets, expressing their anger through violence, rioting, and looting. Authorities called the National Guard to help defend the city. They regularly used tear gas to disperse the looters, and they instituted martial law and curfews; no young black person could wander the streets after dark for fear of being either shot or arrested on sight.

After church, plumes of tear gas still lingered in the air. Even after we rolled up our car windows, our eyes watered and we sneezed and coughed, trying to clear our lungs. "Oh, my God," my mother said, dismayed.

"Look at that!" my father added, pointing at both sides of the street. Wide-eyed, we looked to the desolate H Street NE corridor. A shocking number of buildings were decimated, burned-out shells, their windows broken by late-night looting and fires.

We saw similar rioting in other American cities with large African American populations on the evening news. The images on our black-and-white television screen were startling—the cities were on fire. Never had a people been so united by their helpless rage. It was a frightening time. We rarely went outside after dusk. For weeks, the National Guard was posted on city streets to restore law and order and enforce the curfew. My parents feared we might be accidentally shot and kept us indoors.

By this time, we had moved from the rental house on Madison Street NE to a two-bedroom apartment in Southeast Washington. It was at the end of my third-grade year. The kids in our new neighborhood were tough. Most came from single-parent households, and many were on some kind of public assistance. The need to supplement their income catapulted them into theft, or worse, into gangs and drug dealing.

During our very first week in the new apartment, someone stole Tim's brand-new ten-speed bicycle from the locked storage room. My mother had won it in a raffle and was saving it for when he was old enough to ride it. He never got the chance, because we never saw it again.

My parents moved us to such a terrible neighborhood because they needed to live somewhere cheaper. It was the only way they could think of to save enough money to buy a house of our own. Because both of their incomes were modest, it took a long time to scrape together a respectable down payment.

I regretted leaving behind my pink bedroom at the Madison Street house. Instead, I grew into adolescence sharing a bedroom with my two brothers. My parents bought us a three-tier bunk bed set. As the oldest, I got the top bunk bed. Tim got the middle bed, and Kenneth got the bottom one. I suppose it was the best my parents could do in that crowded two-bedroom apartment.

That neighborhood was rife with crime and occupied by people who probably had lived there most of their lives. We viewed the neighborhood as temporary and never really fit in as a two-parent family. Our apartment was robbed once, and my brothers sometimes got shaken down for cash when they went to a corner market for my mother. We grew wary of staying outside after dark.

But, as with most things, even that horrible place had one good feature—a swimming pool, which we used regularly. All three of us learned to swim in that pool by watching other children. My parents could not afford swimming lessons or summer camp, so we made do with what we had. My brothers learned to swim faster than I did. I believe the younger you are, the less fear you have. But one day when I was nine years old, I decided to put my fear aside and jump into the deep end of the pool.

My brothers were being unusually kind that day. Normally, I was their tackle dummy. But this day, they swam to opposite sides of the deep end of the pool and encouraged me to jump in. "Don't worry, we will catch you," Kenneth said, hanging on the pool ladder on one side. He was six years old at the time and swam like a fish.

"We are not going to let you drown," Tim chimed in, his arm outstretched like he was ready to swim to my rescue if I came up sputtering and waving for help. He was only seven years old himself.

I was all of four feet tall standing on the diving board, looking down at eight feet of water. I had never swum in water I could not stand up in. I was afraid, but I took a breath and jumped in, deciding to take my brothers at their word. The shock of going under the cool water held me still for a few seconds. Then I began to appreciate the aquamarine peacefulness and silence. I kicked my feet experimentally, touching nothing and scaring myself—just a little. I focused on holding my breath, and I looked up at the surface several feet above my head. I used my arms to help pull myself toward the sunlight. Once my head breached the surface I could breathe again, so I treaded water for a few seconds to get my bearings. I saw Tim on my left side, holding the pool ladder, and Kenneth holding on to the one on the right. He looked a tiny bit closer, so I put my head down and swam as fast as I could to the ladder Kenneth was holding.

When my hand gripped the ladder and I began climbing out of the water, my brothers cheered for me. "We knew you could do it!" Kenneth yelled.

"I never had any doubt," Tim added, grinning.

I had trusted them to keep me safe. I felt warm and loved that day—a most unusual feeling when it came to my brothers. They normally showed affection by wrestling with me or giving me a knuckle sandwich. But I never feared deep water after that again. It was no wonder they both became lifeguards as teenagers. They inspired confidence in the water. For me, it was the beginning of a lifelong love affair with water and swimming.

It was a good thing we learned to swim as children because, on his good days, my father shared one of his passions with us—fishing.

He woke us before dawn; we dressed in the dark and piled into whatever used sedan we owned at the time for the long drive down to the Chesapeake Bay. We rented a not-quite-seaworthy motorized dinghy, but my brothers loved it and climbed eagerly aboard. My mother joined in, showing false enthusiasm in the name of family harmony. I came aboard last, skeptical but resigned because they could not leave me home alone. While they threaded squirming bloodworms onto their hooks and dropped their fishing lines overboard, I sat there, ignoring them all, nose buried in a book as the waves bobbed our little motorboat up and down on the bay.

When the sun rose high and the morning mist burned away, my father usually said it was time to head back to land because prime fishing time was over. One time, when he started the outboard motor, it slipped from its mooring and fell to the bottom of the Chesapeake Bay. We were a few miles from the nearest shore.

Wide-eyed, my father turned to our mother. "You think I should dive in and try to get it?" he asked her, trying to sound brave, but his eyes looked worried. We had no idea how deep the water was in the middle of the bay.

"No, don't do that!" my mother said, frightened at the thought of his drowning while trying to drag a heavy motor to the surface—if he could even find it in the murky water. It was bad enough we were stranded with no radio, no telephone, and no help.

"They probably are going to expect us to pay for that motor," my father said softly, clearly worried that he could not afford it.

"Well, we have to worry about that later," my mother said. "Right now, we have to figure out how to get back."

I eyed the long distance to the nearest shore and knew we could not swim that far without exhaustion. My father, my brothers, and I could swim, but my mother could not swim well at all, especially in deep water. She never learned how to breathe while swimming. She could only swim a short distance while holding her breath. That would not work in this dire situation.

My parents looked around our little boat for whatever supplies they could find. After some careful shifting of seats so we did not capsize the boat, we found two wooden oars. "Maybe I can row us back in," my father said. He took the oars, settled himself on the boat's middle bench, and began slowly rowing. As I watched the muscles in his back move with each pull of the oars, I thought of the Marine he used to be. He had to be strong then. He is still strong now, I thought, gratefully.

Gradually, the shore grew closer. It took a couple of hours, but we made it back to the pier, relieved to hop off the boat and onto solid ground again. When my parents went into the little shack to explain what happened to the motor, the owner took their word that the motor had not been secured well enough to the boat. He had seen my father rowing in for miles before we stepped ashore. He did not charge them and waved them off.

My parents were so relieved, they never questioned his motives. In hindsight, I think he may have been worried about his own liability, sending the public out in a boat that was not seaworthy and dangerous to operate. He was probably just glad it never occurred to them to sue.

Not long after that, history took precedence in our lives. Four years after President Lyndon Johnson signed the Civil Rights Act of 1964, which forced several reluctant states toward equality for all, the next shoe to drop was mandatory school desegregation. The federal government finally got fed up with the Southern states dragging their heels on implementing the Supreme Court's *Brown v. Board of Education* decision of the 1950s, and started pressing local jurisdictions to comply.

We had no idea what to expect. As a people, we believed we should stand up for equal rights, but our biggest hero had been killed senselessly in Memphis, Tennessee, for rattling the cage of oppression to shake loose more freedom. What would happen next? It did not take long for us to find out.

My brothers and I got swept up in forced busing to help the school district better integrate its schools. I spent only half of my fourth-grade year in the Southeast elementary school near our home. I had a lousy teacher who spent all morning talking in the hallway to other teachers. If anyone dared whisper to another child out of sheer boredom, she came back into the classroom and made us all write, "I will not talk in class" 100 times. When my parents received the notice that we would be bused across town to an all-white school, I was relieved to get away from her. I had not learned anything in her class.

When notified about the abrupt change, our parents were understandably nervous. They spent their entire education in segregated schools. Like everyone else, they watched television news, witnessing cities across the nation erupting into violence as furious white parents pelted buses of black children with rocks, trying to prevent the races from mixing in public schools. In some South Boston neighborhoods, they saw white parents armed with clubs, rocking buses full of terrified black children, trying to tip them over.

We were slated to transfer to Fillmore Elementary School, a small red-brick schoolhouse in Georgetown, the toniest neighborhood in Washington. As children of the South, my parents were conditioned by a life where lynching people was not unusual and segregation was the norm. They knew it could get nasty if the Georgetown parents decided to oppose our enrollment at Fillmore that semester.

My parents passed their fears on to us; we were nervous on our first day. Getting up before dawn peeked over the horizon, my mother made sure each of us was neat, clean, and dressed in our best school clothes. She hoped we would make a good first impression on our new teachers and classmates. From one end of the city to the other, our new school took an hour to reach. I had butterflies in my stomach that morning when we stepped off the bus in front of the all-white elementary school. Because of what I had seen on television, I was waiting for people to start throwing bottles and rocks at us. We kept looking up and down the brick sidewalk to see if a crowd of white parents was on its way to attack us. But there was no crowd that chilly January morning at 35th and R Streets NW. There was only silence. We later learned the few white parents who objected to their children being educated with us decided to put them into private schools instead. The white children who remained evidently had parents who hoped for the best, or were open-minded enough to give integration a chance.

Our busload of sixty children filed into Fillmore and went to the classrooms assigned to us without making a sound. The white children stared at our brown faces, but were mostly polite. A few even smiled as we sat down. The teachers called the roll to make sure all the black children were in the right classrooms, and then began their daily instruction as if nothing special had happened. It was such a smooth transition that when I told my anxious parents about it that night at dinner, they were relieved. They had believed we would be stoned or worse. Thankfully, none of that happened.

Within a few days, I made several white friends and began to enjoy my new school immensely. I loved being challenged by school-work that was more advanced and comprehensive. I soaked it up like a dry sponge plopped into a bucket of water. These years turned out to be some of the very best of our early education. We were proof that the old segregationists' creed of "separate but equal" was anything but. At Fillmore, our supplies were more plentiful, our teachers were better, and our subjects were more challenging. We were learning more than we ever had before, thanks to desegregation.

One of my best memories is from fifth grade with Mrs. Johnson, an African American teacher who, with just a few encouraging words, opened my eyes to a career path from which I have never deviated.

Mrs. Johnson insisted that every student write a short story and hand it in on Fridays. Over the weekend, she would grade them and read from some of the best ones on Monday morning during English class. She often read my stories out loud. My face would grow warm, the equivalent of a black person blushing, then flush with deep pleasure. One Monday afternoon, Mrs. Johnson pulled me aside after class. "Gail, your short stories are wonderful," she said. "You should consider being a writer or a journalist when you grow up."

With that, she planted a seed in me that bloomed and became my obsession. At eleven years old, I knew exactly what I wanted to do with my life. I have never wanted to do anything else. I have always been a writer, first as a journalist, then in corporate public relations.

This is why good educators are so important. If it is the right kind of positive reinforcement, their influence can affect a child's entire life. Having such a good public school was critical for us. We were African American children with parents of modest means who could not afford private school. They didn't have the money for the Girl or Boy Scouts or to send us to a sleepaway camp. School was it for us. It was the centerpiece of our development into productive citizens— it was critical that our free education be as good as possible.

I liked Georgetown. It was such a cosmopolitan part of the city. Both historic and hip, it attracted an international crowd, plus heavy hitters in Washington whom I found fascinating. One day in fifth grade, Mrs. Johnson told us we were going to have an important visitor that afternoon. I didn't think much about it, more focused on finishing my papier-mâché mask and getting the paint just right so it could be hung in the exhibition hall at our school. I turned in my purple masterpiece and waited for that afternoon, when we would see them all mounted for display.

After lunch, Mrs. Johnson called the class to attention and gathered us in a line to follow her to the exhibition area of our small school. I took a seat in the auditorium/cafeteria and waited with all the other children for our important visitor. A few minutes later, a group of men wearing earpieces and suits came into the auditorium. Right after that, Vice President Hubert Humphrey walked in, smiling and waving to us. My eyes widened, but I said nothing as the other kids chattered excitedly.

Our principal smiled widely as she escorted Vice President Humphrey toward our exhibit of amateur masks. Suddenly, he stopped at mine. My heart did a little uneven flutter in my chest.

"Who did this one?" he asked, looking at the assembled students.

I raised my hand nervously. He smiled when he saw my hand. "Why don't you come up and tell me more about it?" he said, beckoning me to join him.

I walked up to him almost in a daze, glancing only once at the Secret Service agents standing at attention all around the room. When I got close enough, the vice president leaned down so he was eye level with me. His smile seemed genuine. Up close, I noticed how red his skin looked, but otherwise he looked as he did in all the news pictures I had ever seen of him.

"That's a very pretty mask," Vice President Humphrey said. "What does it represent?"

"It's an African mask," I replied, surprised my voice came out so even. "Something a warrior would wear."

"I see that now," he mused. "Yes, it's very good. Congratulations."

If my skin were not brown, he would have seen me blush at his compliment. My face suddenly felt warm, and I grinned, showing my crooked smile.

He stood back up and moved on to other papier-mâché masks, so I went back to sit down before my teacher could urge me to return to my metal auditorium chair. I was stunned for a minute, amazed I had been singled out by the second most powerful man in our country, if not the world. I never forgot that couple of minutes of limelight. It made me doubly glad I was a student at that Georgetown school. I am certain the same thing would never have happened to me at my horrible elementary school in Southeast Washington.

That night, my mother clapped with glee when I told her what happened to me at school that day. She took any tiny accolade we received as proof her children would grow up in a better world and have opportunities she never did.

I loved that elementary school so much. I especially loved all my new friends. The freedom to be myself was refreshing, to study and excel without fear of being beaten up for it, like I was at my old school. One of my best friends during these halcyon days was a girl named

Julie. Her father was the ambassador to Thailand. She told us he had been recalled to Washington during some unrest in Bangkok, so her family moved back to the United States after living abroad for many years. I could tell living among diverse people had opened Julie up to the idea of having friends of all colors. She always treated me as her equal, which at that fragile time in our nation's history was the ultimate compliment.

Julie invited me and a few other girls in our class to a sleepover at her house on a Friday night. I was wildly excited when my mother allowed me to go. She rarely let me go to sleepovers, probably because of the terrible neighborhood we lived in. But she believed my Georgetown friends were nothing like the kids in our neighborhood. She was right.

When the day of the sleepover finally arrived, I packed a small overnight bag with my pajamas and other essentials and brought it to class. After school that afternoon, about five of us followed Julie home to her house a few blocks away on the cobbled streets of Georgetown. We chattered excitedly the whole way, anticipating the hours of fun ahead of us. It boosted my self-esteem enormously to be viewed as just one of the girls. Even though I was the only African American girl invited, everyone treated me the same as everybody else. After my short lifetime full of segregation and mistrust between the races, it was a gift.

That evening at Julie's, we ate too much junk food, played games, and watched television, giggling a lot as young girls do. I fell asleep staring at all the pictures Julie's family had taken in Thailand. It looked like an exciting and exotic place to a little black girl who had never left the United States. I promised myself I would go to Thailand one day when I grew up. Such a little bit of exposure to lives so far removed from my own helped open my mind and gave me an education I am still grateful to have received.

Many years later, I thought of that sleepover as I booked a twentieth wedding anniversary trip to Thailand with my husband. Julie was not at the forefront of my mind, but she was somewhere there in the background, smiling at me as my husband and I blended into the hyperactive crowd in Bangkok, and as I snorkeled in the serene Indian Ocean offshore Phuket Province and the Phi Phi Islands.

My glimpse of Julie's world may have cemented my need for international travel, but she was not my first influence. My mother's sister Comila moved to Turkey with her husband, Nathan, when I was five years old. He had enlisted in the US Air Force. Turkey sounded so far away. I could barely picture it as a child. My aunt always brought me gifts from overseas, which made it a bit more real to me. She repeated the practice when they moved to Japan, further exposing me to a wider world with infinite fascinations.

They moved back to the United States when I was eleven. Aunt Comila paid for my first airplane ride after inviting me to stay a couple of weeks at her home on Cape Cod, Massachusetts. I was so thrilled looking out that airplane window. I saw the ground far below, houses just dots on a vast landscape. The trip reinforced my determination to travel the world when I grew up, just as soon as I could afford it.

I loved the two weeks I spent with my aunt and uncle on Cape Cod. My aunt loved having a little girl around. They were childless at that point, but they later adopted a son, my cousin Orrin, who grew up to be a wonderful father, husband, and musician.

Aunt Comila had some peculiar notions about what upper-class folks were like. She clearly wanted me to have the best that life could offer, so she used to correct me and make sure my table manners were good, my long hair was properly combed and braided, and my clothes were neat and clean. But her funniest instruction ever was, "Wear a clothespin on your nose. You want your nose to come more to a point."

I looked in the mirror at my wide, stubby nose, wondering about what she said. It looked okay to me. It fit in fine with my almond-shaped eyes and ordinary mouth. "If you don't have a clothespin, just pinch and pull the ends of your nose whenever you remember," she said in her shrill soprano voice. "That way, when you grow up, you will have a cute, pointed nose."

A pointed nose like whom, I wondered? White people? Is that

who she thought I should emulate? Her advice puzzled me. I knew no amount of pulling on my nose as an eleven-year-old was going to change it much, but I humored her while I was visiting, pulling on the end of my nose whenever she looked my way. Every time I pulled on it, she would smile with pride and trill, "Yes, that's it! You're going to be such a pretty woman when you grow up!"

She encouraged me as often as she critiqued me. I missed her when I had to leave the lovely shores of Cape Cod and head back south to Washington. It was depressing to go back to that two-bedroom apartment. It was too crowded for our family, let alone our Labrador retriever, Sandy, whom we tried to keep there for a few years.

I loved Sandy. One of my mother's students had offered her the dog and she accepted it. But Sandy was meant for hunting and running in the great outdoors. He was not meant to be confined on a second-floor balcony sleeping in a makeshift doghouse. The poor thing used to bark a lot because the neighborhood kids would throw rocks at him whenever we were not around. After Sandy gnawed on my mother's brand-new sofa, then started running away from home, we had to give him to another family. We couldn't afford to move yet, and Sandy needed a house with a backyard.

Affordability was always a sore point in our small Southeast apartment. We never had enough money for anything as my parents scrimped and saved to buy a house. We were still living there when I turned thirteen and my menstrual period began. As preteens, our parents had treated us as if we were all the same gender. I was just one of the boys. But it grew awkward for me when I reached puberty. Small breasts suddenly sprouted on my chest overnight, and I became embarrassed to undress in front of my brothers in the room we shared. My mother noticed and allowed me to start sleeping on the living room sofa instead. I used our hallway bathroom to dress in privacy. Unfortunately, puberty also brought on more sickle cell crises for me as my red blood count dropped suddenly once a month. But the disease's impact on my bones was the worst side effect in my early teens.

When I was fourteen, I remember listening to a favorite song on the radio. I tried to sit cross-legged on the floor—only I could not do it. Weren't kids supposed to be their most limber at such a tender age? My right hip felt jagged, and forcing it to rotate into a squat position caused me severe pain. My right hip bone refused to cooperate, and I had to sit with my legs straight in front of me.

A few weeks later, my family went on its first, and only, camping trip to Canada. Preparing for that trip was one of the few times I ever saw my father excited and happy about anything. "I am Canada bound!" my father sang as he moved about our apartment enthusiastically packing our belongings. He had likely never left the country or taken a vacation that did not involve visiting relatives. That was a common practice for people of my parents' generation. Any trip out of town was usually reserved for visiting family. He and my mother had rented a camper for the first time in our lives. I have no idea who came up with the idea, but my father had a trailer hitch installed on our sedan and he towed that camper round-trip from Washington to Canada.

The camper required some assembly; the tent half popped up and the bottom half remained a solid metal trailer. Two large double beds anchored the tented sides of the trailer, while a long cushioned sofa, which doubled as kitchen seating, sprawled along one edge. That was my bed for the duration of our two-week camping trip. My parents shared one double bed while my brothers shared the other. Once assembled, the camper was quite cozy with a small stove, refrigerator, and portable toilet.

We stopped about halfway on our trip at a campsite in Erie, Pennsylvania, so my father could rest and drive the rest of the way to Canada. We got an odd vibe when we pulled up to the registration office at the camp. The proprietor took our money and pointed out where we could hook up to water and electricity for the night but was not at all friendly. Apparently, we were also the first black faces our fellow campers in Pennsylvania had ever seen. As we set up the camper and settled in, everyone at the campsite kept to themselves and did not speak to us. At one point, two little boys invited Kenneth to join their game, but his face fell with disappointment as their mother pulled them away and turned her back on him. My parents, used to this kind of chilly reception from whites, told us to stay close to our camper as they set about building a campfire and preparing dinner. We went to bed early that night since we were all tired from the day's long journey.

When my father roused us early the next morning to begin breaking down the camper, we gaped at the deserted campground. Every white family must have packed up and left during the night rather than camp close to us. The empty campground was eerie, but the feeling of total rejection because of our skin color was worse.

My parents shrugged it off, telling us to hurry and get ready for the day's travel. Once on the road, we resumed our car games. My mother drilled us on state capitals every time we spied a car license tag from another state.

We stayed a couple of days at Niagara Falls, then continued north to a campsite in Ontario that boasted a cold, clear lake. Our reception there was completely different than it had been in hostile Pennsylvania. The Canadians were warm and welcoming. Within a couple of days, we had befriended several campers and spent lazy afternoons swimming and fishing. At night we laughed, sang, and danced around the campfire.

On one of these balmy summer days, I was playing with some other kids my age who were taking turns riding a bike. When it was my turn, I fell and could not get up.

"Gail, get up, honey," my mother said when she saw me on the ground.

"I can't, Mommy!" I said. "I'm trying. I really can't."

No matter how many times I tried, I could not get the bicycle pedal to rotate but two-thirds of the way around its track before my hip stuck in place, grinding bone on bone inside my right hip socket. The right side of my pelvis burned with pain, and as I writhed on the ground, I knew that this pain and my inability to sit cross-legged on the floor were related. I tried several times to push to my feet, but the pain in my hip left me gasping. My mother had to come over and help me stand up.

She was alarmed, but we finished our vacation in Canada. As soon as we returned home, she took me to see an orthopedic surgeon, a German woman at the HMO in Washington. The surgeon looked grim after examining me. She *tsked, tsked* over my X-rays, sucking on her protruding front teeth.

In a very stern voice, she told my mother that my hip had collapsed on the right side.

"Her hip is deteriorating, probably from her sickle cell disease. It will only grow worse with time," she said. "Eventually, it may become difficult for her to go to the bathroom," she added, squatting awkwardly over an imaginary toilet seat to demonstrate. "If she were an older patient, I would recommend surgery to replace that hip. But she's still too young and her bones are still growing."

Instead, she prescribed something much worse: bed rest for an entire year. She thought taking my body weight off that fragile hip might give it a chance to heal. I was stunned. I was only fourteen. She may as well have sentenced me to prison.

For the next year, I had to use crutches just to hobble to the bathroom. Whenever we left our small apartment, my parents pushed me around in a wheelchair. To say I was crushed to have to spend my ninth-grade year in bed while a public school tutor came in daily to teach me is an understatement. At the time, it seemed like the end of the world.

But I did get some good news: I was able to leave the hideous Anacostia junior high school I was forced to attend after being yanked out of my cozy Georgetown environment. I was relieved to be away from classmates who, to my young mind, all seemed to be either gang members or teenage mothers—or sometimes both. After two years of wrangling red tape, my mother finally managed to get me back into a Georgetown junior high school with a stellar reputation. My little brothers were still attending Fillmore

Elementary School, which was just down the street from my new junior high. I got to spend two glorious weeks at Gordon Junior High on Wisconsin Avenue NW, and I made some new friends before my surgeon, once again, put me on bed rest.

One night during my endless bed rest, my father returned home to our small apartment, weaving and clearly drunk. "Walk!" he slurred at me, his lips curling into a sneer. Although this kind of nightly abuse was not uncommon, he rarely singled me out. "Walk, I said!" he shouted, probably remembering his days as a drill sergeant in the Marines.

But I did not immediately jump up and follow his orders, which must have, deep down, broken his heart. Instead, his only daughter remained helpless and confined to the bed, crutches leaning against the headboard, wheelchair parked in a corner. It was not yet time for my nightly transfer to our living room sofa, where I slept at night.

"I can't," I said, and tears sprang to my eyes. "I wish I could, but I just can't."

Disgusted, he turned away from me and walked unsteadily down the hallway to the kitchen. Eventually, he sat down somewhere and passed out. His snores told me the episode was over for now.

No matter how frustrating it was for my parents to see me bedridden, I did not need my father's added pressure. It was bad enough my body was failing me so young. Didn't he think I would much rather be healthy and attending my new junior high school? What teenager would ask for this—being on house arrest because her hip collapsed under her? I saw no friends during my confinement. Who would come anyway? The girls I used to know in Georgetown? Or the few I knew at that dangerous junior high down the street? Neither was a realistic option for me, so I was isolated with only my immediate family for company.

Books were my only other companions. When I wasn't studying the four subjects I needed to graduate, I was devouring fifty-cent Harlequin romances at the pace of one a day. I used them to escape my dreary, bedridden life. Through them, I could travel the world, have adventures, and fall in love with tall, handsome strangers until I turned the last page.

On weekends, my parents sometimes took me along to the mall or on other errands so I could get out of that small apartment. They stuffed my wheelchair into the trunk of our car, and I joined my family for outings. But I was, to say the least, extremely embarrassed to be seen like that. Teenage self-image is fragile enough without being stared at and called "a cripple" by the crueler teenage boys who hurled the insult at me whenever I emerged in public. I watched the spittle fly out of their mouths as they jeered at me. I had to grow a thick skin and a stiff spine to endure their taunts. I tried to ignore them with as much dignity as I could.

My mother advised me to hold my head up and pretend they did not exist. I followed her advice and did my best to endure it. By keeping my eyes focused on the future I was determined to have, I found an inner strength I never had to flex before. This focus kept me motivated to study hard and earn the excellent grades I would need to go to college and get away from my unhappy home life as fast as possible.

While I healed in bed, my parents continued to save money and look for a single-family home that they could purchase. Finally, my mother found an all-brick house in Fort Washington, a suburb in Prince George's County that was being developed in 1971. It took her a little bit of time to convince my father we could afford it, but we moved in just before I was allowed to get out of bed and begin high school.

Friendly High School was newly built and 98 percent white when I hobbled in on crutches, carrying a backpack for my books. All eyes were on me as I slowly traversed the long hallways on my first day in September of 1972.

Every day was a physical struggle for me. After a year in bed, I had to build up my endurance, and the route to school was an obstacle course for a girl on crutches. Early each morning, I walked three blocks to my neighborhood bus stop. I climbed the school bus steps slowly, hopping up each one, using my stronger upper body to maneuver the crutches, then swinging my lower body up the steps before awkwardly making my way down the bus aisle to the nearest empty seat. Once we reached the school, I slowly lowered myself down the bus steps, then got into my swinging rhythm—crutches, legs, crutches—on my way to class, doing my best to fit in.

I tried to ignore the stares. Once in a while, I would get a smart aleck, usually a teenage white boy, who would christen me "Crip," short for "crippled," just to get a laugh out of all his friends.

I could have turned inward, sinking into a woe-is-me depression, wallowing in the pain of my disease. But instead I turned outward, to the world. Even at that young age, I sensed that trying to pull others toward me was a better way of enduring my difficulties than was isolation, particularly in the social cocoon of high school. I soon made several friends of my own, which allowed me to ignore the bullies. I never told any of my new friends the real reason I had to use crutches. It was too difficult to explain sickle cell disease to people who had never heard of it, so I would just say I had brittle leg bones and leave it at that.

I walked a tightrope in that school. As an outgoing African American girl, I tried to have both black and white friends. Many of the black kids in that school were not used to blending with whites, but due to my Georgetown years, I was quite comfortable. Most of my friends were white, a choice that became most noticeable in the school cafeteria.

When my lunch period came, I gathered my tray of food and stood uncertainly at the entrance where all the tables were filled with kids. The blacks, who tended to all sit together, were from a rougher, lower-income part of the region. Few of them had gone out of their way to befriend me when they learned my family lived in a wealthier neighborhood of Fort Washington, which, at the time, was more than 80 percent white. My white friends, who admittedly were a collection of brainiacs, if not outright nerds, always waved me over with a friendly smile and asked me to sit with them.

I often received a scowl in response to my tentative smile at the blacks' table, so I made my way toward the brainiacs, where I knew I would have some amusing lunch conversation. Making that choice made me an outcast with most of the black kids. I still interacted with one girl of color who was like me, but we were rare in that school.

Walking in the halls on my way to class, I often overheard some of the rougher black girls saying I was "acting white," which stung and confused me. I have never understood that. I could not change my color if I tried. Why is being smart and getting the most out of your education a "white" trait? It implies that to be black is to be dumb, which is absurd. So I did not see anything wrong with making friends with people who shared my views on high achievement through education. Although I couldn't see it at the time, I understand now that the black children's response to me was mostly informed by fear and insecurity in an environment where they knew their skin color was not a prized commodity.

I threw myself into a range of school activities and ignored my disease as much as possible. Because sickle cell disease compromised my immune system, I often developed strep throat and had to miss several days from school. A few times the strep was so bad, it tumbled me into a sickle cell crisis and I missed even more days of school, stuck in some god-awful hospital. I learned to dismiss my illness from my mind so I could focus on my studies, going on with my life after each crisis as if nothing had ever happened. Although my sickled cells represented a potential time bomb and caused me regular anguish, I still convinced myself that the mortal threat was still years into my future, even if my pediatrician's diagnosis was correct.

By my junior year, I was no longer using the crutches, and my French class was planning a one-week trip to Paris. I wanted to go so badly—the trip would quench my growing thirst for international travel—that I pleaded with my mother for permission.

"No," she said. "I can't let you go. What if you get sick? Who is going to help you way over there?" My mother had always been overprotective, but I was walking normally now after years of crutches and bed rest, and was beginning to despise the short leash she gave me. Right then and there I vowed never to let my disease keep me from doing anything I wanted to do—especially traveling the world—when I was the one making the decisions. If she had said we could not afford it, I would have understood. I had heard that all my life. But she used my illness against me—*that*, I could not forgive or forget.

By the time I was a senior, my brother Tim had joined me at Friendly. Seeing my popularity, he sometimes sneered at me and dug up that old childhood insult: Goody Two-Shoes. I excelled in my classes, earning grades that always placed me on the honor roll. I was elected class vice president that year, and I published several articles and some poetry in the school newspaper. I was one of the Morning Mouths, a handful of students who broadcasted school news every day over the loudspeaker system. I was also active in the French club, the yearbook staff, and the drama club, and I appeared regularly in school plays. I was very social and loved interacting with my friends.

Tim joined me on the school newspaper staff for a while, writing sports articles I was proud to see his name next to, but he soon lost interest and fell in with a crowd of delinquents and drug users. He could never compete with me academically and did not try. He brought home Cs and Ds with utter indifference.

He could not compete with our baby brother either. Kenneth was a gifted high school football player who was handsome and friendly; he had half a dozen girls vying for his attention all the time.

Tim never found solid footing between me and Kenneth. Our stellar roles in the family were firmly cemented before he could decide who he wanted to be. Instead, he goaded our mostly good-natured baby brother past his fury point, until their fists started to fly. Tim liked that Kenneth viewed him as normal enough to fight without holding back. I used to fear they would knock out my poor mother when she threw herself between them, begging them to stop. But most of the time, Kenneth stuck to his jock friends and Tim to his druggie friends—the two crowds rarely intersected.

I was so focused on graduating in the top 5 percent of my class, I paid little attention to their squabbles. On graduation day, I wore the gold National Honor Society ribbon on my cap and gown and sat with the other high achievers in the front row of my 500-member graduating class. My smile was even wider than usual because of the surprise scholarship I had received a few days earlier. My guidance counselor, a heavyset white man I rarely noticed, had recommended me for the Goal Setter Award. It was only enough to cover the cost of my books for four years, but I was so pleased he had seen something about me worthy of reward, especially because I hadn't realized he was paying attention to me.

I was accepted at every college to which I applied. I chose Syracuse University because it allowed me to pursue a double major. I wanted to study broadcast journalism and international relations because they both spanned my career interest in becoming a foreign correspondent one day.

Those spring days at the end of high school were a blur of parties and the senior prom.

I was determined to go to my senior prom even though no one invited me. In fact, my date card was pretty empty throughout high school because of the peculiar social structure. Only 5 percent of the student body was black; most of those students were female. The pool of eligible African American men was small, and it was made even smaller because the popular black athletes dated only white girls. The black girls who wanted to date black men were left single, or they dated boys from some other school. Only one black girl at Friendly dared to openly date a Jewish guy.

Left unescorted for my school's most prominent social event, I decided to act. One day between classes, I boldly walked up to a shy, quietly handsome African American boy named Elmer and invited him to be my date for the prom. I was a modern woman, right? So why shouldn't I do the asking? Elmer was taken by surprise, but he agreed to be my date, looking down with a shy smile as we exchanged addresses and telephone numbers.

On the big day, he arrived on time at my house in his used car. I was wearing a white Grecian-style gown, and he had on a rented tuxedo. He was nervous as he pinned the corsage on my dress. I pinned a flower on his lapel as well.

My mother was even more excited than I was. She made Elmer and me pose for a photograph to capture the moment. She had never seen her daughter on a date and had started to worry about me. (My crooked teeth did not help. My parents had not been able to afford braces for me yet. I would get that much-needed metallic grin just a few weeks before I left for college.) I told my mother not to expect me until almost dawn. She accepted my planned itinerary with equanimity and none of her usual overprotectiveness.

I had big expectations when Elmer and I joined a group of my friends at a prearranged dinner at a fancy restaurant in Crystal City, Virginia. I ordered duck à l'orange for the first time in my life. After dinner, we all went dancing at the prom, then attended some after-parties before finishing up with breakfast at someone's house. I had a wonderful time. Elmer was a perfect gentleman all night and deposited me at home around 4:30 or 5:00 a.m. My mother was still waiting up, eager to hear everything. I could tell she was living vicariously through me and was so excited, she couldn't sleep. I filled her in on all the details, yawning widely. She lay on my bed listening avidly, as though we were girlfriends, as I got undressed.

Even though everything went so well, Elmer and I never saw each other again. I was okay with that. It had been a means to an end for me. In a couple of months, I was going away to a college very far away. My mind was on that and nothing else. I could barely contain my excitement. I had looked forward to this point in my life for so long. I could barely wait to get away from home and begin my "real" life.

PART 2

Taking Off

CHAPTER 5

Ain't No Stopping Us Now

SYRACUSE, NEW YORK, 1975–1979

WE ARRIVED AT THE ROOM TOO LATE TO CLAIM THE WINDOW bed—no surprise, given the long line of cars that stretched for at least six blocks, snaking its way toward Sadler Hall. As each car pulled up to the entrance, frantic students and parents tumbled out, laden with an assortment of freshman essentials from stereo systems to fuzzy footwear. Upperclassmen wearing orange T-shirts helped move things along the best they could, giving instructions and directions, but it was still a painfully slow pace for new students to claim their assigned college abode.

When we finally located my open double room on the second floor, I saw that Linda, my roommate, had placed her stuff on the window bed. Evidently, she had dropped her stuff to claim the prime space before leaving to explore the campus.

I really did not mind, though my mother complained under her breath that I did not get the best bed.

"It's fine, Mom," I said, trying to jolly her along. I settled my things on the windowless side of the room before peeking out the open doorway to see how far away the communal bathroom was down the hall. I had never really liked undressing in front of strangers, especially in school gym showers, and I knew my new living arrangement would take some adjustment. I had new flip-flops for the showers to protect my toes against other people's athlete's foot and a plastic carryall for my toiletries that allowed water to drip easily away from my shampoo and conditioner bottles.

I had brought a small black-and-white TV that my cousin Evelyn gave me as a high school graduation present and a brand-new electric typewriter to help me compose papers for my classes. In 1975, these were prized possessions. I knew Linda would bring a radio. During the summer, we had exchanged letters, making sure we did not duplicate any items given the scarcity of storage in our tiny room.

My mother fussed around the tiny room a bit, putting matching sheets and a new bedspread on the single bed nearest the door. She wrote my name on my waste bin and claimed drawers and closet space for my clothes.

After helping me put some of my things away, my parents, dreading the long drive home, started making reluctant moves to leave. Suddenly, my mother grabbed me and hugged me tightly. I was the first of her baby birds to leave the nest, and at forty-one years old, she simply was not ready to let go. "You be good," she whispered in my ear. I understood that "be good" meant "stay out of trouble" and "do your best in class," both of which I planned to do anyway.

My father hugged me and kissed my forehead. He mumbled something I did not catch, but I could tell he and my mother were both afraid to leave me alone so far away from home. It was the first time we had ever been separated by so much geography for such a long period of time—I would not be home until Christmas. They were feeling uncertain. Would their baby bird be able to fly success-fully—or would she be forever grounded by her disease?

Still, as soon as I closed my door behind them, I leaned against it, sighing in relief.

"I am finally free," I whispered to myself. I continued unpacking and waited for my new roommate to return. All I knew about her was that her name was Linda and that she was from Schenectady, a town in upstate New York that, by the sound of it, was likely very white. I did not know if she knew I was African American or not. My name—Gail Campbell—did not give my ethnicity away. Neither did living in Fort Washington, Maryland—at least not in 1975.

But when she returned to our room, Linda was all smiles and I knew we would get along. She was one of twelve children, she told me, so she was used to sharing. We got to know each other a bit as we unpacked, then went to get a meal later in our dorm's dining hall. She told me she had grown up Catholic, had attended an all-girls Catholic school, and her German American family was politically conservative.

"Linda, I grew up in Washington, DC, and its suburbs," I said. "Where I come from, you can fit all the Republicans in a telephone booth, so let's not discuss either politics or religion, and we should get along just fine."

Syracuse was cold, and getting used to the climate took time. From October to April, the snow fell incessantly—in feet, not inches—and on some nights, the polar cold dipped below 0°F. I had never experienced anything like it. I learned the hard way it was too severe a climate for fashion boots—my toes almost got frostbitten my first semester. I became real friendly with the lined, insulated rubber boots sold at L.L. Bean. Most students had to walk to classes, so we bundled up in parkas, insulated gloves, and boots like we were going on Arctic expeditions. I lived in thermal underwear six months out of the year. I was excited to be at Syracuse, but the climate wasn't ideal for someone with sickle cell. Cold water or weather could cause my veins to constrict and lead to the onset of a sickle cell crisis.

It took a few weeks before I could admit to Linda that I had a life-threatening illness. I knew she would have to know since we were living in such close quarters. I always hated the way people looked at me after they knew. Sometimes, it was with pity. Sometimes, just surprise or even shock. I had to risk it, though. I did not want to frighten her too much when I suddenly went into a sickle cell crisis. With the stress of classes and the extreme weather, I knew it was inevitable, and I wanted to prepare her before it happened, as she would likely be the person who had to call an ambulance to get me to a hospital. Linda took the news very well, considering she had never heard of sickle cell anemia before meeting me.

The inevitability of a crisis could create a certain amount of stress by itself. I tried to put it out of my mind and focus on my work, but it still sat there, weighing on my mind. There really was nowhere I could go to escape it. So I tried to submerge myself in the newness and excitement of my new world.

I made it through the first few months of school without incident. Then, one night in October, my friend Maura dragged me to a Halloween party at a fraternity house. Unbeknownst to me, the frat boys had spiked the fruit punch with grain alcohol, which did not agree with me at all. Maura had to help me home, but I was beyond intoxicated—my body felt like I had the bends as I lay alone on my side of our room. Linda was out, not yet back from a date.

A few hours later, the bends turned into a crisis. Linda still wasn't home yet, so I had to walk across the hall to knock on my friend Elaine's door. I took a minute to explain to her that I needed immediate medical help, then lay back down because I was in so much pain.

Elaine ran down the hall to ask our resident advisor, Rachel, to call an ambulance, since none of our dorm rooms had telephones. The ambulance crew eventually arrived and hustled me onto a stretcher. They carried me out of Sadler amid many girls, dressed in pajamas and robes, staring at me in the hallway. Maura followed the stretcher long enough to tell me she would come to the hospital as soon as she could to see how I was doing.

I ended up at the SUNY Upstate Medical Center nearest my college campus. The interns and residents attending medical school there were not that much older than the undergraduates on campus. That night, the dark-haired resident on duty in the emergency room looked at me like a wise guy. He read my blood results and said, "I see you've been partying tonight. Your blood alcohol level is way up there." He sounded completely unsurprised. I was there from the party school after all, so he had seen his fair share of intoxicated students.

For me, it was quite unusual and never repeated again—not after he told me that alcohol makes my blood more acidic, which makes it sickle even more. I guess no one had seen a reason to pass along that tidbit before this point. I was virtually a teetotaler after that, even as I got older.

Maura and a few of my college friends came to see me at the hospital once doctors had gotten my crisis under control with narcotics, fluids, and an oxygen tube in my nose. I stayed hospitalized for a few days before returning to my dormitory.

By now, word of my disease had spread like a forest fire throughout the dorm. I was sure my crisis would change the way my dorm mates looked at me forever; it would turn me into a repository of pity. I vowed to myself that I would work to turn around that perception, overwhelming them with the potency of my vitality. I answered dozens of questions from concerned friends. Eventually, they were calmed by my matter-of-fact attitude, and my closest friends rallied around me.

They forgot all about it until the next time it happened. By then, they were more practiced and knew what to expect. It became as well-executed as any emergency drill. I signaled the need, and the closest friend would call an ambulance. That I always seemed to rally and return from the hospital almost good as new seemed to reassure them. Although I was often paler and thinner when I returned to school, I was able to rebound within a few days. I had to study a bit harder to catch up on whatever lessons I missed, but that was my life. There was no changing it.

The next year, Linda and I signed up to move to Lawrinson Hall, the dormitory next door to Sadler. It was a coveted high-rise, and it was coed, although the girls and boys lived on alternate floors because of the communal bath and shower rooms. Linda and I shared a split double room with a lovely view for the first semester. Then her older sister needed a roommate, and Linda felt compelled to move in with her. Maura, meanwhile, lost her roommate to a sorority, so I moved into Maura's spacious corner room.

No one could make me laugh like Maura. She was witty and very social. I would often return to our room to find Maura brewing a cup of tea and dancing around in her robe to her favorite Joni Mitchell album. Our study habits were like a study in opposite extremes. I spent a lot of time at Bird Library, nose buried in my books, fulfilling all the requirements of my double major. Maura spent a lot of time futzing about, and by the time she settled into studying, it was late at night and she would nod over her book, falling asleep, horn-rim glasses askew on her nose. I knew she wanted to major in social work like her mother and elder sister, Susan, but her father, who was a prominent obstetrician in Worcester, Massachusetts, wanted her to do something else. I don't think she ever decided exactly what, though.

She was one of nine kids in a rowdy, fun, Irish Catholic family. She embraced me and took me home to meet her family, many of whom embraced me as well.

That semester, I straddled the worlds of my white friends and my African American culture. My dear friend Elaine, whom I met the very first day of college, was a native Baltimorean and encouraged me to join the Delta Sigma Theta sorority. At Syracuse, the Deltas were prominent as a social service organization that did a lot of charitable work in the community, but they were also social powerhouses in the small world of African American life on campus. Their members were usually attractive and dynamic African American women with big plans for their futures. Each year, the sorority held an event to look over potential recruits, and Elaine insisted I go.

"Come on, Gail, it will be fun!" Elaine said gaily, tugging me along.

During my weekly call home, I told my mother about attending their tea.

"Gail, I always wanted to be a Delta!" she said, to my surprise. "When I was in college, the Zetas gave me a scholarship, so I felt obligated to pledge them, but I would much rather have been a Delta."

After talking to her, I looked at the Delta recruitment process with new, less skeptical eyes. Apparently, becoming a member of this group carried some gravitas I had never appreciated. There was also one more African American sorority on campus, but the women in Delta seemed more like me.

Elaine and I must have made the cut because, a week or two after the tea, we were tapped for membership. We were invited to become pledges for a grueling seven-week period of being "on line," which meant I had to travel in line with seven other young women, dressed in red and white, as we ran around together all over campus. We had to learn the sorority's history, rituals, and songs. We also had to practice "stepping," song and dance routines we would later perform publicly at step shows, where we competed against other sororities and fraternities. Being at the mercy of big sisters telling us what to do any hour of the day or night was nothing less than torture.

The stress of keeping up with all my classes and all of Delta's demands began to weigh on me. I was growing exhausted. It did not help that a young man named Peter had chosen to begin wooing me at the same time. I had to sneak out to meet him for a date in the afternoon just so I could make my Delta pledge meeting at night.

I knew something had to give. It was not going to be my grades, because Delta demanded a high grade point average. It was not going to be Peter, either. My love life was just starting to improve. So that left Delta—or at least what I perceived to be some of the sillier activities of pledging in those days.

One late, snowy night, one of the big sisters demanded we bring her a snack. She lived on top of a hill and expected me and my fellow line sisters to trek up there together. I didn't want to go, but they pleaded with me. So the eight of us trudged through three feet of snow all the way across campus to bring her something utterly unnecessary at that time of night. By the time I got back to my dormitory, I had a fever and the beginning symptoms of bronchitis.

The next day started with more grueling demands. By the time our evening meeting rolled around, I was light-headed with fever and not feeling at all well. I took a seat next to the other pledges, who sat in a row facing our stern-looking big sisters. I slouched down in my chair, placing my head against the back of it, exhausted.

One of the big sisters looked at me sharply. "Gail," she said, "sit up and cross your legs like a lady!"

My eyes narrowed. "My own mother can't make me do that," I said, possibly delirious with fever. "So *you* can forget it!" I did not change my slouch one iota, daring her to do something about it. At first, that big sister looked shocked. Then she frowned with disapproval—I don't think she ever forgave me, because we were never close after that.

Though I probably wasn't the perfect line sister, I was officially inducted into the Kappa Lambda chapter of Delta, along with my other line sisters, a few weeks later. Apparently, the pledge captains and lieutenants felt they had tortured us enough. We were now full-fledged members of the sorority.

The Deltas stressed civic involvement, so I chose volunteer work that suited my personality and beliefs. I worked a few hours every week at the local Planned Parenthood office. Early on in my life, I decided that I did not want to have children and risk passing my disease to another generation. While working at Planned Parenthood, I briefly flirted with the idea of having myself sterilized to ensure no pregnancies, even though I was not promiscuous. But something always held me back from taking that irrevocable step. Hope, maybe.

Because I could never bring a child into the world, I was prepared to live my life alone, hopefully traveling the world as a foreign correspondent. I was doing everything I could to prepare myself for that kind of career. It was never an impossible dream. All I had to do was finish my coursework so I could get on with it. I wanted to finish on time and finish strong so that I could get a good job that would help me explore the world. Falling short of that was not an option.

Being a Delta at Syracuse threw me into a fishbowl among the African American students on campus. Since we were often the source of many campus parties and entertainment, they watched everything we did. I can be very social when I want to be, but I prefer my privacy. Living in the limelight of sorority life was not for me. By my junior year, I moved off-campus to a coed house with Linda, as far away from most of my sorority sisters as I could get. I still showed up for official duties and volunteer work, but I kept my life private. I disliked the way they gossiped about each other, whether it was about boyfriends or hairdos and outfits. I never had sisters to gossip with, and my brothers didn't behave that way.

All my housemates were white, so keeping my two social worlds separate was easy. The house we shared, which was little more than a boarding house, reminded me of the house on *The Munsters* because it was so dark and forbidding. Linda and I shared one room, but everyone else had their own rooms and most went their separate ways, rarely socializing together. Maura's brother Paul was one of my housemates. He often teased me about different things, having met me through his little sister, but for the most part we kept to ourselves.

It was a tough year for me academically, as the Newhouse School of Communications demanded we focus on our specialties just as my international relations classes intensified. The Maxwell School of Citizenship and Public Affairs, the school that housed the International Relations Department, was no joke. It has produced many of the nation's leading policy wonks, so it's no surprise that studying world history and multiple political systems was mandatory. I also had to perfect my French, which I had been studying since the fourth grade. It was a prerequisite to speak more than one language, and I had to pass oral examinations with a high proficiency to prove it.

One professor, an expert in Eastern European studies, was so demanding that I could barely pass his class. At the same time, my new living arrangements were not always conducive to studying. One housemate in particular liked to blast his stereo while doing drugs with his friends. To cope, I spent most of my time at the library, but there were not enough hours in the day to absorb the copious amount of reading and political analysis necessary for his class.

There had been several rapes reported on campus; walking home late at night was not the safest thing to do—especially in the wooded area near the boarding house. I managed to remain safe, even though my head was always buzzing with information for all my classes. Of course, with all that uphill trudging in the brutally cold winter weather, stressed to the max with thirty pounds of books in my backpack, I ended up in the Upstate Medical Center just as my first semester final examinations were starting. This crisis made me so sick for so long that Linda became worried and called my parents.

By the time the hospital was ready to discharge me, all of the other students had already cleared out for winter break. My parents drove up from Maryland to take me home. By that time, my depression was extreme. I had missed all my final exams and could not believe my disease had betrayed me, again, and at such a pivotal time. I shut down, feeling hopeless. I did not eat or sleep much, and I could not ease my anxiety. When my parents arrived in my hospital room, I was thin and listless. I barely responded when they spoke to me. My father was alarmed. He thought maybe I had been physically attacked, but the doctors assured him that was not the case.

The extreme pressure I put on myself to succeed and waste not even a penny of the tuition my parents had to borrow pushed me over the edge, and I just snapped. It was like my mind was trying to escape a body it could no longer count on. I felt detached from my life and viewed the world through a cocoon that just barely softened its sharp edges enough for me to cope.

I barely remember our long ride home. My parents tried to talk to me and would not stop asking me questions. My replies must have been odd, because my mother looked alarmed several times. While I don't remember the conversations, I *do* remember the looks on her face. Of course, the disease had to be in the back of her mind—was this how it would look when sickle cell started dragging me down?

At home, I often had nightmares that jolted me awake, clinging to my mother's hand in terror. She was so worried; she took me to see a psychiatrist, who prescribed some mood-altering pills. They pulled me out of my depression, eventually, and I was able to return to school in time for second semester. My parents could barely afford my tuition with my brothers now also in college. They suggested I take the semester off, but I refused, fearing I would never finish my education if I did. It would also ruin my plans to graduate as soon as possible and begin my *real* life—the one I hoped to have far away from them and the constant squabbles that were the mortar of life at home.

I did not need their added financial stress, so I tried to forget about it as I returned to Syracuse to begin the monstrous effort to make up for my illness. I had to carry thirty credits—or ten classes—that second semester. All of my professors from the first semester allowed me to make up my final exams due to my lengthy illness, which meant that in addition to extra classes, I had to study long and hard to score well on those missed exams. It was such an uphill battle, I almost snapped again under the pressure.

I did poorly on the final examination for my Eastern European history and politics class. The professor, tough as he was, did offer to let me retake the entire course since I had been ill, but I just could not imagine doing that with all my other schoolwork. I accepted the first D of my life. The college sent our grades directly home, and when my mother saw the D, she called me, alarmed. She had never seen one before, not from me. A teacher to her core, she barraged me with disappointed chatter.

"I know, Mom, I know," I said. "But I just cannot take that class again." I assured her that all my other grades were As and Bs, so my overall GPA should be enough to graduate on time. "You know what I have been through," I added. "I cannot succeed at everything."

In the fall of 1978, I returned to Syracuse for my senior year. To say the least, I did not have romance on my mind. Junior year had kicked my butt, and I simply didn't have time for dating. It was just as well. By then, I was tired of the men on campus and their Casanova games. The ones I had dated were like fireflies—lit up and interesting one minute, dark and dull the next. I had no interest in romance. I wanted to graduate and get my journalism career started. Elaine called it my "I hate all men" phase.

Of course that's when *he* walked into my life.

One rare sunny Saturday afternoon in October, my good friend Agnes visited me from Smith College. We were walking down one of the campus's main thoroughfares when a nice-looking African American man approached on the opposite side of the street. I had never seen him before. As we passed each other, I paused to say hey and nod at him. There were so few students of color at Syracuse; we tried to acknowledge one another when passing by. It gave us all a sense of unity to know we were not alone in that snowy, mostly white, northern city. However, this guy looked down and kept walking. Agnes and I looked at each other with eyebrows raised.

"He must like white women," I said, and she burst out laughing. We had both been through *that* before, especially with athletes. We shrugged, quickly forgot about him, and continued our weekend plans.

The next semester, I worked on campus at Shaw Dining Hall to support myself. Because I didn't financially qualify for the university's student aid program, which gave the best jobs on campus to the neediest students, all that was left was grunt work. I punched meal cards as students entered the hall, served meals behind the food counter, and prepared food in the kitchen between mealtimes. It was only bearable because I could bring leftovers home, which made my housemates happy and kept my own grocery bills low.

During one of my infrequent calls home, my brothers let me know our parents were working three jobs apiece trying to keep up with all our tuitions and the mortgage payment. Throughout our lives, they had never seemed especially skilled at financial planning, and were not always candid with us when money was tight.

I found out how bad things were at home when I traveled for an hour by bus to a Syracuse suburb to see my orthodontist. I had been wearing braces for three and a half years in college—my parents could not afford them before that. The orthodontist's billing clerk called me into the office. She told me the monthly payments my parents were supposed to be making to cover my dental expenses were several months overdue. I was mortified; I promised to begin making the payments myself and left.

When I got home that evening, I called home and spoke to my mother. "Why haven't you been paying my orthodontist?" I asked. "They called me into the office and told me they haven't been paid in months!"

"Oh," she moaned, breaking into tears. "We just can't afford it."

I hung up, depressed about my home life and glad I was hundreds of miles away. Tim told me later that our father's drinking was getting out of control again, and they never knew where his paychecks were disappearing. I was more determined than ever to make my own way in the world and never ask my parents for another dime as long as I lived. Clearly, I held my fate in my own hands. It was up to me to finish paying for my college education and anything else I would ever need.

Being so industrious junior year had helped. By keeping my head down and taking so many credits, I only needed six more in my last semester to earn my dual bachelor's degrees in international relations and broadcast journalism. I arranged to pay my own tuition with the help of a small scholarship I received from the Corning glass company. I was also able to get my braces off of my teeth a little earlier than anticipated. That helped me pay off my parents' debt and not incur any more.

Since I was on my own financially, I needed every hour at the dining hall I could get to pay for rent, food, and tuition. I had my new white smile intact when I worked behind the cafeteria counter one afternoon, dishing up food for the students. I wore an apron and a hairnet to keep my long hair away from the food. My bare face was shiny with perspiration, and I was blowing a stray hair off my forehead when a man strolled in and slowly pushed his tray toward me. I looked up and caught his eye—he was the same man I had seen that time with Agnes who would not speak. Up close, his dark brown eyes were warm and crinkled slightly when he smiled.

While we were staring at each other, I felt a frisson of something, a tickle along my spine. It was like my soul shivered inside me. I had never met this man. But somehow, I *knew* him. More importantly, *my* soul recognized *his*.

Lynda, one of my sorority sisters, was in line just behind him. She saw the way we were staring at each other and stepped forward to make introductions. "Gail, do you know Howard Woolley?" I shook my head. "Oh, well," Lynda said. "Howard, this is my soror Gail Campbell."

I stared at him over the long glass partition that separated us. "Hi," I said, and smiled shyly.

"Hello."

His was the deepest, sexiest voice I had ever heard. That voice sent another little shiver up my spine. I felt flustered and embarrassed, knowing I did not look my best behind the steamy cafeteria food counter. My oversized apron and plastic gloves completed my flour-sack chic. Glamorous, I was not.

But that voice started me daydreaming. I thought he was a decent-looking guy when I first saw him walking around campus, but I was usually more attracted to the inside of a person, rather than his exterior.

I had never been drawn to pretty boys. A couple of people told me they thought Howard looked a bit like a popular dreamy actor of that time. I wouldn't go that far.

Howard becomes most attractive to me when he opens his mouth. When he speaks, he becomes something so much more than handsome; he becomes irresistibly sexy. His deep velvet baritone rumbles right through me, deliciously tickling everything along the way, from my ears down to my toes.

If he could sing, he'd be the next Barry White or Lou Rawls.

All these thoughts ran through my head lightning fast, but I came back to myself several seconds later. On his side of the counter, Howard smiled at me again, nodded, and moved on down the food line before heading out to the cafeteria to find a seat. I wondered if his soul shivered as well. I could not help grinning as I looked down and finished serving other students in line. This, I thought, was certainly going to be interesting.

When I lived with Maura as a sophomore in Lawrinson Hall, she watched me look out our window and sigh at the boys playing ball games on the open field fifteen stories below our corner room. Our room had two walls of large windows overlooking a beautiful vista of the mountains on the horizon. Maura said she could never get my longing look out of her mind as I watched those college boys playing ball down below. She claimed I would sigh and say, "You would think just one of them would like me." My empty social life was temporary, as it turned out. I began dating Peter a few months later, but when it did not last, Maura was determined to play matchmaker for me.

During February of our senior year, the Deltas were planning a fundraising ball. Some of my friends were worried because I did not yet have a date. It was traditional for all the Deltas on campus to be escorted. My sorority sisters and I were the hostesses, and in our small social circle, it was unthinkable to show up solo at such an important public event.

I mentioned all this to Maura, who'd been there when our dormitory room was littered with red fabric scraps for the suit I was making to wear at a campus step-dancing competition, a requirement of all new pledges in my sorority. Maura called it my "Easter suit" because I ended up finishing it on her mother's old sewing machine in Worcester when she invited me home during spring break.

Linda and I lived around the corner from Maura during senior year. We were rooming with a third girl named Karen, who was in grad school. Neither of us knew her well. Some mornings at breakfast, Linda and I would raise our eyebrows at who came out of Karen's room after obviously spending the night with her. Once, an older man, apparently one of her professors, walked out of her room with a guilty smile. We didn't get it. Karen lived in plaid shirts and khakis, never wore any makeup, and somehow managed to be a femme fatale.

Even though Maura lived nearby, we saw each other only rarely since our classes were located in different parts of the campus. When I did see her, she nagged me about some guy who lived in her boarding house. As far as I knew, her house held a motley collection of students renting a bedroom apiece, but they had little in common beyond sharing a kitchen and a couple of bathrooms. Yet there was one guy living there she thought I should meet.

"Gail, you would like him," Maura said, with that Irish twinkle in her eye. "He shines his shoes!" Maura was short, curvaceous, and had the cutest bow-shaped mouth and long dark lashes. With her waist-length blonde hair and beautiful blue eyes, Maura never lacked for dates. Her type usually wore scuffed Top-Siders, khakis, and shirts rolled up their forearms. They all had Roman numerals after their last names, old money, and family yachts docked off Cape Cod or the Hamptons.

"He shines his shoes!" I exclaimed, looking at her like she was crazy. With her privileged Irish Catholic background and private schooling in Massachusetts, Maura likely had never seen a man shine his own shoes before and must have thought it was unique. I guessed that in her world, boyfriends had a butler shine their shoes before they escorted some debutante to a country club dance. "Maura, why would I care about some guy who shines his shoes?"

"Aww, Gail! He's really nice," she pleaded in her New England accent. "I just know you'd like him."

I stared at her. I knew and loved Maura with all my heart—she is one of my dearest lifelong friends. During the years I had gotten to know her, she had proven to be a liberal New England woman, so while the history of shoeshine men in the African American community immediately jumped to my mind, I am sure it didn't jump to hers, and I did not believe she was being racially insensitive by emphasizing that fact to me. However, Maura *was* a born social worker, so I hoped this was not one of her latest do-good projects I would soon live to regret. I decided to give her the benefit of the doubt.

"Okay, Maura," I said. "Only for *you* would I do this. You know I've had rotten luck with blind dates before," I said. I agreed to let her set me up with her housemate so I would have an escort to the Delta Ball.

The housemate turned out to be *him*! The man with the deep, velvety voice named Howard. The same guy my sorority sister had just introduced me to at the dining hall. He lived in Maura's house! His room was on the first floor near hers. How could I have gone so far through my senior year without knowing that?

One day shortly thereafter, Howard showed up in my meal line—a pure coincidence. In the course of punching his meal ticket, I invited him to be my date for the Delta Ball. He accepted shyly and I filled Maura in. She was thrilled!

But our first date was almost our last.

A few days before the event, Agnes called to tell me she was bringing five more Deltas with her for our ball. They were all sorors from Smith College, which did not allow sorority activities on campus, so they had pledged off-campus. A contingent of Deltas was also arriving from Cornell University, which had the same rules. With so many women coming without dates, I felt obliged to begin inviting single men to the ball on their behalf, hoping they would have potential partners for dancing.

As I punched meal cards in the dining hall, I began reminding young men that the Deltas were having a ball in February and that it would be nice if they attended. Many nodded agreeably and moved on into the dining hall.

The night of the ball arrived, and I was getting dressed with all my friends from Smith College, who planned to sleep over at my house before returning to school the next day. We all wore either red or white, Delta's colors. I had chosen a slinky red gown with a cutout of a rose trailing down my lean torso. My makeup looked good, my hair was behaving, and I was anxious to begin my date with the new man Maura thought was my ideal match.

Only Howard did not show up.

The clock kept ticking, and I started to worry we would arrive at the ball late. So I called Maura. "Have you seen Howard?" I asked. "We are all here at my house waiting for him. We're going to be late if he doesn't come soon."

"What? I'll go find him," Maura promised, hanging up.

She must have done some scurrying because she called me back a little while later to say she had found him at the Laundromat. "I told him you were waiting for him to go to the ball," Maura said. "He said he'll be right over as soon as he gets dressed."

Howard finally showed up at my house almost an hour late. He was dressed in a suit and a turtleneck sweater. I was appalled since it was a formal event. All of the ladies at my house were wearing ball gowns that brushed the floor. He could see the displeasure on my face. "Never mind," I told him. "Let's just go."

We piled into cars and headed to the ball. I said very little to him on the way, and as soon as we arrived and got settled at a table, I jumped up and started taking pictures—it was my duty as the chapter's photographer. When I returned to the table, Howard was dancing with Clarice, one of the Smith girls. Agnes was dancing with a freshman named Mark, and the other ladies had managed to snag dance partners. There were various drinks sitting around the table but nothing at my spot.

The only person left sitting at the table was my ex-boyfriend, Peter.

He looked at me, cleared his throat, and said, "Would you like to dance?"

I gave him an icy stare. "Hell no."

Our breakup had been messy. Apparently, the young lady he left me for had left him. He attempted a reconciliation my junior year, but I rebuffed him. It was way too late now to mend fences.

A few minutes later, Howard and Clarice returned to our table. They picked up their drinks and began chatting as if I were not sitting there. "I wouldn't mind having a drink," I said, looking at Howard, who was supposed to be *my* date.

"Oh, what would you like?" he asked, turning away from Clarice to look at me. I told him, and he ordered it for me. Somehow, we got through the evening. I don't even remember dancing with him. I just remember seething all night.

The next day, I ran into Maura on campus. "How was your date?" she asked, her face lit up with anticipation.

"Don't ask," I said. "And don't ever mention that man's name to me again as long as I live!"

"What happened?" she asked. I gave her the short version and continued on my way, trying to put Howard out of my mind. However, Maura, our self-appointed Cupid, decided to intervene. After talking to Howard, she finally put together what happened.

On the day of the ball, Howard encountered Mark, a freshman from Texas. Howard told Mark he was going to the Delta Ball. "I'm going, too," Mark said. "I'm going with this babe named Gail."

"I thought I was going with Gail," Howard said. Mark shrugged his shoulders and kept walking, his stride confident, his ego as big as his home state. Howard told Maura that he thought I was two-timing him before we had even gone on a date, so he went to do his laundry and forgot about the ball.

I was thunderstruck. Mark and me? Was he kidding? I wouldn't be caught dead dating a freshman. I was a senior! Then I remembered. Mark was one of dozens of young men I told about the Delta Ball when I was punching their meal tickets at the dining hall. Apparently, he had taken what I intended to be a casual group invitation as a personal one. "No, Howard was the only one I ever invited to the ball with *me*!" I told Maura. "Mark is completely delusional."

Maura said Howard also didn't like my jumping up and down all night leaving the table to take pictures at the ball. "But that was my job!" I protested. After all, I was the sorority's photographer! Maura said it had all been a big misunderstanding and encouraged us to try again.

So we did.

We went to a party given at a local nightclub by the Phi Beta Sigma fraternity. We got up every time the deejay began playing "Ain't No Stoppin' Us Now" by McFadden & Whitehead, humming the words under our breath as we swayed together in unison, rocking side to side to the catchy beat. If there is such a thing as having a theme song for a relationship, that song is ours. It seemed to sum up that phase of our lives perfectly. We were poised on the brink of a future together. We felt invincible and ready to tackle anything.

I introduced Howard to Elaine, who attended the party with her steady boyfriend, that night. The nightclub was too dark to make out anyone's features. But it didn't matter. Howard's voice entranced people. Elaine almost melted on the spot. Howard leaned in close so he could be heard over the loud music in the club and shook her hand, saying, "Hello, how are you?" in his deep, caressing tone.

"Gail," she breathed into my ear when he walked away to get us drinks, "he is *sooo* fine."

"Fine" was the highest praise for a man or woman. It meant

attractive, eligible, and acceptable on all levels. To the young ladies of quality we perceived ourselves to be, it was the Holy Grail. Unlike some of our acquaintances, we were always in search of future mates, not just temporary tumbles in the hay.

Elaine was not alone in succumbing to his charms. Howard told me later that several women who ignored him during his first few months on campus took a keen second look when he started appearing in public as my new boyfriend. Whoever Delta women dated was the subject of much scrutiny and even more gossip on campus, so other women sat up and took notice. Some girls asked me where I met him, giving him the full body once-over. "Around," I responded, always very circumspect about my private life.

Howard was still relatively new to Syracuse, so it was not surprising that some women didn't know him. He started as a junior when he enrolled as a transfer student, and although we were the same age, he was behind me by one academic year.

The African American men on campus would do about the same thing to Howard. "So, when did you hook up with that Delta?" they asked slyly, giving his shoulder an approving brotherhood bump.

Until I met Howard, I tried to keep my love life a secret. I almost never dated fraternity men, who gossiped like magpies. With an off-campus apartment, it was a little easier to maintain my privacy than when I had lived in the fishbowl of dormitory life. But keeping our relationship under wraps was not feasible on campus. Besides, I did not want to keep it a secret because I was in love for the first time in my life and I did not care who knew it. He must have been feeling the same because we went everywhere holding hands. People said we just glowed when we were together.

"The first time I met Howard, I could tell you two were *in love*," our friend Lorraine, who is now dean of the Newhouse School of Communications at Syracuse University, once told me. She has known us for more than thirty years. She was one of my editors when I worked as a reporter at the *Baltimore Sun*. "You don't see true love that often, but you two found it. It was hard to miss. It's like you two light up when you are around each other," she said.

Many other friends say the same thing. But none of them know the trials we have been through as a couple.

My illness has always brought a level of stress and commitment to our relationship that no one can fully understand. So it is ironic that my illness is the very thing that compelled me to fall for such a wonderful man in the first place.

I believe I truly fell in love with Howard in a hospital emergency room. We had only been dating a few weeks when I had a sickle cell crisis. All of a sudden, I didn't feel right. Within minutes, I was in extreme pain. I knew I was having a crisis. I was moaning and perspiring. I really didn't want Howard to see me in that state, but I let him call an ambulance and accompany me to the hospital.

"Please," I begged him. "I'll be all right now that I'm here in the emergency room. You can go now."

I didn't want him to see me suffering so much. I was the very definition of ugly. I looked like a bag lady. I was sweating so much from the pain, my hair was matted to my head.

"No," he responded. "I'm not going to leave you here all alone."

He looked so worried. He kept rubbing my face to reassure me and looking around for a doctor or a nurse. I could tell he was frantic to get me some relief.

"Really, it's okay to go," I pleaded. "I'll be all right. It's really late. You need to go home and get some sleep."

"No," he said. "I'm not leaving you."

"I don't want you to see me like this," I finally said, crying from both pain and embarrassment.

He stopped looking for a nurse and walked over to where I lay in an uncomfortable hospital cot. He leaned in close to my face, taking my hand in his warm, comforting grip. "You look like a princess to *me*," he said, kissing my dry, parched lips.

I fell for him right then and there.

This man was special. Somewhere inside I had known he was the one when I first saw him in that cafeteria. But with this, he proved it. My illness did not frighten him away. He didn't seem to care what I looked like, my eyes and nose red from crying. My hair was matted to my head, my clothes were wrinkled and disheveled, and I was tossing and turning from so much pain.

My illness had caused me so much agony, my conscience would not let me subject such a special person to even a small amount of that pain.

"You have to let me go," I whispered to him in tears. "I am not the right woman for you, not if you want children someday." My mind raced frantically. "I can't have children because of my illness. I refuse to pass this disease on to the next generation." Severe pain can make you a little crazy, but I remembered he told me he only had sisters and a couple of male cousins who either had daughters or were childless. "There won't be anyone to carry on your family name."

Yes, it was a wildly premature topic for a newly involved couple, but I live a very tenuous life, and situations like that are intense for me. I truly thought a breakup would be easier for him before we got too entangled. I knew I had to do the noble thing and stop it, before he got hurt later. But I couldn't say the words while he looked down at me with his heart in his eyes.

"I can't," he said, tears brimming. "I love you too much to let you go."

After I recounted that story to a reporter for *Ebony* in 1990, the magazine published an article calling Howard "a knight in shining armor." Yes, it is one of the world's most overused clichés, but in his case it is appropriate. He has been my knight in so many ways.

I knew Howard was pretty serious about me by the spring of my senior year, when he wanted to take me home to meet his mother during spring break. We caught a ride to New York City with one of his housemates, who lived relatively close to Howard. Howard had coached me a bit about the big city. He saw me as a sheltered girl, almost like Rebecca of Sunnybrook Farm. He told me I was whole-some, a trait he apparently treasured after his time with previous girl-friends, who were all street-smart New Yorkers.

As we entered the city, Howard's housemate decided to take 42nd Street. It might look like the set of a Disney movie now, but we're talking 42nd Street thirty years ago. There were hookers everywhere. One even came up to our car and pushed her bare breasts against the side window. It was like an X-rated carnival, a red-light district on steroids. My mouth fell open. Howard shooed her away from our car window as his housemate doubled over with laughter.

Eventually, we reached Howard's home in Jackson Heights, Queens. His mother lived in what appeared to be a massive city of co-op apartments, a concrete labyrinth. He had to ring a buzzer to get someone to let us into the lobby of the building.

I was nervous as I straightened my clothing, preparing to meet his mother. For any potential mate, this was a moment fraught with significance—and possible peril. I knew from our many conversations that Howard's mother was the center of his life. She had raised him and his sister Joy alone after his father Kelly passed away, when Howard was only twelve. I knew her opinion would carry a world of heft in any decision he made about a life partner.

I tried to be myself, as Howard had encouraged, and seemed to be getting along fine in my conversation with her. Suddenly she rose from the dining table. She looked down at me. "You rate," she said with a nod of approval. Then she walked away. But I felt a deep sense of satisfaction, an elation that bloomed in my chest. I had passed.

Two years later, on a sunny Valentine's Day in a small church near Andrews Air Force Base in Camp Springs, Maryland, Howard and I married.

PART 3

Soaring

CHAPTER 6

Life of a Reporter

MOST JOURNALISTS DO NOT WIN PULITZER PRIZES. MOST OF us just toil daily, sniffing out news like bloodhounds, unrecognized and unrewarded for our efforts to enlighten the public. I knew this when I was a journalism student. My first journalism class at Syracuse had over 500 students in it, and on the first day, the professor warned us that "only two will actually make it in the business." I had been bitten by the journalism bug in high school, when the Watergate scandal was exploding in my hometown. That was what sent me to Syracuse, along with a flood of eager young students in my generation—a yearning to follow the path that had just been blazed by Woodward and Bernstein.

My professors at Syracuse made sure my classmates and I did not believe we were the next Woodward and Bernstein, and told us that a Watergate story only came along once in a reporter's career, if ever. Nevertheless, I was optimistic as I walked across that stage on graduation day, holding degrees in both broadcast journalism and international relations in spring of 1979.

As I tried to break into the highly competitive journalism business after graduation, I was grateful to be able to return to my summer job working for Tourmobile, giving guided tours of Washington and

Arlington Cemetery in both French and English. Although Tour-mobile did not require it, I prepared a full tour in French to complement the English one I had to memorize for my job.

French tourists could easily see the bright red button that said "Français" on my lapel and would immediately break into rapid French when they caught sight of it. When they were overly eager with their questions, I sometimes had to slow them down, but they were so relieved to find someone bilingual in America, they forgave any small grammatical errors I might have made.

As an African American female speaking French in the United States or abroad, I was constantly mistaken for everything but an American. "Are you Haitian?" tourists asked. "Or from Martinique?"

"No," I said. "I'm American."

"Really?" the astonished tourist often said. "We didn't think Americans knew any other language but English."

"Some Americans do," I would say.

And then, dying of curiosity, the tourist might ask, "Where did you learn to speak such good French? Your accent is flawless."

"I learned right here in the USA." I tired of having to repeat this answer so often. I did not bother to mention that I had been studying French since I was in the fourth grade and continued to study the language in college as part of my degree.

That summer after college, my last with Tourmobile, I was voted "Tour Guide of the Year" by my colleagues. I think it was mostly by the all-male bus drivers who seemed impressed with my extra efforts to make the tourists feel comfortable.

Once, while we were stopped at a traffic light and I was rattling away in both languages to fill the dead time, a mounted US Park policeman rode his horse over to my open window.

"Hi there," he said, smiling, his eyes hidden by sunglasses.

"Hi," I replied, puzzled, thinking maybe we had broken some traffic law or another.

He leaned forward, close to my window. I leaned closer to listen.

"Can I get your number?" he said smoothly. "I'd like to call you for a drink sometime." He pulled the reins on his horse as it pranced impatiently, unnerved a bit by the teeming traffic on Constitution Avenue.

The entire busload of eighty-eight tourists was gaping at us. I was tempted to gape with them at this guy's nerve. "Uh, I'm working here," I said, polite but discouraging.

"Come on," he said. "It'll be fun."

"I don't think so," I replied, turning away from the window.

Thankfully, the light changed to green and the bus pulled away. The policeman wheeled his horse around and rode away. My bus driver smirked and said, "Never saw *that* one before."

"That makes two of us," I quipped before turning to resume my tour.

The Tour Guide of the Year honor came with a monetary prize and was presented to me by the company president at a staff party. I was quite surprised, actually. Maybe the drivers did not see the other tour guides going to so much trouble, but I was grateful to be singled out for the award.

While I worked at Tourmobile, I sent out resumes to TV stations and newspapers along with tapes of myself on camera reading the news and writing samples from my time as a college newspaper reporter. My journalism professors had advised me to start my career in a small market, such as Kentucky or Idaho. But that wasn't for me. I only sent resumes to markets where I thought I might possibly live, like the Southeast, mid-Atlantic, and Boston.

I ended up reaching out to dozens of media outlets. I even walked into a Washington station one day armed with my samples. The human resources person didn't exactly laugh at me, but I didn't get a job. In fact, I didn't get a single callback from anywhere, not even from backwater markets in the rural South. I was too naïve to realize that sending a tape or a photo of my smiling brown face probably did not go over well in many Southern markets.

Finally, after several months of applying for jobs, I got a break.

My cousin Tonya had been working as a dictationist at the *Washington Star*, one of my hometown newspapers, for a few years. She put in a good word for me with her bosses and the editors called me in for an interview. They only interviewed me for a dictationist's position. I would have preferred to start as a reporter right away, but they felt I was too green to start as a reporter in such a major market, even though I had just graduated from one of the best journalism schools in the nation.

The senior editor was frank during our interview.

"I hate hiring people like you," he said, "because you are bright and ambitious and will not stay." I looked at him innocently and thought it best not to reply.

They offered me the job, and I accepted. I was glad they offered me any position at all. I wasn't a reporter, but it was a real journalism job, I got my foot in the door in a major market, and I never had to do what my professors had told me to do. I knew I could do the job while keeping my eyes open for a better opportunity. I also knew I could push to cover stories other reporters didn't want to do—school board meetings, planning board meetings, neighborhood events, and the like. I could collect a few bylined articles to shop around elsewhere.

However, a dictationist's job was to write down exactly what the correspondents dictated. As a dictationist, I was not to edit their stories in any way, even though my fingers and brain itched to correct their poor grammar. That was the copy editor's job, I was told. After a few months of taking dictation from journalists—some of them world-famous—I yearned to begin my own career as a reporter. As predicted, I did write a few bylined articles that no one else wanted, but for the most part I took dictation from foreign correspondents, and that was not what I wanted to do with my life. I wanted to be a foreign correspondent myself. Listening to an aging reporter's whisky-sodden slurring on the other end of the telephone while he fumbled with his notes in a Middle Eastern phone booth was not the best way to spend my time as I tried to maneuver in the competitive journalism marketplace.

So, after just six months of dictation, I jumped ship when the *Baltimore Sun* offered me a job as a reporter. Of course, I started at the bottom rung, earning a mere $180 a week. Luckily, I rented an apartment in a seedier part of town for $200 a month, leaving money for food, gas, and my car payment, but very little else. I moved in with nothing but my girlhood bed, a bookshelf from home, and a kitchen table. But I was finally beginning my life.

All the senior reporters told me I had to pay my dues, which at the *Sun* meant covering the gritty police beat. In some cities, the police beat would not be too taxing, but in Baltimore, which was at the time the murder capital of the United States, it was grueling work. All the reporters claimed they had done it before climbing the ladder to more interesting beats.

As a rookie, I had to work nights from 4:00 p.m. to midnight. My only days off were Tuesdays and Wednesdays—I did not have a single weekend or holiday off for more than a year. Luckily, Howard was still finishing his senior year at Syracuse, so I had little socializing to do anyway and could devote all my energies to the job.

For those first few months, I trekked from precinct to precinct, reported from some very scary neighborhoods late at night, and wrote crime stories that would have given my mother nightmares. Once, while covering a warehouse fire at the old industrial docks near the Inner Harbor—years before it became the showplace it is now—I passed Oprah Winfrey on the street. She was covering the same story for Baltimore's news channel 13, where she worked at the time. We made eye contact but kept walking, as competing news reporters sometimes do. She wore her hair in an Afro then, and no one had any clue she would one day become a famous one-name celebrity. She was just another reporter that night, sifting through the smoky ruins of the warehouse, trying to glean some news from any witnesses or authorities she could find, just as I was.

A friend once asked me how I wandered those terrible neighborhoods at night, alone.

"Aren't you afraid?" she asked me.

"Sure I am afraid, but I have to do it anyway," I said. "If I don't do the assignments they give me just like a man would, my editors won't respect me. If I only cover things 'like a woman would,' that leaves me very little to do."

There were times when I did question my judgment about moving to Baltimore. Even though it was only forty miles away from Washington, the two cities were so drastically different. I felt disoriented. People I had never met before in my life would call me "hon." More than once, I knocked on a door in one of the city's most infamous row-house neighborhoods, and a guy wearing a wifebeater T-shirt yanked it open. One of those times, I identified myself as a reporter for the *Baltimore Morning Sun*, as it was called then, but the man asked me, "Where the cameras at?"

"I am a reporter for a newspaper," I said.

"Yeah, yeah," he said, scratching his belly. "But where the cameras at? When they coming?"

I felt a wide gulf between myself and some of the people I met in my pursuit of news. My accent, education, demeanor, just about everything about me, spelled "out-of-towner" to these people. Even the way I pronounced *Baltimore*, stressing each of the three syllables, marked me as an outsider.

The work itself could be brutal. I sat in a small basement office of the city's main police station, trolling the offices of homicide detectives and narcotics cops, poring over police crime logs, trying to find some news. I had to listen to the police scanner constantly squawking in my office, learning to discern the codes that meant it was time to run out and chase a story. I felt myself desensitizing and dehumanizing. I had to grow a tough outer shell to survive the violence around me and maintain some emotional distance between my work and personal life. The murder and mayhem became routine.

This was the very same beat my colleague David Simon took on a few years later. Only he thrived in it. Then he turned his experience into award-winning television shows like *The Corner*, *Homicide: Life on the Street*, and *The Wire*. David perceived that gritty life in Baltimore as an opportunity for must-see TV. I could never see beyond the misery of it. Perhaps I had too many inner demons of my own to see the opportunities David did. I congratulate him on his vision and am very proud to know him. In any case, we were both subjected to an archaic system that thrived in newspapers like the *Sun* during the 1970s and 1980s, where the editors believed cub reporters had to pay their dues for several years before they could do something more glamorous like be a foreign correspondent in an exotic locale.

One night, I interviewed a homicide detective about a particularly gruesome murder. A woman was chopped to pieces and stuffed into a dumpster. The homicide detective munched on his corned beef on rye as if we were discussing the weather. The subject matter did not bother his appetite one bit. He just ate, giving me Technicolor details about this poor woman's worst nightmare. For him, it was just another night on the crime-ridden streets of Baltimore. I did not want to become like him.

After a year of the night-shift crime beat, I was looking and feeling pretty beaten down. One evening, an African American desk editor happened to notice how wan I looked and pulled me aside.

"Gail, are you okay?" he asked.

"I'm okay." I did not want him to think I was failing at the business of journalism.

He clearly did not believe me. His raised eyebrow told me as much. He tried again to get me to talk to him, but I was cautious because I did not want to be perceived as a whiner not cut out for the job. Still, as I walked away to begin my night shift, I could tell he was worried about me. I think he thought I would quit before I even got a chance to get some much-needed news-gathering experience. It was difficult to attract good African American reporters to the newspaper as it was. Losing one of the very few in the *Sun*'s newsroom would not look good to his superiors or the news industry at large.

He must have done some talking to some people behind closed doors because in short order I was given a reprieve and reassigned to cover a quiet suburban county bureau instead. The paper paid my moving expenses and hired a moving van to take my meager belongings from my Baltimore apartment to one in Columbia, Maryland.

I got stuck in a sleepy suburban bureau where there was a dearth of interesting news. It was a steady but unfulfilling diet of county council meetings, school board decisions, and domestic court cases. To amuse myself, I dug up quirky little stories I hoped would resonate with a wider audience and gain more visibility. Once, I ran across a Greek woman who had lost her mangy old German shepherd named Bunny. She explained she had left her car in front of a dry-cleaning store with the engine running so her fourteen-year-old dog could stay warm while she ran inside. Someone carjacked her vehicle and drove off with the dog in the back seat. Frantic, the woman ran out of the shop, shouting for help. After several fruitless hours searching, and filing a police report with an indifferent county police officer, there was still no sign of her car or her dog.

For most people, the story would have ended then, but not for Bunny's owner, and not for me. The woman owned a Greek restaurant in Baltimore and viewed Bunny as her only child. When she invited me to her spacious rambler in the green hills of Howard County, she showed me that the dog had her own bedroom, access to the family swimming pool, and every doggy toy imaginable. The poor, distraught owner posted flyers around the county, then hired an airplane to drop more flyers over a four-state area. The flyer had a picture of her dog, her tale of woe, and her telephone number so anyone who saw the dog could call her.

I wrote a story about her plight that my editors thought was so funny they placed it on the front page of the paper. It ran with a picture of the woman looking sad, holding up a picture of her beloved Bunny. For some reason, the story tickled the public's imagination, hit the newswires, and raced across the country as fast as the technology of the 1980s could take it. The woman received hundreds of calls from people who thought they might have spotted her dog. Finally, one call from West Virginia panned out. Bunny had been spotted limping along a rural road there. A Good Samaritan coaxed Bunny into his home, fed and watered her, then called the owner to come pick her up. Apparently the carjackers had dumped the elderly German shepherd out of the car and kept driving to parts unknown.

The owner was so elated to be reunited with Bunny that she told everyone within earshot that I was her hero. When I met with her for a follow-up story, she hugged me tightly and begged me to come to her Greek restaurant for a free meal anytime I wanted for the rest of my life. If that sounds like I am exaggerating, I am not.

A few days after that, I walked into the newsroom in downtown Baltimore amid snickers. The laughter got louder as I got closer to the metro desk. By the time I reached it, my colleagues were laughing so hard, tears were streaming from one man's eyes. "You have a present," my fellow reporter and rewrite man Mike said, barely keeping a straight face. "It's from your dog lady."

Then he unveiled a flower bouquet shaped like a poodle. Most of the newsroom erupted in gales of laughter all over again, middle-aged men holding their stomachs because they were laughing so hard. My face flushed with warmth.

"Where would you like it?" Mike asked, a cigarette dangling from his mouth, the smoke causing him to squint. He followed me all the way to my desk, setting the doggy bouquet down on one of the many piles of paper that adorned it. "I thought I had seen everything, but this tops it," Mike said, grinning from ear to ear.

I later took that poodle bouquet home to show Howard, but removing it from my newsroom desk did little to stop the mirth. Months went by before my fellow reporters stopped asking me how my friend the dog lady was doing. Thank goodness, there was always some bigger story coming along to take their minds off the past.

During my time at the *Sun*, I covered a couple of geographic areas and general assignment beats. Once, while covering Howard County in central Maryland, I unearthed a story about an eighteen-year-old girl who died in the arms of her date while dancing at her high school prom. As I investigated and talked to numerous friends, family, and the girl's doctors, I learned she had a rare form of lupus. But the story was more about the sorrow of a life snuffed out so young.

As I pounded away on the keyboard, it was hard for me not to think about my own disease. I immediately identified with the young girl. I attended her funeral and was struck by the daisies draped all over her casket, left by dozens of her friends, teachers, and family members. I started my story with "Daisies were her favorite flowers. Hundreds of them covered her casket yesterday. . . ." It ended up on the first page of the *Sun*. The colleague who had ribbed me so much about the dog lady story told me, "That was a three-hankie job you did on that story. I don't think you left a dry eye in the house."

I preened. His praise was so unexpected; I felt I must have done something right for once. Even my irascible editor raved—something that happened about as often as a sighting of Halley's Comet. Usually he greeted my daily calls into the newsroom with a bad-tempered "What have you done for me lately?" All the county bureau reporters hated his evil moods. We thought maybe he suffered from migraines, but no one asked him because he was so grumpy all the time. We once had a meeting in a reporter's backyard and joked about hiring a hit man to get rid of him. It gave us some comic relief to spend a few minutes planning the hit—that's how despised he was.

I spent six years at the *Sun*. I headed a couple of suburban bureaus and even did some weekend editing, but I knew it was time to move on when I interviewed to fill a vacancy in the newspaper's Paris bureau.

The editors were polite. They listened as I answered their questions, nodding as if what I said mattered. I made sure I mentioned I was almost fluent in French, had a degree in international relations, and had some news experience that would help me cover a foreign government. They didn't laugh, but I could tell by their expressions they were not taking my candidacy seriously. I knew I was right when a few weeks later they announced that Robert, one of my colleagues, would be heading the French bureau. Robert was a competent reporter, but he spoke no French and was only a few years older than me. He was a white male and therefore had their trust. That was all that mattered. He was more qualified by default.

Sick of the glass ceiling and of paying dues that were never going to be fully paid, I started job hunting. I still had a clear idea of how my career could proceed, and as always, I did not want to get stuck for too long. I needed to get overseas, to travel, see this vast world. That had been part of the plan since my elementary school days in Georgetown. I wasn't going to let my employers' lack of vision be a permanent impediment. I needed to find new employers.

However, sickle cell anemia threw a major obstacle in my way: a hip replacement, my second one, in fact. I planned to job hunt during my recuperation, even though it meant I would be hobbling around on crutches at a job fair held by the National Association of Black Journalists. It was certainly not the most promising look for a reporter eager to impress.

Looking back now, it was a pivotal moment in my life, when I had to find a way to push forward. We all get these at some point in our lives—though we aren't always sure at the time that we are standing at the elbow of a major crossroads. I told myself that I wasn't about to let my hobbled condition scare me from my path. So many of our initial impressions are based on the physical—tall, short, fat, skinny, ugly, pretty—and too often we use these to make character assessments of people. What would my crutches and hobbled state say to potential employers? Would they see me as weak, as less able? Like many women, I liked to look pretty, to present the best version of myself to the world. But there were times when my sickled cells forced me to move beyond that. This was one of those times.

I looked out across the expanse of the convention hall and took a deep breath. Even if I got some withering stares, I couldn't be deterred. This was a moment when I had to call upon my boldness. After perusing the tents of the bigger names like the *New York Times* and the *Chicago Tribune*, I took a chance and stopped by a tent manned by a short, bearded man named John, the metro editor of the *Washington Times*. He was friendly and enthusiastic about my resume and experience. He never once asked why I needed the crutches. He didn't even inquire about them. He was following the letter of the law about privacy and what is—and is not—permitted in an interview.

At this time in the mid-1980s, the newspaper was owned by the Unification Church and not well respected by the mainstream media. The church was headed by the Reverend Sun Myung Moon. He made headlines during the early 1980s because of the mass weddings he officiated in places like Central Park, where he married hundreds of couples at a time. Everyone joked about how brainwashed I would become if I worked for the "Moonies," a pejorative term some people used to refer to the members of the church. However, only a few church members worked at the newspaper, mostly in menial positions. John, who hailed from the *Miami Herald*, was looking for some qualified journalists to help turn the paper into a more professional news operation.

No one was more surprised than me when he hired me and allowed me to choose whatever beat I wanted to cover. I chose City Hall. He agreed and we concluded the paperwork in record time.

The day I walked into the *Sun* metro editor's office to resign is a day seared into my memory. Tom was the head editor. He was smug as he accepted my resignation, his prominent Adam's apple bobbing in his crane-like neck. He made no attempt to talk me into staying, but could not contain his curiosity after I finished my brief resignation speech.

"So, where are you going?" he asked.

"The *Washington Times*."

His eyebrows rose. I could tell he was starting to say something snide about the newspaper, then stopped himself. Instead, he asked me what I would be covering.

"City Hall."

I glimpsed the shock written on his face then, turning on my heels, left his office. The City Hall beat in Washington meant covering the notorious Mayor Marion Barry, who was more famous than Baltimore's mayor was at the time. For an ambitious news reporter, it was a dream job likely to yield great exposure and many front-page stories.

Word of my resignation and new job spread quickly through the newsroom. I was already consigning the *Sun* and all its frustrations to the past, looking forward to my future. A few of my fellow reporters and friends came over to my desk to ask me if I was sure I wanted to "ruin" my career by working at the "Moonie paper." I knew there would be no growth without risk, so I was comfortable with my decision.

"The *Times* is offering me an opportunity the *Sun* never will," I told them.

A few days later, someone threw together a cake and punch party for my final day at the *Sun*. I laughed a bit with friends but didn't stay long. Eventually, I gathered my purse, pulled the crutches under my arms, and started to hobble out of the newsroom for the final time. Frank, one of the editors who had interviewed me for the Paris bureau job, suddenly stood up from his seat at the international desk. When he started to applaud, several others in the newsroom also stood up and applauded. As I paused to look back at my *Sun* colleagues in surprise, most of the reporters and editors were clapping and smiling. It was the first and only standing ovation I have ever received in my life.

I was so shocked by their generous farewell, I don't remember taking the elevator down to the lobby or getting into my car. Suddenly, I was grabbing my steering wheel for support as tears rolled down my cheeks, overcome with emotion. It was the first time I cried because I was so touched by a gesture. I felt like Sally Field during her acceptance speech after receiving the Oscar for *Places in the Heart*. She gushed to the audience, "You like me, right now you like me."

CHAPTER 7

You are soo bee-yoo-tee-fool!

DECEMBER 1988

THE AIRPLANE JARRED ME AWAKE WHEN IT LANDED, SLIPPING a bit on a dark, icy runway.

I was bleary-eyed after a fitful sleep and several hours trapped in the confines of a stuffy airplane cabin. On the leg from Washington's Dulles International Airport to Frankfurt, Germany, my connection to Moscow, the endless wails of a US Army wife's three-week-old baby made sleep impossible. The poor young woman was new to motherhood; her efforts to quiet her child were futile. The red-faced infant wailed incessantly, leaving my teeth on edge and the rest of the cabin passengers restless.

Sleeping in Frankfurt's massive, austere airport was also impossible. My layover was several hours long, and I spent it sitting in a sleek, hard, plastic chair, a seat too torturous for me to even doze in. Wary by nature, I never fall asleep in public. Anything can happen to a woman traveling alone. Add unaware or unconscious to that, and you are just asking for trouble.

Once I boarded the Moscow flight, I caught a few hours of sleep. After more than fifteen hours of traveling already, I was so tired, I was dazed. Luckily, the flight was half-empty and I was able to lie down on several connecting seats. I can only sleep when fully horizontal and have never slept well sitting upright on airplanes. Even though it made international travel exhausting, I loved traveling too much to give it up.

I was thankful, but not surprised, that there were so few passengers aboard the flight to Moscow. For one thing, it was the middle of winter. No one in their right mind visits Russia in the winter unless it's for business reasons. Also, at this point in history, only Soviet citizens and those with the proper visas could venture beyond the Iron Curtain.

Looking out the frosty window, I couldn't make out much. I saw a dark, frozen runway and miles of white snow disappearing into an inky blackness on either side. Once I stepped off the plane into the bitter night air, I realized just how cold it was—cold, wrapped tightly in more cold, then topped with a frigid wind that could slice right through you with a pain so intense it felt like a burn. It was at least twenty or thirty degrees below zero. I had never been so cold in my entire life. It took my breath away and made my eyelashes stick to my face during the short walk to the overly warm airport terminal.

Although I tried not to think about it, I knew that extreme cold could more easily trigger a sickle cell crisis. But I was on assignment for my newspaper, an opportunity I couldn't let pass. This was the kind of trip—putting my wits and guile to the test on assignment in a foreign land—I had been dreaming of for years.

I was wearing a thick, white shadow fox coat and hat from Norway that Howard had given me as an early Christmas present. I figured if the little creatures could survive Norwegian winters, I could survive this Russian one wrapped in their skins. The icy wind burned my face, and I pulled my long fur collar up and over my cheeks as I joined the other exiting passengers making their way to the luggage carousels to collect their bags before navigating the long lines of Soviet customs.

Maybe the novelty of my brown face surrounded by all that white fur did the trick, but I got through customs in record time. The customs official glanced at my face, then quickly at my passport photo. Next thing I knew, he had stamped my passport book and visa, which stated I was in the USSR for a short, business-related stay.

Bags in tow, I exited customs and looked around for the group of journalists I was scheduled to meet. But standing there in the airport's cavernous entry hall, I did not see anyone who looked familiar. No one held signs with my name—or the name of the American businessman who had sponsored us all to witness his first steps to establish a business in the Soviet Union under perestroika and glasnost. I paused and looked around the hectic airport. Soviet citizens were rushing here and there to meet arriving passengers or do what people do at airports.

Standing uncertainly in the middle of that chaos, I gave myself a mental pep talk. "You are an independent woman," I told myself. "You do not need anyone to tell you what to do or where to go. You have the itinerary the host sent you in advance. You know where you are supposed to be staying in Moscow. Maybe you are supposed to meet everyone at the hotel."

Mind made up, I waltzed out the front door of the airport into the evening air with my luggage and hailed a taxi.

The driver jumped out, stared at me for several seconds, then eagerly moved to help with my luggage. He took my bags, shoved them into his small trunk, and gestured for me to get into the rear seat of the cab. The car's little heater bravely blasted, doing its best to keep out the freezing Moscow air. I asked the driver if he spoke any English.

"Da," he said, nodding.

"The Rossiya Hotel, please," I said, proffering a piece of paper with my itinerary written on it in English. I had forgotten that he likely read only Cyrillic script, so it was just as well he waved my paper away before driving us toward the hotel.

I looked out the window with wonder. I had been fascinated by the Soviet Union. During my youth, it was a closed fortress; little real information got out to those of us in the West who wondered how people lived every day. During my studies in international relations, I spent most of my time focused on two geographic regions: the USSR and Africa. I learned all about the USSR's republics and its eleven time zones. I even bought English–Russian and Russian–English dictionaries, thinking I would sign up for a Russian language class, but ultimately, French took precedence. It would not help me much here in the USSR, but French had proved useful during my travels in Western Europe.

I gazed at the icy Moscow streets as my mind wandered. I recalled plowing through Leo Tolstoy's *War and Peace* and the works of Alexander Pushkin and Fyodor Dostoyevsky. Being a romantic, my favorite Russian tomes were Boris Pasternak's *Doctor Zhivago* and Tolstoy's *Anna Karenina*. I admired the genius necessary for these tortured Russian writers to reach literary greatness during the late nineteenth and early twentieth centuries. I thought I might glimpse just a few of the romantic influences that so inspired Tolstoy when he gazed at the same wintry night streets now passing outside my window.

Alas, there was nothing remotely romantic about Moscow in 1988. Instead, the extra wide street reminded me of scenes from dozens of American movies about life behind the Iron Curtain. I could easily imagine seeing tanks driving down the boulevard followed by uniformed men marching in goose step as the Cold War raged on.

Eager to impress my editor, I did my homework for weeks before the trip. I knew that the Soviet Union was engulfed by a multitude of problems. The economy, especially the agricultural sector, was falling apart. The country lacked technological advancements and relied on inefficient factories. Consumers lined up for hours to buy low-quality goods and suffered from a lack of social freedoms.

President Mikhail Gorbachev's new policy of perestroika, literally "restructuring," was designed to reconstruct the political and economic system established by the Communist Party seven decades before. Perestroika promoted demonopolization and allowed some semiprivate businesses to function, like the one I was there to cover. Gorbachev ended price controls that had been firmly in place for more than seventy years. His goal was to create a semi-free market system and mimic some, but not all, of the successful capitalist practices used in Germany, Japan, and the United States.

Unfortunately, the Soviet economy was still a long way from thriving. Sick of a worn-out economy, the people revolted with strikes and civil unrest in many parts of the country. Everywhere I looked, I saw people standing in long lines, unsure of what merchandise would still be available for purchase by the time they reached the front. They waited for the chance to purchase vodka, bread, and poor-quality goods few in the West would bother to spend money on.

Meanwhile, Gorbachev was busy promoting glasnost, or "openness," his social and political reforms to bestow more rights and freedoms upon the Soviet people. His goal was to include more people in the political process through freedom of expression. This led to decreased media censorship, which allowed writers and journalists to expose news of government corruption, the depressed condition of the Soviet people, and criticism of government officials.

I knew all this was going on behind the scenes as I watched one squat, gray, utilitarian building after another—uniformly ugly to my Western eyes—perched on either side of the road. I was used to gracious, tree-lined streets and traffic circles, courtesy of Pierre L'Enfant, who had designed Washington in a style similar to his beloved Paris. Everything in my field of vision looked so industrial—no graceful curves, edges, or arched doorways.

Although it was snowing, the road seemed clear enough for the taxi to roll over the packed snow. I supposed when snow was a daily occurrence, it didn't stop traffic or people going about their daily activities. Still, there were very few pedestrians braving the frigid air this late at night.

The taxi driver pulled up in front of a building large enough to take up an entire city block and stopped. We had arrived at the Rossiya Hotel, built by the Soviets in 1964. I stepped out of the taxi and pulled my white fur close in the blistering cold. The taxi driver struggled to pull my luggage from his trunk. It was extra heavy because I had packed it with several bottles of spring water, which I hoped would help me stay hydrated and stave off a sickle cell crisis during this sub-Artic trip.

I didn't want to get trapped in some Soviet hospital, trying to explain what was happening to me to people who did not speak English and had likely never treated anyone with my disease. Since I had no idea whether the drinking water in Russia would be potable, I wanted some bottled water on hand until I could find a place to purchase more. I had also packed a hefty supply of dried fruits, nuts, and snack crackers filled with peanut butter or cheese, just in case the local cuisine was not to my liking. I have always been a picky eater and I feared what I would find on my plate once our Russian hosts began to entertain us.

I paid the taxi driver with what I hoped was the correct amount of rubles. As he drove away, it began to lightly snow. Already, there were six-foot piles of snow stacked along both sides of the road. There was no telling how much more snow I would see before my journey here ended. Chin held high, I waltzed into the hotel lobby, exuding confidence as I approached the front desk.

"Do you have a reservation for Gail Campbell?" I asked the desk clerk, smiling to look as open as possible. I assumed he spoke English since he worked at the city's largest hotel, which was centrally located in the heart of a tourist district, just a short walk from Moscow's famous Red Square. He did speak English, but said he did not have a reservation for me—at least, not under that name. I had given him my maiden name since I used it as my byline on my newspaper stories. It was a modern, feminist thing to do, and my husband—who grew up in a family full of women—had no objection.

"How about a reservation for Gail Campbell Woolley?" I asked him, since my married name appeared on my passport and other official documents.

"No," he said, checking his computer screen. "No reservation under that name either."

"Are you *sure*?" I pressed him, knowing this gigantic hotel had more than 300 rooms.

"No," he insisted. "We have nothing for anyone with that name."

"How about a reservation for Charles Sutherland?" I asked. Perhaps the room was under our host's name.

"No, we do not have a reservation for anyone by that name either."

"Well," I said, "do you have any rooms that I can check into now?" If I spent the night, I could figure out how to catch up with the journalists' group tomorrow.

"No, madam," the officious clerk said. "We are fully booked."

This was a big wrinkle in my plans. My itinerary stated that the Rossiya Hotel was the first stop on our ten-day tour of this country, so I could not understand what had gone wrong. As I stood puzzled at the desk, a family of three that had been standing just behind me moved closer.

"Excuse me," the man said with a Texas drawl. "It appears you are having some trouble here. It's probably some kind of misunderstanding, but it's way too late for you to be wandering alone around Moscow at night looking for a place to stay. Why don't you come up to our room and wait awhile? Maybe they will find out what happened to your reservation in the meantime."

I looked at the man, *really* looked at him, trying to gauge his intent. He was middle-aged, with a wrinkled face and graying hair. Beside him stood his wife and teenaged daughter, both looking at me with concern.

Now, most of the time, I am not a gullible person. If anything, after years as a journalist, I am downright cynical and wary of people's motives when they approach me for something. In most situations that involved a man with an offer for me to come up to his room, I would have been quite suspicious and turned him down immediately. My husband is fond of telling me that I have a "no" face, which was why he was hesitant to approach me at first when he saw me at college. He says anyone reading my body language knows not to approach me with any foolishness.

That thought ran through my mind as I gazed at the face of the Texan. The man's wife must have seen what I was thinking; most people who know me best tell me I have a face so expressive you can tell what I'm thinking quite clearly. She stepped forward, saying, "Oh yes, please join us. It's way too late for you to be wandering around out there all by yourself." Her Texas twang was as pronounced as her poufy hairstyle, a 'do I associated with Dallas housewives.

Her eyes appeared earnest. It *was* late. And this family seemed sincere. I did not know a soul in Moscow. There were no cell phones, so I did not have my contact's number. I only had an itinerary and some basic information about where the US Embassy was in case of trouble.

"Thanks," I said, letting a smile warm my face. "That's very nice of you. I will join you for a little while. Then I will call the front desk again to see if any of my colleagues have arrived to check in. Maybe they can explain what's going on."

I picked up my luggage and dragged it behind them to the elevator, where we exchanged the usual small talk. On the eleventh floor, we stepped out of the elevator and I followed the family down the hall to their room. They had a suite with two bedrooms with a sitting area in between them. The man invited me to sit down on the sofa. After we were all seated and chatted for a while, the wife said she was going to order some tea and refreshments and asked me if I would like some. The room was sweltering. It must have been 80°F in there, so not only was I exhausted, I was thirsty—and I had no idea when I would eat or drink next.

"Sure," I said, "thank you. That would be nice."

When the refreshments came, we nibbled on the snacks and drank the tea, chatting casually. I had been with the family for less than an hour when the telephone in their hotel room rang. The father, who was also a businessman exploring commerce possibilities in the Soviet Union, answered it.

"Hello?" he said, then was quiet while listening to the speaker on the other end of the line. "Uh, yes. Yes, she is," he said, handing the telephone to me. "It's for you."

"For *me*?" I asked, quite surprised. "No one knows I'm here in your room. I just met you and your family!" I took the telephone like it was a snake about to bite me and lifted the earpiece to my ear. "Hello?" I said, clearly puzzled.

"Hell-oooo," a man said carefully, like he was unused to speaking English. "Eeez dees Gail Woooolllleeey?"

"Yes," I replied.

"Dees eees Eeee-gorrr," he said, rolling his r's in that Slavic way. "We have been looking for you. You were not supposed to leave the air-o-poorrrt."

"I didn't know that," I said. "I didn't see anyone at the airport to meet me, so I thought I'd catch up with everybody here at the hotel."

"We are not staying at the Rossiya anymore," Igor said. "We booked a different hotel for your group."

"Oh. Nobody told me," I said. "Wait a minute. How did you know where I was? Nobody saw me come to this family's room."

"Are you a black wooman een a white fur coat?"

"Yes," I answered slowly, really cautious now.

"*Everybody* saw you!" he said wryly. "We don't get many black women in white fur coats running around Moscow in the middle of winter. Wait there! Do not move. We are coming to get you!"

I hung up the telephone, then looked at the family and gave them the news. I was not the only one who felt uneasy.

"How did he know to call *our* room?" the Texan asked me.

"I guess what they say about Russia is right," I said. "The KGB or something like that has a million informants. According to Igor, everybody I passed on the way here told him my whereabouts."

"Hunh," the Texan said. "Ain't that something?"

I thanked the family for their kindness and hospitality and made my way back down to the lobby of the Rossiya Hotel. A few minutes later, Igor arrived with a busload of American journalists and guests of our host. I climbed aboard, and the driver stowed my luggage underneath the bus. I took the first available seat on the bus as there were several other people, most of whom I did not know. It turned out Igor was our translator and guide for the duration of our press tour. Most of the others were journalists like me from various media outlets who had been invited to witness the "wonders of glasnost."

I had chosen a seat next to a female journalist from Florida. When we arrived at the decrepit hotel where we were deposited for the night, she ended up my roommate. Although it was the late 1980s, the hotel's technology was better suited to the 1960s. The elevator had been designed for a different building; someone had stuck a handwritten note on the elevator panel with the symbols "+1" so we knew to press eight if we wanted to go to the ninth floor. In the hotel room, there was a neon pink plastic telephone. It reminded me of something a young girl would use growing up in the 1950s back home in the United States.

After examining our Spartan lodging, my roommate and I settled down for the night. After my twenty-two-hour journey, I was too tired to unpack my very heavy bag, but I did open it enough to remove some of the bottles of water. I had forgotten to ask Igor if the water was potable. I also removed some of my snacks—I had a feeling raisins and nuts were going to be my staples on this trip.

The next morning, I came downstairs to the buffet our host had prepared, my first chance to taste Russian cuisine. A hefty woman wearing a scarf around her head set out our breakfast. Using hand motions, she encouraged me to take a seat at one of the tables set for our group, then offered me warm plain yogurt, coarse dark bread, and some boiled eggs. The yogurt was disgusting, so I asked the hostess for some butter for the bread. I survived most of the next ten days on bread and butter and, as anticipated, the snacks in my suitcase. Lunches and dinners were not much better—gray mystery meat floating on top of greasy gruel. Quite often, we faced acres of salmon and caviar at meals, because the Russians were trying to impress us. I got tired of that diet very quickly. There were no fresh vegetables or fruits. I understood they would have been hard to come by in the dark winter months.

The ten days we spent in Russia were a whirlwind of meetings. For those of us who did not speak Russian, a translator was available.

At one point, when I was sitting at a table wearing earphones while a translator simultaneously spoke English inside my headset, I felt like I was at the United Nations.

I was the only African American journalist present in the group, which caused quite a sensation as I traveled around Russia. Everyone turned to stare at me in my white fur coat and hat. During some leisure time, I wandered over to a mall not far from the Rossiya Hotel to purchase some Christmas presents for my family. As soon as I stepped into the mall, a group of young people stopped in their tracks to stare at me.

One bold young Russian boy yelled out in English, "Are you an African princess?"

"No," I replied. "I am from America."

Another boy, emboldened by his friend, asked, "Do you know Michael Jackson?" I realized if I kept answering their questions, I would never get to my destination, the department store GUM (pronounced "goom"). So my smart aleck side peeked out.

"Sure," I said. "We have lunch every Tuesday." And I walked into the store.

GUM was a revelation. I had expected something like Macy's or Bloomingdale's. It was more like a vast warehouse with people standing in long lines. I walked to the head of one line only to discover the merchandise on display was cheap, reminiscent of what a dollar store in the United States might carry. With Christmas only a couple of weeks away, I searched in vain for items that might be suitable gifts for my family. I finally found a scruffy fur hat that reminded me of a muskrat pelt. I bought it for my father, thinking he might use it to work in the yard or do other cold-weather chores. The fur quality was inferior to anything I had ever seen, but at least it was from Russia, and no one else in Dad's neighborhood would have a Russian hat like it.

It was harder to find a gift for my mother, but I eventually bought a set of stackable "nesting" dolls; the smaller ones were stuffed inside progressively larger ones, eight dolls in one. I also bought her a scarf I thought might be suitable to wear with her everyday coat.

My mother was very apprehensive about my going behind the Iron Curtain. She has always worried that my health will fail me when I am visiting a place where no one will understand what I am saying. However, on this trip, the only alarming moment came when I could not call home because of some prefabricated rule at my hotel.

"You cannot call the United States until next Tuesday," the desk clerk said, sounding bored.

"Why not?" I asked. "It's Thursday!" I knew Howard would be worried about me because he had not heard from me since I left home several days earlier. I had no idea Russian landlines were so tightly controlled.

"We do not get a line to call the United States until Tuesday."

No amount of protests or bribery would sway her, so I went back to my room, disappointed.

When Tuesday rolled around, I got up early to make sure I was the first one in line to call the United States. I dialed all the international codes and our home number. After a couple of minutes, I heard the faint ring thousands of miles away at our house. The answering machine came on, Howard's booming voice informing me no one could take my call right now.

"There are only certain days I can get a telephone line to the US from my hotel," I began to explain, then stopped because Howard would think this was as unbelievable as I did. I assured him I was okay and would call again whenever possible.

Even more unbelievable was the variety of Russians I encountered. As we traveled through the country, I was approached several times by strange men who propositioned me on the spot. It got so ridiculous after a while that one of my traveling companions, a Hollywood producer who had come to find opportunities for filming in Russia, offered to help me rebuff their advances. But even my new friend could not deflect a determined Russian officer who marched right over to me during an official reception, clicked his heels, and bowed over my hand to give it a lingering kiss.

"You are so bee-yoo-tee-fool," the officer said, rising from my hand so he could puff out his chest full of medals. "I love exotic women."

Before the officer could continue, my producer friend caught my eye. Seeing the beginning of panic on my face, he knew this officer was yet another uninvited suitor. So he marched over to me and said loudly, "We have to be going now." He grabbed my arm proprietarily and escorted me out of the reception.

I thanked him for his chivalry. "I just don't understand it," I said. "I am clearly wearing my wedding ring. They know I'm not single. Why do they keep trying to pick me up?"

"I don't think they care," he said. "They see an attractive woman and they go for it. Just give me a holler if you need me to help you out of a jam again."

A few days later, our party boarded the night train to Leningrad. Each of us had our own sleeping compartment. Once I reached mine, I took off several layers because the train was at least 80°F and I was beginning to perspire. As the train got underway, I looked out my compartment's window and saw a frozen wonderland. It reminded me of the train scene in the film adaptation of *Doctor Zhivago*. So did the little old lady sitting at the end of our train car, dressed in a scarf and an old-fashioned dress, huddled near a wood-burning stove. I know I romanticized Russia more than I should have, but not even my rose-colored glasses missed the underbelly of desperation I detected in some of the people.

About a half hour later, the little old lady knocked on my door. When I looked out she was motioning to a cup of tea, offering it to me prepared the Russian way: in a glass cup with a spoonful of jam in the bottom to sweeten it. I thanked her, accepted my cup of tea, sweetened just the way I like it, and closed my door to savor it as I watched the frozen tundra roll by outside my window. Before long, I was sleeping soundly in my cozy compartment.

When I woke the next morning, our escorts hurried us off the train and onto a bus that would take us to our hotel. I looked up to see an immense bust of Lenin, for whom the city was still named. It was too large to miss, standing in the center of the station.

Russia in the middle of winter was dark. Daylight this far north only lasted four hours a day. The rest of the time, night and cold enveloped everything, even people's moods. The weather hurt my face and took my breath away. The guide told us not to linger outdoors because it was -40°F. I had never been so thankful for my fur coat and hat, but I could not manage to keep my feet warm enough. In mere seconds, the cold penetrated the leather and the several layers of wool encasing my feet.

At the hotel, everyone hurried inside to check in. I headed toward my room, making sure my luggage was all there. When I looked up, I noticed a group of swarthy, darker-skinned men looking at me curiously. They appeared to be from one of the southern republics, like Azerbaijan. A few waved and smiled at me. One bolder man followed me all the way down the hall to my room. I looked at him suspiciously over my shoulder when I reached my door.

"What do you want?"

He held up his room key, jiggling it at me. I assumed this was his shorthand for yet another proposition.

"I am married!" I said, holding up my left hand, where my wedding rings gleamed in the hallway's subdued lighting.

"So am I," he said, in broken English. "I won't tell if you don't."

I shut the door in his smug face and started unpacking.

Once I got settled, I looked out of my hotel room window. Despite the darkness outside, I could see what appeared to be a vast expanse of white. At dinner later that evening, I asked our translator about it.

"That's the Baltic Sea," he said.

"But it was frozen," I exclaimed. "I didn't think saltwater could freeze."

"It will if it's cold enough," he replied, without a hint of humor.

CHAPTER 8

The Dark Decade

THE TWELFTH-FLOOR APARTMENT WAS NICE ENOUGH. IT HAD one bedroom, a full bath, a living and dining area, and a small, but usable, kitchen. The living room even had a sleeper sofa, in case I had guests. By New York standards, it was quite spacious and located in a desirable neighborhood.

There was only one problem. I did not like New York City. I never have. I will never sing "I Love New York" because I don't. I find the city too crowded, too noisy, and way too expensive. I think most people I encounter on the streets are rude, pushy, and always seem to be rushing somewhere. Many lack the common courtesy found so often south of the Mason–Dixon line and in America's heartland. I especially do not like the mountains of garbage on the streets or the cat-sized rats I see gleefully jumping in and out of them on even the nicest Manhattan streets.

But here I was, in New York City, on my first week on the job working for Mobil Corporation. I was excited and nervous about my sudden career change from reporter to public relations professional. While a reporter's life might have been a bit more exciting than the corporate world, being a PR executive for a huge multinational was still in the realm of what I had trained for at Syracuse.

I didn't see myself as veering off my path. I also knew the corporate salary would help Howard and me to accumulate the cash we needed to see the world.

I was hired to work in the company's newly built headquarters in Fairfax, Virginia, but my boss wanted me to spend the first month of my employment at its old headquarters in New York—a place the company had called home for more than 100 years before deciding to move—to familiarize myself with the company. Mobil put me up in a residential hotel at 2nd Avenue and 39th Street in Manhattan. It was close to the United Nations building and a three-block walk to my office on 42nd Street.

Elaine, a former newspaper colleague who was living in Greenwich Village at the time, felt the same way I did about New York City. She had moved to New York for a plum job at *Time* magazine. We had dinner together my first week living in the city. She sympathized with my distaste for the place. We had spent five years working together in the National Press Building right in the heart of downtown Washington when I was covering City Hall. That was a pleasant area. She was from Ohio and thought the pace of Washington suited her better, too.

Elaine told me that on her first day at *Time*, she got lost trying to find her new office, so she carefully chose someone from a crowd of pedestrians to ask for directions. "I picked out this well-dressed white businesswoman carrying a briefcase," Elaine said. "I thought to myself, 'she looks safe enough. It should be okay to ask her for directions, right?'"

But the woman, despite Elaine's politeness and cute, dimpled smile, shouted at her to "Go to hell!"

"My mouth fell open," Elaine said. "I was so shocked!"

So typical, I thought, shaking my head. I have never wanted to live in the city, even when my dear husband, a New York City native, pleaded with me to consider the idea when it became apparent we would share our lives together after college. I only agreed to the temporary apartment in Manhattan because my boss at Mobil promised it would only be for a month. The company was still in the process of moving the entire corporation to Fairfax to escape the city's high taxes and high cost of living, which discouraged their best and brightest employees from accepting promotions to move to headquarters.

As part of my employment negotiations, my boss had also promised to buy me either airline or train tickets to and from Maryland every weekend—I thought that would be the only way I could endure the wretched experience. Howard grew up in working-class Queens and was ecstatic to have a chance to stay in the heart of Manhattan. Instead of me traveling home, he ended up coming up from our Maryland home every weekend to visit me and his beloved city.

During his first weekend visit, one week after I started, we acted like tourists, even taking an elevator to the top of the Empire State Building to revisit a view we had both seen several times during our courtship. We spent some time at the top, peering at the four-way views of the city.

But we both forgot that the thin air at the top of the Empire State Building was not good for me. Having sickle cell disease has always meant being oxygen deprived. At such a high altitude, the air was even thinner, with less oxygen. Between this, whizzing all over Manhattan with my excited husband, and the stress of starting a new job in a new field, my body succumbed and I tumbled into a sickle cell crisis late Sunday night.

The timing could not have been worse. Howard had left already to return home, my parents had not yet arrived for their preplanned stay, and I was supposed to go to work the next morning. I had only spent a couple of days there the prior week, and it would look terrible not to show up for my first full week.

I immediately called Howard. He was too far away to be of much help, so he told me to call his friends since high school days in New York City, Bill and his wife Cheryl. They were both physicians in New York and might be able to advise me. I called Bill and Cheryl at home, explaining what was happening to me. It was after 11:00 p.m. and they were in bed, but as doctors they were used to responding to emergency calls in the middle of the night.

They told me to call an ambulance. Cheryl told me the ambulance technicians would likely take me to the closest hospital, which I had heard had a less than stellar reputation.

"No!" I said. "I don't want to go there. Isn't that where they send crazy people?"

"They also do patient care there, Gail," Cheryl explained. "It's a public hospital."

"I don't want to go there!" I panted in pain over the telephone. "Isn't there anywhere else I can go to get decent treatment?"

Cheryl suggested I ask them to take me to the more esteemed academic medical center, which was also nearby. "But they might not do it," she said. "Insist though, and maybe they will."

The ambulance crew arrived just before my parents. Since I had a free place to stay in Midtown, my mother could not resist a chance to see a show and some of the sights. They had planned to use the sleeper sofa in my living room and sightsee while I was at work. The minute my mother saw the ambulance, she knew it was for me. She had seen it so many times before and knew the dread in her stomach was real.

As the EMTs loaded me onto a stretcher, I pleaded with them to take me to the academic medical center. They told me that the hospital's emergency room had issued a code red, turning all patients away because they were full. It was 1990 and the AIDS epidemic was in full bloom in New York City. Emergency rooms were overrun with patients and doctors were at their wits' ends. Nevertheless, I forced the issue, adamantly refusing to go anywhere else. The EMTs eventually gave in and dumped me in the medical center's emergency room, despite the staff's protests, and left.

I lay there on a hard cot in agony for hours before a harried emergency room physician stopped by. I pleaded with him for some pain relief, but he was brusque and indifferent and ordered blood work instead. "Please!" I said. "I'm having a sickle cell crisis, and I'm in so much pain from head to toe!"

"Look, lady," he said. "I don't know if you have sickle cell or not until I see your blood work. You could be a junkie trying to get some drugs for all I know." He left me lying on the cot in the hallway. This is a fairly common reaction that sickle cell patients receive in the emergency room—even when the hospital isn't overrun with a different crisis. Medical literature suggests that emergency health care workers tend to undertreat sickle cell patients in the throes of a crisis, as they assume they are addicts looking for drugs. It doesn't help that many sickle cell patients, after dealing with a lifetime of chronic pain, have learned to adapt. Often, sickle cell patients do not look like they are in excruciating pain, at least not the way doctors expect them to look.

The hospital was so overcrowded, there was no sign of when I would be admitted. I could barely sleep for all the loud noise, bright lights, and general chaos of dozens of moaning people. At one point, a nurse spotted my giant diamond engagement ring and my wedding band as I clutched the side of my cot and gasped.

"Lady, you really need to give that to someone to take home for you," he whispered, shocked. "It's not safe here in this hospital."

I nodded, knowing my husband was still on his way back from Washington after having to make excuses at work for a hasty departure. I turned my diamond ring around on my finger so only the gold band of it showed and held my treasured diamond in my palm until my husband could reach me and keep it safe.

When Howard arrived, he jockeyed with numerous hospital officials and finally got me a room after two days of anxious waiting. In all, I had spent seven days in the hallway, with Howard, my parents, and Howard's mother all buzzing around me at different times. I was so miserable, I could barely open my eyes, but I was in way too much pain to get much sleep on that hard cot.

After I was admitted upstairs to a hospital room, it took another week for me to recover. The emergency room doctor had allowed my crisis to spiral out of control by withholding pain medicine for hours until a simple blood test returned and he focused on it long enough to confirm I had an alarmingly low red blood cell count and was, indeed, having a sickle cell crisis. But by then, it was nearly impossible to relieve my excruciating pain. Instead, I writhed and screamed for hours. His initial orders to a nurse to administer a minimal amount of narcotics were ineffective and too infrequent to do any good to abate my pain.

Unfortunately, the treatment I experienced is not uncommon, even today, when emergency room doctors treat sickle cell patients. Research on care for sickle cell patients has shown that they feel their treatment is quantifiably inferior to the general population's.

What he and so many other doctors I have encountered fail to understand is that early intervention in a sickle cell crisis cuts its duration, and subsequently, hospitalization costs. They never recognize that their inattention to sickle cell patients makes a bad situation infinitely worse and shoots the costs of medical care up much higher than necessary. Until sickle cell medications improved in the late 1980s, I was averaging five to six hospital trips a year to receive treatment for painful sickle cell crises. Even at my local hospital, where I was a repeat patient, a middle-of-the-night rush to the emergency room was a roll of the dice in terms of the treatment I might receive. It usually took intervention by my primary care doctor to get the protocols on track to alleviate my pain and bring the crisis to an end in four to six days. Crises that are allowed to get out of hand, like the one I had in New York, can take up to two weeks for me to recover from.

My new boss looked sour when I finally returned to work after two weeks of being absent. I was thinner, frailer, and after seeing his expression, afraid I might not still have a job. But I put my head down and got back to my assignments and waited with dread in the pit of my stomach. First impressions are often everything, and mine had been terrible indeed. After a few hours, he called me into his office with a minor, seemingly unrelated excuse.

"Why didn't you tell me you had sickle cell anemia?" he asked.

"We are not allowed to discuss such things during an interview," I reminded him in as neutral a voice as possible, given the level of my outrage. He clearly had not consulted one of the company's many employee relations professionals before venturing into such a legally tricky area. He sat up straighter, proceeding more cautiously.

"Well," he said, "why didn't you tell me after you were hired?"

I just looked at him, trying to read between the lines of his inquiry. His body language told me little, but I think he must have been embarrassed by some higher-up or another when I was suddenly absent after being employed only a few days. I could think of no other reason for his persistence and ill-advised foray into this sensitive area.

"It is a private matter that does not seem relevant to my job," I replied evenly, turning away and leaving his office.

He became my enemy after that. He made my entire first year at Mobil so miserable, I could tell he was trying to get me to quit. He gave me the worst review I have ever received in my life, telling me I was virtually on "probation" unless I corrected the faults he pretended I had. His real complaint, however, had nothing to do with my work.

"You have a strong personality," he once told me, sitting back in his seat to better witness my dismay.

"What can I do about that?" I asked him, truly puzzled.

"Be aware of it and how it affects others," he said acidly, and dismissed me.

I returned to my office, shocked and tearful. I had never failed at anything so completely in my life. I knew I had been doing my assignments just fine. What he apparently didn't like was the way I interacted with people—him in particular. Being outspoken and being myself got me nowhere fast in that rigid, white male–dominated corporate environment. The men bristled, apparently, and complained to him about me.

But I am not a quitter. So after a few days, I marched back into his office and demanded a private meeting. I could not let such a poor rating stain my record any longer than necessary. So I negotiated with him. I offered to do more and better work, making sure I pleased our clients. He apparently took the word of anyone, coworkers as well as subordinates and superiors, when he formed his impression of me. I had to bear that in mind in order to survive this corporate chapter of my life. This "personality problem" was undoubtedly a collateral effect of the sickle cell, the impatience that I have felt most of my life. I had to squelch as much of it as I could while I was at Mobil. I had to make my white male coworkers comfortable—or at least less intimidated. We struck a bargain: if I did what I promised, earning praise from all corners, my boss agreed to change my poor rating to an acceptable one within six months. I left his office.

I volunteered for extra projects and worked weekends. My boss even looked up in surprise to see me at my desk one Saturday afternoon, deeply focused on whatever assignment I had on my computer. I did have to keep reminding him of our agreement, however. Finally, he could dodge me no longer and told me in passing he had changed my review rating. I sighed in relief. I wasn't used to bad grades; I was deeply stung by this episode. My boss ended up promoting me, but I never got over his first damaged perception of me. Over the next few years, he made numerous overtures to befriend me, but I never trusted him again.

Instead, change became my friend. The company went through several reorganizations during my ten years there. My first boss was swept out with a number of other old-timers as the company trimmed its payroll. In the aftermath, I joined the media relations section, becoming one of two company spokespersons. I enjoyed my time with the senior media manager. He was a good mentor and appreciated my extra effort, especially when I spoke French with the reporters calling from Paris. It was a halcyon period that could not possibly last.

When the senior media manager retired suddenly to take care

of his ailing wife, I was left manning the press desk solo, with not enough experience and too much responsibility. My life became a blur of media queries coming in from every corner of the world. Most days, I felt like I was dancing on the head of a pin, trying to please upper management, who rarely wanted to reveal any information, while still meeting the deadlines of a voracious newspaper, wire, internet, and oil trade press corps with a keen nose for trouble. Every syllable out of my mouth was quoted around the world. A lot of my colleagues were impressed with my position. I just shook my head and said, "High profile just means high target."

Inevitably, this could not continue. I am certain I made some mistakes, especially when I did not have enough information to provide credible answers in times of crisis. Eventually I was assigned a British partner to help with the media desk. Later, they hired a media manager from a competing oil company to supervise us both, and he hired a few more people to help. In this crowd of all-white males, I was ultimately sidelined to a publicity role, which is viewed in the industry as less important than a company spokesperson. I endured it stoically, biding my time.

A couple of years into my tenure at Mobil, I aged past the fault line of thirty-five, which had hung over my head and my brother Tim's for nearly three decades. I had tried to put the number out of my mind over the years, to focus more on living than on dying. It took monumental mental discipline, helped enormously by a job that kept me busy and a husband who loved me dearly. But it was difficult to avoid thinking about it occasionally, reflecting on a life that at times felt like it was being lived with a gun barrel to my head.

It was somewhat astonishing to me then when my brother actually succumbed to the disease at age thirty-five. I was able to rationalize the number by telling myself that Tim and I had lived very differently, had handled that gun barrel in radically divergent ways. I had assiduously attended to my health, taking every step that would prolong my life as long as possible. Tim had descended into a pit of pain and self-destruction, reaching for whatever he could find to send his mind elsewhere.

In Mobil's next departmental reorganization, I was moved to another public relations area that dealt with internal communications. To my surprise, this new "internal" role led to some of my best experiences. I traveled to Caracas, Venezuela, for the Pegasus Prize for Literature, a program I oversaw that awarded a prize to foreign authors and published their books. I also helped develop a multilingual employee site that was heavily used during the negotiations for the Exxon-Mobil merger, as people worried whether they would have jobs or not when it was over.

I survived all these changes, but I never really fit into corporate life. It never suited my free-spirited personality. I always felt I had to repress the best essence of myself. At times, I even felt like I was in a militaristic atmosphere where everyone had to walk in lockstep—or walk away. I chose to walk away when Mobil and Exxon merged in 2000. Corporate public relations was moved to Irving, Texas, and my female boss was kind enough to ask me if I wanted to be considered for a position there.

"No," I said easily. "My husband's career is Washington based and we prefer not to relocate to Texas." It was the easiest career decision I ever made.

With that in mind, it was only a matter of time before Mobil offered me and thousands of other employees lucrative packages to sever our ties with the company. The day I drove out of Mobil's parking lot for the last time, I felt as if a two-ton weight had been lifted from my shoulders. I felt so light, I could almost fly. I didn't know what I would do next, but I definitely knew I would never, ever do that again.

CHAPTER 9

Dot-Com Daycare

I WAS IN BED WITH MY HEAD UNDER THE COVERS WHEN MY bedside telephone rang.

"Hello," I said sleepily.

It was a headhunter. I shook my head to wake up better and listen to what she was saying. She had an opportunity she thought I might be interested in.

Me? Interested? I was only three months into the yearlong sabbatical I had planned to cleanse my palate of corporate shenanigans. I liked having no place to be and no boss to nag me. It was refreshing. Getting away from the stress was rejuvenating my soul, rebuilding my energy for the next chapter of my life—whatever that may be. I made my husband be as quiet as possible when he got up to go to work in the mornings. Sleep was my new best friend. I rarely got up before 9:00 a.m. Now a headhunter was bugging me. This better be good, I thought sourly. I listened with a lot of skepticism and no small amount of caution.

The headhunter explained that a dot-com start-up in the pre-IPO stage was seeking a vice president to head its public relations function. The pay was better than what I had been making in the oil business and the potential payoff from all the stock options was obscene. I sat up to listen more closely.

The call led to a meeting with the senior vice president, who was so pleased by our interview that he immediately took me to meet the president, Robb. If it hadn't been for his prematurely gray hair, I would have thought him a kid in his twenties. His boyish smile and personality made him seem much younger than his actual age, which was in his thirties. He was married with two kids, which made me feel a little less ancient—I was forty-three.

That did not last. By the time I was hired and stumbling around the office, it was clear I was one of the most senior members of the staff. One day, I walked into the office, and young guys with Mohawks and pierced tongues called me "ma'am."

My office was right next door to Robb's, which I found refreshing, since it would make any time-sensitive communications easier. He and several other senior executives told me to relax my dress; the dot-com world was very casual. That night, I joked with my husband that we were now both vice presidents, "Only I wear blue jeans, while you still wear blue suits!"

In 2000, our company was trying to create a virtual assistant, sort of a precursor to today's Siri, only a whole lot more user-friendly. Our product targeted road warriors—businesspeople who traveled a lot and had no administrative support. Our virtual assistant, which was called Confidant, was able to read your email to you, take dictation, make travel arrangements, and ship presentations overnight, among other things. We had a human customer service team to handle specialized requests, but mostly the virtual assistant handled things.

Robb and his cofounders had secured a venture capitalist to invest our seed money, but we were burning through that rapidly as we tried to develop the software necessary to give Confidant her widespread flexibility. That meant the computer programmers and the webmaster were kings and queens of the compound. They worked around the clock. Our company regularly brought in meals and massage therapists for them.

There was a twenty-four-hour game room dominated by a foosball table that was rarely idle. In fact, the noise from the game room got so loudly enthusiastic sometimes, I thought I was working at a fraternity house whose sole qualification for admission was being a member of the millennial generation.

I had been working there about four months when I attended one of my monthly book club meetings.

"How's the new job?" one of the members asked me.

"It's like dot-com daycare," I said. "I watch young people play for a good part of the day, then program furiously at night. The average employee is twenty-three years old. They all call me 'ma'am' because I am probably their mother's age." I told the group that my colleagues often spewed geek talk at me, and most of the time, I tried not to look too dumb while they did it. "But," I added, "I had to ask one of the tech support guys for some assistance with my computer. The whole time he's in my office, I'm watching the piercing in his tongue. It has a little ball on a track that slides back and forth in his mouth. I could not look away from it as he explained my computer problem. Of course, I didn't hear a word he said."

I told them that some days, it was completely surreal and that I had to change the way I viewed technology. "Our firm hires the best programmers they can find," I said, "and some of these people have never seen daylight or interacted with other humans before."

The book club member shrieked with laughter at that one.

My dot-com tumbled in the great dot-com crash less than a year later. We never made it to the IPO, but we were generating client interest. I was able to get us featured on WTOP Radio, the road warrior's number one station in the Washington metropolitan area. Confidant cooperated beautifully, her mechanical tone transmitting smoothly across the airwaves as I asked her to do a simple office task.

Still, it was not enough to counter the dot-com crash. Venture capital dried up like rain in the summer desert. As I packed up my second office in two years, my husband said I needed to stop making a habit of it. "This is absolutely the last time," I said. "I am really retired now!" Then I got back in bed and pulled the covers and my pillow over my head.

CHAPTER 10

Traveling Is Life

WHEN YOU CONFRONT YOUR MORTALITY AT AN EARLY AGE, you become imbued with a quest to see everything that's out there. While most folks might say, "One of these days I'd like to go to China," I'm the kind of person who wants to go to China *now*. Today is the day. Today is always the day.

One of the best ways to forget about my medical dramas, if just for a short time, and to rejoice in being alive was to travel the world. From the early days of our relationship, Howard and I put our minds to seeing as much of this glorious planet as we possibly could, traveling to the ends of the Earth to explore some of the world's most stunning locales. This feeling intensified after I stepped away from corporate America and focused on squeezing even more out of my time.

After thirty-four years of marriage, I sat down one day and counted up all the trips we had taken. I couldn't believe it—I got to thirty-one major trips. We left the country a total of twenty-nine times. Some of those were short hops to Canada or islands such as Puerto Rico, Bermuda, and the Bahamas early in our marriage. But as we got older (and thus made more money), we got more adventurous: Egypt for two weeks, Europe for two weeks on two separate trips to different regions, Tahiti for two weeks, Australia and New

Zealand for almost three weeks, Thailand and Indonesia for three weeks, South Africa for two weeks. I was giddy that we could check off six of the seven continents (and I honestly don't have any interest in Antarctica; it'd be too cold). I believe I've seen every single place on my travel bucket list.

My travels with Howard have provided me with some of the most exciting, vivid, distinct memories of my life—as if they happened yesterday. We had several different categories of trips. There was the veg-out trip, when we needed a total escape from the stresses of work and life. These usually consisted of going somewhere pretty, like the Caribbean. Howard lay out on the beach and I snorkeled—while our minds turned to a happy mush. Then there were the learning trips, when we went to places so rich in history and culture that we'd feel like we were postgrad students conducting research, like brown-skinned Margaret Meads. In some places we were able to do both: veg-out and also learn something while we were there.

We took one of the most epic veg-out trips early in our marriage, in 1985. It was a Caribbean Windjammer Barefoot cruise to the Leeward and Windward Islands, which include Anguilla, St. Kitts, St. Maarten, St. Lucia, St. Vincent, and Nevis. This cruise line outfitted luxury yachts to accommodate several dozen people, who were allowed to participate in crew activities. It was not a high-end trip, but the benefit was that the smaller ship was able to visit smaller islands that the massive cruise lines couldn't reach—places like Tobago Cays and Mustique. We hit a different island each day, and by the second week on that boat, we had ascended to a higher plane of mush-minded veg-out. We were still in our twenties, so Howard and I were all about the fun. In fact, we were the youngest couple on the ship—and the only black people. There were costume parties, a drinking game ("boat race") with women and men competing against each other, good food, an endless array of diversions—or the opportunity to do nothing at all.

At one of the islands, the other passengers were getting excited about disembarking and hitting one beach in particular. Howard and

I soon discovered the reason for the excitement: it was a nude beach. As the bus got closer to the beach, we looked at each other.

"These people are really gonna do this?" Howard asked.

We quickly got our answer. As soon as the bus stopped, the other couples started shedding clothes. Howard and I looked at each other, laughed . . . and started disrobing. We said to ourselves, "When in Rome . . ."

I don't think spending a day at a nude beach would have made it onto my original travel bucket list, but there I was, storing another memorable experience in my memory bank. We saw one of our ship-mates, a fifty-something businessman from California, walking arm in arm on the beach with a lovely blonde woman who appeared to be a bit younger than him. Neither of them wore a stitch of clothing. We talked to him when we got back to the boat.

"Hey, Phil, what's your wife's name?" I asked him.

Phil looked over at us and chuckled. "I divorced her in 1959. I think her name was Mary." Our eyes widened as Phil laughed out loud.

"Well, who was that on the beach?"

"Oh, I just met her on the boat," he said.

That's the kind of trip it was.

I particularly liked visiting French-speaking countries, so I could practice my facility with the language. As a French speaker in the United States, you don't get a chance to do much practicing. I enjoyed our trips to France and the opportunity to speak the language in-country and when we traveled to other countries on the European continent. While traveling the German countryside in the late 1980s with my college roommate and her husband, I was able to negotiate our stay at a bed-and-breakfast by speaking French to the owners. Since no one in our group spoke German, the French language was a bridge that facilitated communication with our hosts. Islands like St. Barts and Martinique and French-speaking African countries were perfect for me, though they didn't necessarily work for poor Howard, whose French vocabulary began and ended with *oui*.

We were transformed by the time we spent in South Africa in 2007. The previous year, we were supposed to go to Australia and New Zealand, but we had to cancel the trip because I had to have hip surgery. I was so afraid that the surgery signaled the end of my globe-trotting. I even called my mother in tears, which was a rarity for me because I never wanted to burden her with my struggles. I was depressed because it seemed that my local doctors had run out of miracles for me. Fortunately, through the talented work of an expert orthopedic surgeon in Minnesota, I was soon literally back on my feet. So the next year I was ecstatic when I saw that Coming Back Together, a Syracuse University African American and Latino alumni initiative, was organizing a trip to South Africa. I told Howard we had to go.

I got together with a dozen or so of the black female alums to do a safari side trip before joining the big group. The safari was epic. We were at the Makalali Private Game Reserve, a high-end lodge with well-equipped huts that were accessible to the animals in the wild. On one of the night safaris, we were in search of the Big Five—rhino, leopard, elephant, cape buffalo, and lion, the five most dangerous animals to humans in that region. We had already seen lions, elephants, and hippos. On the night safari we were hoping to see the leopards, which you can only see at night when they hang out in the trees.

Though our only weapon was my Nikon, our guides were well armed. In fact, when we came upon giant hippos bathing in a pond, one of my friends from Syracuse asked the guide, "Hey, you still got that gun, right?"

During the night safari we came upon an unbelievable sight: a pack of lions crossed right in front of our Jeep, only about ten feet away from us. It was breathtaking. I slowly lifted my camera and got some fabulous shots, forever memorializing these magnificent animals in our scrapbook.

Later that night when we were trying to sleep, we kept hearing animals moving around outside of our hut. I wasn't concerned, but Howard found it a bit disconcerting. While I was asleep, Howard heard an enormous lion's roar that he said sounded like something out of a cartoon. I was sorry to have missed it. The next morning when we called the front desk, we were told that a pack of lions had moved through the area the previous night. "There are lion tracks around your cabin," the desk clerk said. "We'll send someone over to escort you all to breakfast."

Howard and I looked at each other. Lion tracks? Escort to breakfast? We didn't expect nature to be quite *that* close at the game reserve. The lions were making sure we got our money's worth. When the escort showed up, Howard wondered why he didn't have a weapon. "What's *he* gonna do?" Howard whispered to me. I tried not to laugh out loud.

Once we joined up with the large alumni group, we hit some of the must-sees, such as Robben Island, where Nelson Mandela was imprisoned for eighteen of his twenty-seven prison years. It was very moving to walk through the prison spaces, guided by a former Robben Island prisoner. Including Mandela, three former Robben Island prisoners have gone on to become president of South Africa.

We spent some time visiting children at a school in South Africa. They were so adorable! I practically emptied out Howard's wallet when it came time to donate money to the school. I absolutely loved spending time around children, but we decided early on that we weren't going to undertake the risk of having one of our own. I always assumed that I wasn't able to have them, what with all my medical challenges, but not long after we were married an ob-gyn friend of ours told us he thought I could deliver a baby. We talked about it over the course of several weeks, but eventually Howard told me, "Yes, ultimately we could have a household of three people if we are successful—but we could also have a household of one if we aren't successful and I lost you. The gain is not worth the risk to me."

That was the end of that. We never really talked about it again. One weekend years later, a gaggle of my nieces visited and we had so much fun with them. As I watched Howard with the little ones, I felt a few pangs of regret that he would never know what it was like to have children of his own. "Howard," I said later that night, "I'm sorry I can't give you children."

He swept me up into a huge embrace and smiled down at me. "It's not a concern of mine, Gail."

I believed him. So I let it go.

During our wonderful trip to Egypt in 1996, we were reminded of how traveling can be a different experience for African Americans. After going on a few TWA tours, we took an Abercrombie & Kent cruise down the Nile and we were blown away by the stunning views. When we went to Aswan, which is overflowing with incredible ancient sites and stories, we spent time with the Nubians, the ethnic group who, at one time, ruled all of Egypt and who have retained much of their incredibly rich culture. As we circulated among them, they asked me and Howard to come back to their huts, which were their living quarters. We were able to socialize and learn about their lives in a much more intimate setting than I expected. When we got back to the ship and sat for dinner, trading stories with other couples, they were all shocked that we had been invited to the huts of the Nubians.

"Nobody asked us to go back to their huts!" one of the women complained.

Howard and I looked at each other and started laughing. All the other couples were white; as usual, we were the only black people on the ship. They couldn't understand why we were treated differently. But Howard and I knew. There weren't even any words required between us. All it took was a glance. We knew. It was like the time in the late 1980s when we went to a ski resort in Pennsylvania with three other African Americans. The African American piano player in the resort restaurant was happy to see us, and we were pleased to meet him. One night during the cocktail hour, he took a break from his normal set of standard popular tunes and, to our surprise, played the music to "Lift Every Voice and Sing," which is often referred to as the African American national anthem, to his audience of five. Only the piano player and our group of five knew that we were communicating on a different wavelength.

CHAPTER 11

Sand in My Shoes
FEBRUARY 1999, TAHITI

"PUIS-JE AVOIR UN VERRE D'EAU, S'IL VOUS PLAIT? AVEC LA GLACE?"
I asked the bartender, walking into the beach bar at Club Med
Bora Bora.

He glanced up in surprise, turned to get my glass of ice water,
and pushed it across the tiki bar towards me. As I reached for it, he
turned to a Frenchman sitting at the bar having his morning coffee
and a Gauloises cigarette.

"Not only does she speak French," he said to the man, making
sure I could hear, "she speaks very good French." They both cast impressed looks my way.

I looked down, a pleased smile slipping across my lips, and took
a sip of my water. It was no surprise to me I had been underestimated
again. Apparently, the Club Med staff rarely met Americans who
could speak the local language. They assumed anyone who could, and
looked like me, must be Haitian or from French West Africa. But I
was clearly from neither place—Americans emit a unique confidence
that is hard to miss.

In my experience, the French can be snobby about their beautifully melodic language. During my dozen years studying it and visiting several French-speaking nations, I have found that many French

141

dislike that so many people tramp through their countries unable to speak or understand the language. But even more so, they hate to hear the language butchered.

I had just enough time to finish drinking my ice water before I had to hurry down the beach with all my snorkel gear to join a boat full of other tourists headed to the magnificent reefs surrounding Bora Bora. I had loved snorkeling since I first jumped off a boat into the Caribbean Sea on our honeymoon in February 1981. A crewman had jumped in with me and held my hand through the first few minutes until I got the hang of it. My fascination with all the sea life made me forget any fear.

The boat was manned by buff Polynesians wearing ponytails long enough to brush the tops of their glorious, bronzed shoulders. They set sail toward the reefs circling this Tahitian island created from the eruption of a giant volcano still located hundreds of feet below us. It was impossible not to drink in the beauty of this place. I could easily see how it had seduced artist Paul Gauguin and movie star Marlon Brando, who bought his own private island not far from where I was.

I left Howard back at our bungalow. Jumping off boats into forty feet of ocean water was not his thing. We were both happier pursuing different activities when we were at resorts like this, and I knew he had his golf clubs to amuse himself.

Eventually our Polynesian hosts anchored the boat. As I suited up, donning a long, stretchy black aquatic suit designed specifically to shield my skin from the relentlessly blazing sun, my fellow snorkelers stared at me.

"You look right official," one of them said. He merely added fins, a mask, and a snorkel to go with his swim trunks.

"The sun can burn you through the water before you realize it," I said. "And it's not like I need a tan." I usually tried to bring some humor to the fact that I was almost always the only African American on these deep-sea adventures. I have tried for years to get my friends to go snorkeling with me, but nine out of ten of them don't know how to swim very well. My husband Howard is the same, despite taking lessons when he was a child. I guess fear is a hard thing for a lot of people to overcome.

I jumped off the boat into the crystal-clear water. The underwater view was spectacular. I could see forty feet down to the bottom. The peaks of brightly colored reefs were about ten feet below us, and we swam against a relatively strong current to get to them. The current came from the open ocean where there was a natural break in the reefs encircling Bora Bora. There were so many multicolored tropical fish, I did not know which ones to focus on first.

One of our Polynesian guides swam close to me and pointed his finger down at a tiny opening in the reef. I dove down a bit and saw a moray eel. Then he dove even farther and brought up an octopus. When he swam closer, he offered the octopus to me. I raised my eyebrows in question since we were underwater and I could not ask, "Est-il correct de le toucher?" He nodded and placed the small octopus in my hand. It immediately wrapped its tentacles around my wrist. I gingerly rubbed its head. It felt like a wet mushroom. After a moment, the octopus grew agitated and started spewing ink at me. I let it go and it swam quickly back toward the reef.

I surfaced for a moment to get my bearings and blow the seawater from my snorkel tube. I could see some of the other snorkelers exploring various parts of the reef several yards away. I put my head back down in the water, kicked my fins, using strong leg strokes to counter the vigorous current, and made my way toward them.

There was so much to see beneath the undulating aquamarine water, we must've snorkeled for hours. Floating in that warm, crystalline sea was the closest I had ever come to flying outside of an airplane. My body felt free and weightless. It was sheer bliss to spread my arms and legs wide and let the current move me. I knew I could not stop grinning around the snorkel bit in my mouth. By the time I climbed aboard the boat, I was pleasantly tired and as happy as I could ever imagine being.

Tahiti is one of the most beautiful places I have ever seen. Howard and I joked that if we could find jobs, we would stay there forever. It had all of my favorite things—warm clear water, powdery white sand, hunky, French-speaking Polynesians, and a casual lifestyle. What more could a girl want?

We spent two weeks there, one week on the island of Moorea and the second on Bora Bora. Each island had different things to offer. Moorea was a lush tropical paradise, but Bora Bora had some of the best reefs I have ever seen anywhere in the world. I've spent time snorkeling at the Great Barrier Reef off Australia, the Indian Ocean off the coast of Thailand, throughout the Caribbean, and off the Mayan coast of Mexico. But none of them surpassed Tahiti's South Pacific splendor.

My husband has always been a very good sport, accompanying me around the world to pursue my passion for foreign travel and adventure. That was never more evident than during one particular evening when we were seated at dinner with a table full of Europeans. I sat next to a Swiss man. He was fluent in most of the languages being spoken around our table, so he was having a very good time talking to everyone.

Since we had been in Tahiti awhile, I had my ear for the language back, and my French was tripping off my tongue more fluently. It gets rusty from lack of use at home. At one point, while I was laughing at a joke one of the French men told, my poor husband looked at me in bewilderment. "What's so funny?" he asked me. He does not speak another language, so most of the dinner conversation went over his head.

"Nothing really," I said. "The guy over there was just making fun of some of the stuff they do at resorts like this."

The Swiss man to my left, seeing my husband's puzzlement, began translating what everyone was saying for Howard's benefit. Howard relaxed once he could also enjoy the conversations taking place in German, Italian, and French. He had spent several lonely moments during dinner looking down at his plate, unable to converse with anyone but me. Once he was included, he smiled and nodded at each person speaking. Stung by my thoughtlessness, I promised never to let him feel left out again.

The next day, I was surprised when Howard joined me on a shark-feeding expedition that I had signed up for at the beginning of our week in Bora Bora. The boat stopped first at a shallow sandbar. All of us jumped off the boat and petted stingrays, following the directions our guides offered. We kept away from their razor-sharp tails and stayed near their heads, feeding them underneath their bodies where their mouths were located. Howard enjoyed petting the huge manta rays immensely since we were standing in only waist-deep water.

A half hour later, everyone climbed aboard the boat again and we sailed toward the edge of Bora Bora's circular reef. We could see the dark, choppy water of the open ocean beyond the reef. That's where the sharks usually roamed. Half a dozen Polynesian men were with us, and two of them were armed with harpoon guns. We knew they were trying to ensure our safety, but accidents happen when you interact with wildlife.

The guides warned us to stay close to the boat and hang on to the runners along the side. They warned us not to go thrashing about, as that would attract the sharks' attention. Then they threw several large fish heads into the water and waited for the reef sharks to catch the scent. After a few moments, dozens of six-foot-long sharks swam through the opening in the reef and began attacking the fish heads.

One of the Polynesians told us we could start climbing in the water with our snorkel gear. Eager to participate, I was one of the first down the ladder. Immersing myself, I put my face down and saw dozens of sharks swimming just below my fins. It was an adrenaline rush like none I had ever experienced. I loved every second of it.

I put my head up and asked Howard to take a picture of me in the ocean with all the shark fins swimming around me. He took several shots then waved to indicate he had gotten enough.

Then he did something shocking. He borrowed a snorkel, fins, and a mask and climbed down the ladder to join us in the ocean.

"Um, Howard," I said, "this water is pretty deep." I knew he didn't like swimming in water over his head.

"I know," he said, climbing down the ladder.

"You have never snorkeled before," I said. "Not even in shallow water. Are you sure you want to learn how with sharks swimming around your feet?"

"I did not come all this way not to at least try this." Then, borrowing a line from a popular beer commercial, Howard said, "You only go around once." He continued down the ladder, clinging tightly to its rail. I asked some of the other snorkelers if they would move a little so he could squeeze in next to me. He adjusted the mask over his eyes and nose, then stuck the snorkel between his teeth.

"You have to breathe through your mouth, not your nose," I said.

He nodded and put his head under the water to take a look at the sharks. He couldn't quite get the breathing right, and his mask filled quickly with water. Soon, he had had enough. He slowly made his way back to the ladder, never letting go of the boat rail as he moved around the other tourists, and climbed aboard.

I stayed out in the water awhile longer, then climbed back on board with everyone else when the guides motioned that it was time to go. "Wow, you really surprised me!" I said, giving him a soggy hug.

"Yeah," he said, "I was brave all right. Did you see the Polynesian guy with a large horizontal scar on his torso? I bet a shark took a piece out of him."

For the three decades we have been traveling together, the odds have been in my favor. I have gotten seriously ill on only four of more than twenty-five trips abroad. Such was the case on our first trip to Bermuda, where we stayed at a resort on a secluded part of the island. We had decided to try something closer to home for a quick but luxurious getaway.

Midway through the first week of our trip, I went on a catamaran excursion to visit a famous reef near Bermuda. It was a beautiful day for sailing. The sky and water were a crisp azure blue. The sun was so bright, I had to cover my eyes with dark shades so I could still make out details on the charming shoreline. I took some photos of the pink exterior of our hotel as we sailed past it.

When we got within proximity of the reef, the captain refused to moor the boat any closer than a mile from the reef, fearful that his brand new hull might be damaged by the jagged coral reaching close to the surface. Instead, he insisted all the snorkelers swim that mile toward the heart of the reef if they wanted to see it.

Being an avid swimmer and an experienced snorkeler, I jumped in with the same bravado as everyone else. But after a quarter mile of swimming, I knew I was in trouble. I tired much more quickly in the strong current than the others. I breathed heavily through my snorkel to get enough oxygen to my starving lungs, let alone my extremities. My legs began to feel heavy, then painful, so I turned around and headed back towards the catamaran.

When my legs and ankles began to ache sharply, I knew a crisis was coming on. I was taking hydroxyurea, a drug that had decreased my hospitalizations for sickle cell crises from four to six per year to just a handful over the three decades since I had started taking it, in 1987. I feared my body had gotten used to the drug, rendering it less effective. By the time I climbed aboard the catamaran, pins and needles started going through my legs, then into my back and arms. I was in full-blown sickle cell crisis within minutes and too far from shore to tell Howard, who was at the hotel, that I needed help.

Not wanting to alarm the skeleton crew who stayed aboard, I swallowed a couple of the pain pills I kept in my fanny pack for emergencies, drank from a bottle of water the crew supplied, and sat down on some cushions on deck. After fifteen minutes, I knew the pills were not going to work. They did little to stop the onslaught of pain racing through my body. I asked a crewman if I could lie down below deck because I did not feel well. Since we had to wait until the others returned from the reef before we could sail back to shore, I lay there in misery for another hour or two. I lost track of time, but I finally heard the captain pulling up anchor and turning the catamaran around to head back to shore.

Once we finally returned to the resort, I slowly and painfully hobbled to our room. The hot concrete patio singed my bare feet as I made my way across it to our bungalow. Howard was inside our room, and I told him quickly what was happening. Alarmed, he immediately called the hotel desk to find out how to get me to the nearest hospital. Even though it had been several years since I had had a crisis and he was beginning to believe they were rare, he adopted old habits to get me the best care he could find.

The Bermuda resort management team was wonderful. They arranged for our transportation and sent us to a local hospital near the resort. The ambulance crew carefully backed its vehicle down a hill to get as close as possible to our bungalow. Then two men carried me on a stretcher up some stairs and across a wide paved area to put me into the back of the ambulance. Howard jumped in with me, and off we went to face whatever foreign care was available.

In 1986, a year before I started taking hydroxyurea, I had a sickle cell crisis in Jamaica, and neither one of us wanted a repeat of that horrid odyssey. The first hospital the resort sent us to in Jamaica was like something out of *National Geographic*. People were moaning on the floor, swatting flies away from their eyes while one or two harried doctors raced to and fro, overwhelmed. I begged Howard to get me out of there, or I would die for sure. He found a second hospital, a small house with no air conditioning, where ceiling fans stirred the hot, muggy air around but did little to cool the room. I had to plead for more pain medicine every few hours, and nurses would delay it as long as they could—deliberately, it seemed, until Howard demanded the doctor intervene. The nurses were mean and jabbed the needles in especially hard. One rotund nurse's aide sneered at my Americanism, and often dropped my food tray hard enough to rattle dishes.

My first impression of the hospital emergency room in Bermuda was not good either. It was dim and old and seemed a bit disorganized. The young physician who first saw me did not appear to be very skilled. She was obviously a newly graduated doctor with no experience with sickle cell anemia. After reading over my typed medication list, she made snide comments about not having heard of some of my medications before. After giving me a cursory examination and asking a few questions, she left me squirming in pain on the exam table for far too long. As I writhed, sweating in pain, I looked to Howard, my eyes pleading with him to do something. He knew what the look meant. He would have to do battle for me. I was too weakened with pain to do it myself. He left the exam room and went to speak to somebody with authority.

Due to my husband's tireless advocacy on my behalf, we found a doctor who could help me. The Bermudian hospital staff put me in an isolated room since I had been in a US hospital within the year and they feared I might be bringing a hospital infection with me. Then they called a white doctor to treat me. She asked me many questions, sat by my bedside, and then did something I had never seen another doctor do before: she recused herself. She thought it would be better for *me* if she arranged an outside specialist to come in and treat me.

She was right. The Bermudian specialist turned out to be a black doctor who had a son with sickle cell anemia. He knew just how to treat my crisis. He ordered drugs I had never heard of, and he insisted the nurses keep them coming every three hours. He told me he knew how to keep me comfortable. And he did. He even called my primary care physician, just like I requested. Most doctors just looked at me like I was crazy when I suggested they contact my doctor back in the United States.

"You know," the Bermudian specialist said, "your doctor is a very nice man." It was a few days after I had been admitted, and he was in my room to check on me. "I can tell he cares a great deal about you. We discussed your care, and I think we are on the right track."

It was one of the most pleasant hospital stays I have ever had.

Within three or four days, my crisis abated and I was released. I could even return to our resort to finish the last week of vacation.

The day after my release, I was relaxing on a beach recliner next to my husband and staring at the clear azure water longingly. My husband could tell what was on my mind. "Don't even *think* about it," he said. "I don't want to end up in the emergency room again." He put his earphones back on to indicate the subject was closed.

I sighed and reclined, feeling chastened like a kindergartner who could not go out to play.

PART 4

Crashing

CHAPTER 12

The Politics of Pain

I HAVE ALREADY SURVIVED MUCH LONGER THAN MY PEDIATRICIAN predicted. It just shows doctors don't know everything. Once I educated myself about my disease and learned to manage it better by avoiding triggers like frigid cold, infections, fatigue, and too much stress, I evaded many of the crises that I might have had.

My mother had never heard of the disease before the physicians told her about it. She certainly never knew what was wrong with her before that day. It explained so much about the pain she felt as a youth that small-town minds had dismissed as "growing pains."

She had never seen anything about it on the news and never heard it even whispered about in the rural towns where her reverend father moved the family as he sought employment at parishes throughout North and South Carolina. This was not surprising during the early part of the twentieth century. Even today, our illness is not widely known, despite the fact that it is the most common inherited blood disorder in the United States.

One reason sickle cell disease remains so obscure is its lack of publicity. There are no famous celebrities or professional athletes headlining high-profile fundraisers for us, and since sickle cell disease sufferers tend to be people of color, they have not fared well in the politics of pain that characterizes big money fundraising in the United States.

According to the Centers for Disease Control and Prevention, sickle cell disease affects millions of people throughout the world. It is particularly common among those whose ancestors come from sub-Saharan Africa, South America, the Caribbean, Central America, Saudi Arabia, India, and Mediterranean countries like Turkey, Greece, and Italy. Sickle cell disease seems to occur most frequently in areas of the world plagued by malaria, which led some researchers to link the two diseases. It is widely believed that people with the sickle cell trait are less likely to contract severe malaria than people with normal hemoglobin. Sickle cells compromise hemoglobin's ability to carry oxygen throughout the body, which starves the malaria parasite in the process.

In the United States, sickle cell disease affects about 100,000 people. Statistically, it occurs in 1 in 365 African American births and 1 in 16,500 Hispanic American births. At least 70 percent of those afflicted are considered economically disadvantaged, without access to decent health care. By contrast, approximately 2 million Americans—about 1 in 12 African Americans—have the sickle cell trait. They carry one gene and can pass it along to their children, but they do *not* experience any symptoms themselves, so many are unaware of it.

It is difficult to pinpoint the exact number of sickle cell trait carriers because most feel fine and, for most of the early twentieth century, people rarely got tested for it. Many of them unknowingly procreated with another trait carrier, creating the disease in their children, who suffer the consequences of their parents' union every day of their shortened lives.

In the United States, there was no routine testing for the sickle cell trait or the disease until 1972, when President Richard Nixon signed the National Sickle Cell Anemia Control Act and pledged to "reverse the record of neglect on the dreaded disease." He made a public commitment to fund $1 billion in research at the National Heart, Lung, and Blood Institute, part of the National Institutes of Health (NIH). About $10 million of that was dedicated to sickle cell research.

"It is a sad and shameful fact that the causes of this disease have been largely neglected throughout our history," Nixon said. "We cannot rewrite this record of neglect, but we can reverse it. To this end, this administration is increasing its budget for research and treatment of sickle cell disease."

But even with all its promise, the act eventually lapsed and most people forgot about the disease until the next federal initiative. In 2003, President George W. Bush signed the Sickle Cell Treatment Act, a bipartisan bill enacted only because it was tacked onto an amendment to the American Jobs Creation Act of 2004. The act contained several key elements to help thousands of sickle cell sufferers not being treated effectively. For instance, the law provided funding to eligible Medicaid recipients for physician and laboratory services that were not reimbursed or were under-reimbursed by Medicaid. It also let states receive a fifty-fifty federal funding match for non-medical expenses such as genetic counseling, community outreach, and education about the illness, and it authorized an annual $10 million competitive grant program for five years to create forty treatment centers at Federally Qualified Health Centers (FQHC) across the nation for sickle cell patients.

But in reality, these initiatives have suffered significantly, whether it's because of states not opting to take the funds or because the initiatives are not fully funded at the national level. The Sickle Cell Disease Association of America (SCDAA), an advocate for the disease based in Baltimore, Maryland, has tracked the implementation of many of these well-intentioned but unevenly executed laws. Several states have not opted to accept any of the expanded Medicaid reimbursement available. Since the Sickle Cell Treatment Act, the SCDAA has worked with a handful of congressional champions to advocate for full funding each year. Even though it receives broad-based community and bipartisan legislative support, the act has never been fully funded by Congress. The United States Department of Health and Human Services oversees funding and research for sickle cell disease. As part of its mandate, the agency collects and distributes public information on managing the disease. From 1972 to 2001, the department dedicated $923 million toward sickle cell research, but Congress never fully funded this commitment. In reality, it seems, there is a widespread lack of will to fulfill all these good intentions, and as a result, the needs of sickle cell patients nationwide far outpace available health care services.

But it's not all bad news. As a result of NIH jumping in to unravel the mysteries of sickle cell disease in the 1970s, quite a few research labs funded by NIH grants have produced positive developments to help doctors better understand the illness. According to NIH, sickle cell disease is the first human disease to be fully characterized at the DNA level. Medical science knows *why* it occurs, just not how to effectively treat or cure it. However, NIH grants have spurred private researchers and pharmaceutical companies to invent some new therapies.

Nonetheless, scientists still know little about how it progresses. Most studies only have information about the sickest patients. There is limited information about the typical course of the disease or what works therapeutically to treat or prevent its symptoms in the vast majority of patients whose symptoms are not as severe.

Since the 1970s, researchers have discovered some useful information that has changed the way the disease is treated. Hospitals now routinely screen newborns to detect the disease and suggest giving affected infants and toddlers daily doses of penicillin to ward off life-threatening infections that kill children younger than three years old. NIH found that giving oral penicillin daily to patients aged three months to three years reduced bacterial infections by 84 percent. Researchers now know the disease destroys the spleen at an early age, leaving youngsters particularly vulnerable to bacterial infections.

My own spleen shriveled and died when I was a preteen. So did my brother Tim's.

Still, some breakthroughs have been discovered by accident. Such was the case with hydroxyurea, a chemotherapy drug first used to treat leukemia patients that is now prescribed to sickle cell patients, as it was for me. Doctors at Johns Hopkins Hospital were treating a little boy who had both leukemia and sickle cell anemia. After a while, they noticed the hydroxyurea had no impact on his leukemia, but it seemed to improve the child's sickle cell symptoms. Incredibly, the chemotherapy drug created more fetal hemoglobin in the child. These fetal cells collapsed less often into the sickle shape, causing fewer painful episodes and sickle cell crises. These findings were so compelling that, in the mid-1990s, the US Food and Drug Administration fast-tracked hydroxyurea's approval and made it available to the general sickle cell population.

Even before this breakthrough made news headlines, my favorite primary care doctor, an African American man with a kind heart, suggested putting me on the drug. I had been seeing him for twenty-five years, and he was always on the lookout for something to help my worsening health. His practice was associated with the Johns Hopkins Hospital network, so he heard about it early.

For me, hydroxyurea was a miracle drug. It improved my health immensely. I went from having sickle cell crises three or four times a year to not having any for five years! But I knew it could not last. As with all drugs, my body grew accustomed to it, and after a while, I began having occasional crises again, like the one in Bermuda.

My doctor tried juggling my dosage to kick-start the beneficial effects again, but that only worked for a while. Discouraged, I sought out NIH experts to see what therapies I might try next. They put me on a drug that boosts production of red blood cells. It, too, worked for a while, but these days, my body struggles to make red blood cells on its own, and I have discovered nothing new on the current market that can help me.

In the fundraising world, sickle cell disease is not in the running for high-profile, multimillion-dollar campaigns like those run annually for heart disease or cancer. Our illness is still considered relatively rare by the mainstream medical community. But rare is relative in the politics of pain.

There are several rarer diseases in the United States. But the parents of some children with obscure and very rare illnesses are often desperate enough to begin foundations so they can help find a cure. Unfortunately, that is not the case for sickle cell disease. Many of its sufferers cling desperately to the bottom rung of the economic and educational ladder. So the wherewithal, will, and knowledge to begin foundations often elude them. The situation is so serious, doctors call sickle cell disease an "orphan disease" because of its very lack of champions.

The problem? It's a matter of racial politics. Sickle cell is considered a "black" disease. Anything with the label "black" is still viewed with suspicion, if not distaste, by many in this country and abroad. There is already racial disparity when it comes to access to good health care. The Centers for Disease Control (CDC) in Atlanta issued a report saying people with sickle cell disease have less access to comprehensive health care than people with other genetic disorders such as hemophilia and cystic fibrosis. They do not receive regular attention from either primary care doctors or specialists who could monitor the unique aspects of their illness.

In fact, the CDC says an estimated 90 percent of people with sickle cell disease are still unable to attain the resources they need to improve or maintain their health. Even today's proven therapies are not being used adequately. At the time of this writing, only 30 percent of sickle cell patients are being treated with hydroxyurea, an inexpensive drug proven twenty years ago to reduce pain crises, stroke, pulmonary complications, and disability. That means tens of thousands of victims are out there suffering unnecessarily.

The implications are clear. Access to comprehensive health care and research funding is based largely on who gets the disease. Millions of dollars pour in annually for the research and treatment of heart disease, which affects Caucasian males. Very little money trickles in for less-understood diseases that mostly affect people who are black, poor, and undereducated.

The same rule of thumb applies to publicity about my disorder. During my dozen years as a major-city journalist, I noticed firsthand that news editors are, for the most part, predominantly Caucasian males. Their point of view was that stories about white people's problems were much more newsworthy than stories about African Americans. Only crime stories seemed to regularly feature people of color. It was an opinion I could never shake, no matter how often I pointed it out to my editors.

It is common to be underestimated and misunderstood as a person of color. It follows that we are also treated differently in our most vulnerable moments, such as when we are born with an incurable illness. I have spent half a century encountering people in and out of the medical profession who do not care about my disease. It's as if we are "throwaway" people.

It is difficult to retain confidence in the scientific and medical communities when I scan the landscape and understand how relatively sparse resources are being expended. To hold on to too much hope is to indulge a dalliance with fantasy. Year after year, I watch other diseases receive floods of cash while sickle cells' cupboards remain bare. But I hold on to the fantasy. Medical breakthroughs are starting to appear, and this is encouraging. Some patients have found a cure in stem cell transplants. Biotech and big pharma companies have also started to look at drugs to cure the disease. One day a cure will come.

I have been a guinea pig in many research studies at NIH over the last twenty years, helping public health officials understand my disease just a little better. My husband and I also devote considerable personal resources to this cause. Due to my sudden blindness and

continued vision problems even today, we recently underwrote a research study by a doctor at the Johns Hopkins Wilmer Eye Institute
that could change the way doctors examine sickle cell patients' eyes.
Right now, ophthalmologists focus on the center of the eye during
routine examinations. But most sickle cell patients like me have problems on the outer areas of the retina, where it's harder to detect fragile
blood vessels that break and hemorrhage easily and detach the retina.
By determining their retinopathy early, with new, state-of-the-art
equipment, doctors may be able to prevent some of these problems.

If this study is successful, it will help thousands of patients with
the vision side effects sickle cell can cause. But what we really need is
more people committed to finding a cure.

What we need here is someone in show business to help us shine
some limelight on this problem.

CHAPTER 13

Possessed by Demons

AS BAD AS MY DISEASE BECAME AS I GREW OLDER, AT LEAST I knew *why* I had sudden pain in all my joints during a sickle cell crisis. Imagine what my ancestors must have thought when they were suddenly beset by pains wicked enough to cause unending anguish. They must have believed they were possessed by demons or evil spirits. I can only imagine them, squirming helplessly in pain while some witch doctor waved burning herbs and chanted spells over their bodies centuries ago. Most died relatively young without proper medical care, and their deaths were explained away by superstition and tradition.

Depending on whom you believe, sickle cell disease has been present in Africa for at least 5,000 years and has been known by many names in many tribal languages. The disease likely jumped the Atlantic Ocean and made its way to the Americas and Caribbean shores aboard slave ships during the Middle Passage. Some of the millions of captured West and Central Africans likely carried the trait, since Africans with full-blown sickle cell disease usually died in childhood. As slaves were bred on plantations, the disease likely mushroomed over time.

Strangely, the disease remained unobserved in the United States for centuries until 1846, when it was briefly mentioned in an obscure

161

medical publication called the *Southern Journal of Medical Pharmacology*. It contained a paper, "Case of Absence of the Spleen," in which the author describes a runaway slave who was executed and autopsied. The doctor found "the strange phenomenon of a man having lived without a spleen." Spleens in sickle cell patients often shrivel and die, leaving the patients defenseless against bacteria, which is what happened to Tim and me.

Even after the journal article, however, no one made the connection between a missing spleen and sickle cell disease until many decades later, when a few doctors began to connect these dots. In 1910, a cardiologist named Dr. James B. Herrick met a dental student named Walter Clement Noel at the University of Chicago. Noel came from Grenada, a Caribbean island country. He complained to Dr. Herrick about pain episodes and symptoms of anemia.

Dr. Herrick was not very interested in Noel's case, so he assigned it to a resident named Dr. Ernest Irons. Dr. Irons examined Noel's blood under a microscope and saw red blood cells he described as "having the shape of a sickle." The sickle was known only as a farm tool at the time. When Dr. Herrick saw this in Noel's chart, he became more interested in the case because he thought this might be a new, unknown disease. He published a paper in one of the medical journals using the term "sickle-shaped cells" for the first time in medical literature.

A decade later in the 1920s, the role of deoxygenation in sickle cells was discovered by Drs. Hahn and Gillespie. In 1934, Drs. Diggs and Ching postulated that the blockage of small blood vessels might be responsible for the painful "crises" of sickle cell disease. In 1940, Drs. Ham and Castle suggested the exchange of oxygen for carbon dioxide in the small blood vessels causes certain red blood cells to sickle and block these vessels.

The 1940s were also when the long-held theory related to sickle cell and malaria was developed. That's when Dr. E.A. Beet, a British medical officer stationed in Northern Rhodesia (now Zimbabwe), observed that blood from malaria patients who had the sickle cell trait had fewer malarial parasites than blood from patients without the trait. A physician in Zaire also reported that there were fewer cases of severe malaria among people with the sickle cell trait than among those without it. Geneticists believe the abnormal gene mutated over time to help people survive malaria. We now know that when invaded by the malarial parasite, normally stable red cells in someone with the sickle cell trait can sickle in a low oxygen environment like the veins. That sickling process destroys the invading malaria organism and prevents it from spreading through the body. That evolutionary advantage goes haywire, however, when two people with the sickle cell trait create an infant with sickle cell disease. These infants and young children cannot fight off malaria as well because of their deficient immune systems, and many of them die.

In 1948, Dr. Janet Watson, a New York pediatric hematologist, noticed that newborns had very few sickle cells, possibly because of their fetal hemoglobin. She first suggested a link between higher fetal hemoglobin levels and fewer problems with symptoms in sickle cell patients. At birth, blood in the human body contains mostly fetal hemoglobin, the main protein that transports oxygen to fetuses as they develop in the womb. Within twelve weeks after birth, fetal hemoglobin production shuts down in normal, healthy people.

In sickle cell patients, however, that switch does not occur as efficiently, resulting in higher than normal fetal hemoglobin levels for much of their early childhood. This prevents some children from having sickle crises during their developmental years. Even though the protective role of fetal hemoglobin was discovered in the 1940s, finding drugs to simulate that effect in the human body would take decades, and when it happened—as with most revelations surrounding my illness—it occurred entirely by accident.

The hereditary nature of sickle cell disease was suspected, but it was not demonstrated until 1949 by Dr. James V. Neel. A couple of years later, the disease's association with hemoglobin was discovered by Drs. Linus Pauling and Harvey Itano, and Drs. Ibert Wells and

Seymour Singer. They introduced the concept of a "molecular disease," a disease that can be traced to a particular molecule, such as hemoglobin for sickle cell.

In 1955, a Dr. Daniel Tosteson noted abnormalities in how ions are transported in and out of sickle cells. The next year, Drs. C.L. Conley and Rose Schneider developed a test to identify various forms of sickle cell disease and other conditions developed due to defective hemoglobin. It wasn't until 1956 that the actual amino acid substitution that causes the disorder was isolated and identified by Dr. Vernon Ingram. He pinpointed the sickle cell mutation at position six on the beta-hemoglobin protein chain.

As of this writing, doctors at the Mayo Clinic, NIH, and Johns Hopkins Hospital say bone marrow transplants, also called stem cell transplants, offer the only potential "cure" for sickle cell anemia. But finding a donor is difficult and the procedure has serious risks associated with it, including death. That's why stem cell transplants are reserved for the most desperately ill sickle cell patients.

Doctors replace the bone marrow of a sickle cell patient with healthy bone marrow from a donor, usually a healthier sibling. But the diseased bone marrow must first be depleted with radiation or chemotherapy. This process so sickens such patients, they lose their hair. They must be kept in isolation because their immune system is severely repressed, and they can easily catch a bacterial infection. If the transplant is successful, the adult patient begins making normal bone marrow and no longer has sickle cell disease.

As my health worsened in my forties, I tried to get a stem cell transplant myself. Kenneth volunteered to help me and we both went to NIH to be tested. Unfortunately, we were not a complete match in critical areas needed to move forward with the transplant. It was a bleak day, I admit. It was the first time I felt a little of the lost hope my late brother Tim must have experienced. There would be no miracle cure for me. I would live out my days suffering from this disease. I was deeply shaken.

Without other siblings as potential complete matches, I am doomed. So many factors must match, similar to an organ transplant, that doctors are reluctant to proceed without a perfect donor. There is no national registry for this type of procedure yet, so people cannot volunteer to be bone marrow donors. All I can hope for is that some researcher will find another way to turn off the sickle cell gene and help others live a better life someday.

Without a cure or a reliable form of prevention, there is only treatment—and there haven't been any major breakthroughs in how to treat a crisis in recent history. For most of my life, a sickle cell crisis has been treated the same way, with intravenous fluids, oxygen, and shots of strong painkillers like Demerol or Oxycontin every few hours. In the early days of this century, researchers at NIH looked into why people with sickle cell anemia have low levels of nitric oxide in their blood. Nitric oxide is a gas that helps keep blood vessels open and reduces the stickiness of red blood cells. They recruited volunteers to come in during a sickle cell crisis and treated them with nitric oxide. They treated others with a placebo. After a few years, the study ended without a satisfactory conclusion. It was never proven that nitric oxide could prevent sickled cells from clumping together and causing painful crises.

While all this research might seem pricey, the cost of letting the disease linger for decades longer is even more expensive. A 2010 study by NIH researchers illustrated the massive cost to the health care system and, ultimately, to the general population, which must bear the cost of providing care to the indigent. The study narrowed its focus to just one state for one year. Researchers discovered that 85.7 percent of 7,202 hospital admissions for sickle cell crises in Illinois initiated in the emergency room. Total charges for sickle cell–related hospital admissions that year were $30 million. Multiply that by dozens of states with African American and Hispanic patients pouring into emergency rooms, decade after decade, with unexpected episodes of excruciating pain, and you begin to get an idea of how expensive it is to let this disease go without a cure, or at least better treatment than is currently available.

Like all chronic illnesses, frequent emergency room usage is a primary driver of cost. A different study found that children with sickle cell disease who were insured by Medicaid used emergency rooms more often than those with private health care insurance (57 percent versus 45 percent). Since the majority of sickle cell sufferers tend to be economically disadvantaged, most hospital stays for a crisis begin in the emergency room, the most expensive place to treat it.

Johns Hopkins Hospital, recognizing this trend, opened a Sickle Cell Infusion Center in 2011. Patients in the Baltimore-Washington area going into sickle cell crisis can avoid the emergency room altogether and go directly to the center, where intravenous fluids and pain relief medications are administered much sooner than in emergency rooms. This helps avert longer crises and saves medical costs.

Now that screening newborns for sickle cell disease is universal in the United States, parents and their medical caregivers can prevent potentially fatal complications of sickle cell disease during infancy. Once an infant is diagnosed, NIH recommends parents give their children antibiotics to fight off many of the predatory infections that can kill them during their first few years.

After President Nixon declared sickle cell disease a public health priority in the 1970s, there was a push in the African American community to get genetic counseling so carriers of the sickle cell trait would not produce children with one another, helping to prevent the disease. That backfired a bit, though, when some members of the black community viewed that initiative as genocide. Today, carriers of the trait continue to produce children with other carriers, which is why sickle cell disease continues to crop up in hospital emergency rooms across the nation, unchecked, and treated as it has always been for the almost six decades I have been alive.

The fact that I can push back with substantive facts about my illness makes me something of an anomaly, which is most clear to me when I meet a physician for the first time.

"Well, you have obviously gotten very good medical care and educated yourself about your disease so you know how to manage it," an NIH doctor once said to me. "Not everyone does that." Most doctors I have met are like this.

I am an educated, professional, African American woman of middle age, well spoken, well read, and widely traveled. And while I know hundreds of other African Americans very much like me, there are few people with all those attributes who also suffer from this relatively rare illness. Patients the doctors see at NIH, and those whom doctors see at publicly funded urban clinics, are largely poor, black, and undereducated, and they possess little knowledge about their illness. Many drag their young children to the clinic with them, obviously deaf to entreaties about genetic counseling.

I have been lucky enough to have private health insurance for most of my life, and Medicare once I finally conceded to having a disability in my late forties. I have mostly worked with suburban doctors to manage my health care, but even the doctors in these well-funded facilities are not always on the cutting edge when it comes to sickle cell. When they have been stumped by a recent development in my disease, I have been forced to venture to city clinics with a large African American clientele to get the most recent treatment information. These clinics see patients like me every day and have more opportunities to treat sickle cell. That is not the case in the predominantly white suburbs where I have lived most of my life.

Other than our disease, I have little in common, socially or economically, with most of my sick brethren whom I encounter at these clinics. Many are recent immigrants from Africa or the Caribbean. Others are Americans who were never well enough or economically able to complete their education and obtain decent employment. Several of the patients I see waiting there for hours seem to have succumbed to depression or have such a poor self-image, they stopped trying to improve their lot in life years ago. Many are unemployed and rely on public assistance.

Sitting in these waiting rooms is one of the most depressing things I have ever done. The hopelessness in the air is palpable. It threatens to swamp my normally positive attitude. I am well educated and was once employed in relatively well-paid positions, so I feel remarkably out of place in the group therapy sessions the clinic social workers urge us to attend.

At one such session, everyone was complaining about never being able to get a job, while I surreptitiously looked at my watch, knowing I had to get back to work—I was at the dot-com firm at the time. It was such a waste of my time, I never went back. All that negativity bothered me. I have always believed the "mind over matter" mantra. I can do almost anything if I put my mind to it.

Yes, some of my worst sickle cell crises happened after I stretched beyond my endurance, trying to grasp something impossible. But I can live with the pain because I know I at least *tried*.

CHAPTER 14

A Convergence of Calamities

I HAVE BEEN TOLD THAT I AM A SERIOUS PERSON. MY HUSBAND sometimes jokes with me that I'm too busy forging ahead to slow down for the frivolous. If that is indeed true, I suppose that's another personality trait you can attribute to this dastardly disease. Score another for sickle cell.

But when I stepped away from the world of work in my forties, I began to gain an appreciation for the beauty of the moment. Spending summers by the beach with my husband at my side, I saw that a hearty, full-bellied laugh with my beloved offered just about the most sublime pleasure this life has to offer. In all those years of pushing forward, I was propelling myself toward these special moments. I'm happy that I've lived long enough to realize that, to understand to what extent time can reward those who don't lean on her too heavily. When I eased off the pedal a bit, wonderfully sensate secrets revealed themselves. I discovered that the roses did, in fact, demand to be smelled—if you stood still long enough.

Howard and I made a conscious effort to explore the world near and far. That exploration included the Outer Banks region. We have owned Dreamcastle, our house in the beautiful Outer Banks, for more than twenty years. We finally have the time to spend months there, now that Howard has retired from his career as a telecommunications executive.

When we first came to the Outer Banks in the early 1990s, we used to see the horses wandering the dunes near our house. But in 1995, wildlife activists herded the horses north and behind a fence to protect them. Although the wild horses had been living on the Outer Banks for centuries, modern technology—specifically, the millions of cars swarming the Outer Banks during the summer months—had thinned their herds; cars often killed them accidentally along the roads.

The mustangs first came ashore from Spanish galleon ships in the 1500s, when the ships ran aground on the shallow sandbars dotting the coastline. In order to free the ships, the sailors had to decrease their weight, and they jettisoned anything too heavy. Often their horses qualified; overboard they went, to allow the ships to sail on. The horses swam for land and have remained, breeding and living happily on the Outer Banks for generations. As of this writing, there were 130 mustangs roaming the northern North Carolina dunes.

I was excited one morning as we drove north along Route 12 on our way to see the wild mustangs of Currituck County. I missed seeing this important part of Outer Banks life, so we signed up, like tourists, to take the off-road tour to see them again. It was a rainy and overcast morning, a bit chilly for May. During the ride, Howard reminded me it was the first anniversary of my leg amputation. May 18.

"It is?" I asked, wrinkling my brow. "I didn't remember. I knew I had the surgery a year ago in May, just not exactly when." I thought about my right foot and its eighteen-month battle against that virulent infection. I couldn't remember many details, as the doctors had kept me drugged up most of the time. "Did we say a proper goodbye to my foot?" I asked, growing teary. "It was a good foot. It deserved something. I hope we said something." I started becoming visibly upset as I remembered parts of the ordeal.

"Yes," Howard said, "about two days before the surgery, we said our goodbyes to your foot. You started it off yourself. You said, 'Thanks for being a good foot and carrying me all over Syracuse University so I could meet Howard. And thanks for taking me all over the world. You were a very good foot. I am sorry you have to go.'"

"I did?" I asked, crying openly now. "I'm glad I did. You have to show respect for something when it dies. Especially when it's a thing you treasure more than you know. It *was* a very good foot." I told Howard my family did the same thing when my favorite dog Pepper died. A good dog deserves a good funeral. "We even had a funeral for our goldfish in the backyard when I was younger," I said. "So I can't imagine I would have forgotten something as special as my foot," I said.

"You didn't forget," Howard assured me. "We both said goodbye to your foot and let it know how much we cared about it."

"I'm glad I didn't forget to say goodbye to my foot. That would have been terrible," I said, sniffing. "I hope I told my foot I tried everything humanly possible to save it first. I hope I said that."

"You did," Howard assured me, reaching over to grab my fingers and squeeze them.

"I'm just sorry I don't remember it better," I said. "Those pain-killers—I can't remember very well."

"Well," said Howard, "Elaine was there with me all day during the surgery."

"That's right," I said.

Our friend Elaine, the one I met my first day at Syracuse, was born without the bottom half of her right arm. She grew up wearing a prosthetic, but she made it seem so natural I did not find out it was not her real arm for at least two months after meeting her.

So, decades later, when I was faced with an impossible dilemma, I turned to her for advice. Elaine wasn't an amputee, but she knew more about living without a limb than anyone else I had ever met.

The doctors made it quite clear that we had already tried every-thing else. In 2011, I had an ankle fusion surgery at a prestigious out-of-town hospital to repair my right ankle, which had been damaged over the years by my disease. During recovery, I developed a staph infection called MRSA, which started ravaging the dead bone in my foot. I likely caught the infection in the hospital—probably during the ankle surgery—as it often spreads in hospitals, particularly among patients like me who have had multiple surgeries and have artificial joints.

MRSA is resistant to many of the antibiotics used to treat normal staph infections. For my treatment, I suffered through numerous rounds of debridement, which removed infected tissue from the wound, and took harsh antibiotics that slowed, but never killed, the infection. Again, my traitorous sickle cell disease was working against me. After decades of oxygen deprivation from sickle cell crises, there was so little blood flow that the antibiotics could not reach the source of the infection inside the tiny capillaries of my dead ankle bones.

I went to three different hospitals and doctors across the nation trying to save my foot. None of them could eradicate the infection. For months, nurses, like my home nurse Sheryl, known as the "wound whisperer," would come to clean out the necrotic tissue inside my ankle. I had to hold my own leg down while I screamed from the fiery pain. The nurses all said it was very important not to jerk my leg while they picked at the dead tissue with a sharp elongated metal tweezer. Even though Sheryl was gentle, it felt like someone was peeling off my flesh, scraping acid-laced sand along my inflamed nerve endings.

I tried not to look, but sometimes my morbid fascination got the best of me. I saw the yellowed, grainy tissue surrounded by angry red flesh; we are not meant to see inside our own bodies. Looking inside that gaping hole in my ankle was both repellent and intriguing.

The nurses all told me debridement promoted healthy tissue if they removed tissue contaminated by the infection. Sheryl reminded me the reason my incision had never healed in the first place is that healthy tissue will not grow over an infection. The incision on the outside of my right ankle never closed like the incision on the inside of my ankle because it had probably been infected from the first scalpel incision.

But debridement didn't help much, and the only thing the antibiotics killed was my spirit. Between the infection and the harsh antibiotics, my whole body felt sick. I was getting weaker and sicker with each passing day, and growing weary of the lengthy fight to save my foot.

With every passing month, I watched my right foot dying before my eyes. The toes curled over and were paralyzed, and they turned gray from lack of circulation. There was a hole the size of a tennis ball in my ankle from all the surgeries to "clean out" the pernicious infection that kept returning.

There was still one more option: a painful external fixation surgery that only a few doctors would even attempt. During this kind of surgery, doctors would place a device around my traumatized ankle, a kind of scaffolding that would hold my bones in place while they healed. I was told to expect a full year of recovery after such a drastic procedure, and even after that, my foot and ankle were unlikely to fully recover. But I would still have them intact. I was willing to try it.

I met with a surgeon at a well-known Washington hospital, one of the few doctors who performed the external fixation surgery. After examining my extensive medical records and seeing that my last ankle surgery had been done by a well-known ankle guru, he raised his eyebrows. "Oh, so you're coming to *me* as the last resort," he chortled. "Well, I will give it a try. But if I get in there and it looks like it's not going to work, I will tell you the truth."

We scheduled the surgery for the middle of May 2012. I went into the operating room praying it would work. When I came out of the anesthesia, the person I trust most in the world was standing at my bedside, holding my hand gently.

"Hi," Howard said to me quietly in the recovery room.

"Hi," I replied groggily. I looked down and pulled up the sheet.

I saw metal poles sticking out of my leg and what looked like metal scaffolding built all around my ankle and calf.

"Did it work?" I asked, looking down at the contraption encircling my right ankle and shin.

Howard took my right hand in both of his.

"No, it didn't work," he said slowly, shaking his head. Looking sad, he leaned down to kiss my parched lips, dehydrated because I had not been allowed to eat or drink before the surgery. It was a sign of his deep love for me that he kissed my parched lips anyway, letting me see the disappointment in his own eyes.

Tears filled my eyes. My mind reeled with the news. I had tried everything. I had endured more than half a dozen surgeries on my ankle and indescribable pain for eighteen months.

For what? For *this*? To have someone hack off half my right leg anyway? I was certain the doctors, after receiving their payday from all my operations, were ready to move on to the next patient. Meanwhile, I would be left with an amputated ankle, and there was nothing I could do about it.

"Damn it!" I thought. "Don't I ever get a break?"

When I became aware again, I heard Howard speaking quietly. "The surgeon said the infection has begun moving up your shin," he said. His deep, radio-quality baritone soothed my frayed nerves.

When the surgeon visited me later, he explained he had discovered the scaffold technique wouldn't work for me. "I guess the MRSA had all kinds of places to hide in the dead bone in your ankle," he said. "It's almost impossible to get it all out."

He recommended we see his colleague, a wound-care specialist and surgeon, as soon as possible to amputate my leg. He urged us not to wait.

We followed his advice and contacted the specialist. He is known in the medical world for using state-of-the-art techniques to save the torn, mangled limbs of combat veterans. When he and his team of residents visited me in the hospital in Washington, one resident began mentioning ways we might still be able to save my foot and ankle. He suggested using bariatric chambers and other techniques; both Howard and I appreciated his effort. But the doctor kindly shushed him. He had already consulted with my previous surgeon and knew my ankle had extensive internal damage.

Peering at me through his eyeglasses with his gentle blue eyes, the doctor patted the side of my hospital bed kindly. "If we don't take your foot and ankle now," he said quietly, looking me straight in the eye, "the MRSA will spread and eventually kill you."

It was the same thing my other doctors had been telling me for more than a year. I had steadily resisted hearing it, living in denial. The pain in my ankle was indescribable. That I had contemplated even more pain for that last procedure now seems incredible to me. Trying to save my foot almost cost me my life.

I thought of all I had already been through. After all of those months enduring dozens of torturous debridement procedures and several surgeries to remove metal, bone, and anything else doctors thought might be contaminated with MRSA, I was miserable. The harsh antibiotics had taken a toll; my skin looked gray and old.

My soul screamed at me to stop living in denial. And one day, I did. It was the day I looked in the mirror and saw death in my eyes.

"Face it," I told my mirror image. "Your foot was already dead. If you wait any longer, the rest of you will be too."

So with a heavy heart and tears in my eyes, I contemplated signing the consent form to allow the surgeon to amputate half of my right leg. My closest friends kept in touch during those awful months, clearly worried about me. But it was Elaine, one of my oldest friends, whom I reached out to, asking for her support through the hardest time of my life. She visited me in the hospital, even though she was juggling work, church, and family obligations. But when I needed her most, she was there for me.

One day, she and her husband Timothy helped Howard bring me home from yet another hospital stay to surgically clean out my ankle wound. Elaine quietly kneeled in front of me as I sat on a kitchen chair. "Gail, look at me," she said. "Look me in the eyes." I did. Her face was solemn and more serious than I had ever seen it in our decades-long friendship. "Do not wait too long to agree to the amputation," she said. "Do it while it is still possible to do it below the knee."

She explained that every prosthetist she ever knew had said that it's much better to work with a below-knee amputee, as it's much more difficult to adapt to prosthetics after an above-knee amputation.

"I want you to promise me you will not wait too long," Elaine said, grabbing my knee. "Promise me."

Looking into her eyes, I saw all the love and worry my dear friend felt for me. We had known each other since the very first day of college at Syracuse University—almost forty years ago.

"I promise," I whispered, growing teary. "I promise I won't wait until it's too late."

I signed the consent papers a few days after that.

On the day of surgery—May 18, 2012—Elaine spent the entire day waiting at the hospital with Howard to keep him company and offer reassurance. She counseled me about amputation and living with a prosthetic. On this subject, I bowed to her expert opinion.

When I woke up after the amputation surgery, the first faces I saw were hers and Howard's. I was groggy and in pain, so I do not remember everything we said to one another. I do remember looking down the bed and seeing my legs were covered by a sheet. On the right, the lump stopped about halfway down. The left lump continued almost to the end of the bed.

I mourned my right foot and ankle like a dear friend was lost to me forever. I fell into depression for several days.

Hospital social workers came. Prosthetic company representatives came. Volunteers who had lost limbs came by trying to cheer me up by showing me a perfectly decent life was possible after amputation. Psychiatry interns came, asking me inane questions that seemed to serve no purpose.

"Can I see a *real* doctor please?" I asked loudly before they finally scurried away, their chirpy voices sliding like razors along my nerves. When the real psychiatrist, a bearded older man, finally came to my room, he sat down facing me and we talked for a few minutes.

"Are you depressed?" he asked.

"Yes," I replied, looking him in the eyes.

"It would be surprising if you were not depressed after an amputation you did not want," he said calmly.

"How long will I feel like this?" I asked, woefully sure my life as I had known it was over.

"It varies," he said. "It depends on the person. After all, you are mourning a lost part of yourself."

"How will I know if my depression is really serious?"

"If you ask us to remove your *other* leg, then I will know you have a problem," he said, trying for humor.

I did not laugh or crack a smile—I merely looked at him with dead eyes. Then he got serious. "It is natural to be depressed after a traumatic loss," he said. "If it continues for a very long time, please feel free to call me again. But I do not think there is anything wrong with you."

There was plenty wrong with me, but I knew he meant mentally rather than physically, so I let that go without comment.

I don't remember how long I was hospitalized after the amputation, but after that, I spent two weeks at a rehabilitation hospital in Washington. Then I was sent home to live in a wheelchair until a temporary prosthetic could be made for me.

Although my memory of those weeks is made blurrier by anesthesia and depression, I do recall meeting a prosthetist in the hospital the day after my amputation. "Will I be able to swim again?" I asked him, groggy from all the drugs doctors were pumping into me so I could stand the initial postsurgery pain.

"Eventually," he replied. "You might want to focus on walking first."

I turned my head away, dismissing him. All I could focus on was how I was going to enter the water at the beach if I could not walk across the sand. How was I going to swim in our pool at Dreamcastle with one and a half legs?

Swimming has always been a passion for me; it is my favorite exercise. Even groggy after anesthesia and surgery, it was the very first thing I worried about.

The prosthetist said we had to wait until my stump healed before I could begin using a temporary prosthetic. He said getting a leg for swimming would come much, much later.

CHAPTER 15

Falling in the Shower

THERE I WAS, LYING IN THE SHOWER STALL, SOAP STILL IN hand, as the water continued to patter all around me. For a moment, I was stunned. The plastic chair I was using to help me shower had suddenly cracked beneath me; I landed with a thud on the tile. Since my amputation, I had been using the chair to remain independent in the shower. Now, I only felt helpless.

I started to cry, mostly out of frustration. Yet again, I had reached a fork in the road, a metaphor for my life. I could choose to move forward as a disabled person with half my right leg intact, or I could sit there on the floor looking ridiculous, crying and feeling sorry for myself.

"That's just not the Gail way," I told myself. I had to figure out how to get up by myself. It was up to me, and it was both as simple and as difficult as that.

So I brushed away my tears and finished showering on the floor of the stall without another sniffle. When I finished soaping and rinsing myself, I turned off the water and shifted to my knees. I used my stump to help my full leg bend enough to help lift me up. My body has always been strong, with wide shoulders, strong arms, narrow hips, and long legs. Using my upper body, I managed to pull myself up into the seat of my nearby wheelchair. But I was backward, so I turned around, properly seated myself, and put my long leg on its footrest and my stump on its stump rest.

I sat there for a moment, huffing and puffing. I was proud; I got myself out of a scrape without anyone's help.

After that, we borrowed a toilet-seat riser with sturdy legs and arms that doubled as a shower chair for the handicapped. But we did not know that at first. Howard and I learned a lot about how to cope by making mistakes.

My narrow hips and long, thin legs turned out to be one reason my hips and knees were so vulnerable to fracture as I grew up. I had my first hip replacement at only twenty-seven years old. It took the doctor at the HMO—my husband and I could not afford any better at the time—more than seven hours to replace my old hip. Afterward, I woke up in so much pain, I screamed a lot. It did not help that I was also in traction. I was so uncomfortable lying on my back, my thigh lifted high off the bed in a trapeze-like contraption. While I recovered, the medical staff had to knock me out with intravenous drugs just to quiet me for a little while.

It turned out the HMO doctor had forced in a metal hip joint that was much too large for my small bone socket. On X-rays, you could see where he had to wrap wire around my greater trochanter just to hold the bone in place around a spike that looked too huge for my narrow femur. Forcing that piece, rather than one that actually fit me, ended up fracturing my femur. As a result of his ineptitude, I was in traction in the hospital for a month. After more than thirty days, the insurance company forced the doctor to send me home, but I was still in so much pain, I could not climb the stairs of our town house to get up to our second floor bedroom.

A colleague and friend from the *Baltimore Sun* came over and helped Howard move our bed downstairs to the dining room. I set up my recuperation quarters in our dining room for several weeks, within a few feet of the powder room I would have to use, sweating and swearing every painful step of the way on crutches. I was in agony for much of that time, my deep bone pain unrelieved by the pain pills my doctor prescribed. I tossed and turned so much at night, I disturbed my husband, who had to rise early to commute more than an hour to work in Washington.

The *Sun's* Howard County bureau editor, whom I was working for at the time, was genuinely kind and understanding, considering my very long absence. The graphic artist for the weekly paper was also kind. She was an elderly lady who came by to visit me, pulling a chair close to my bedside in the dining room. She taught me how to crochet to make the endless hours in bed more bearable. This was an era before the internet, so I had little to do except read whatever books I could borrow or buy through the mail and watch our little black-and-white television.

Once I recovered enough to return to work, I did a little investigation of the HMO doctor who had almost crippled me. It turned out he had been sued by some of his patients in the past. I immediately changed doctors before undergoing my second hip replacement on the opposite side. I was up and walking the next day and I was able to return to work within weeks, not months. I never visited a doctor at an HMO again. I vowed never to join another one with managed care so tightfisted that the doctor would not even order parts in different sizes to ensure a proper fit.

Altogether, I have had seven hip replacements, two knee replacements, and a faulty ankle fusion surgery, which resulted in my leg amputation. The amputation was necessary to save my life, but it definitely changed me. I was depressed for six months. I sought counseling and rehabilitation to help me through it. But it forever changed my image of myself. I have not been as optimistic since.

Gone was the beautiful young woman who readily smiled despite a life of crippling pain.

I always walked with a limp because of my multiple joint replacements. But with a prosthetic leg and a left hip that had fractured from the pressure placed on it during my right leg's turmoil, I could barely walk at all. That fracture rendered weeks of rehabilitation exercises useless. The muscles could only strengthen so much with a faulty foundation.

I spend a good deal of time in a wheelchair when I don't want to be bothered with my prosthetic leg.

However, I did learn to drive with hand controls. It was an exciting day in January 2013 when I passed my driver's test at the Maryland Department of Motor Vehicles. I regained some of my independence. But my everyday life is that of a disabled person.

It is amazing how few places in our country are really handicap accessible. Despite the Americans with Disabilities Act, this country still has kinks in the system. For instance, restaurants may have one toilet stall with grab bars and a bit more room for wheelchairs, but there is often no way for someone in that wheelchair to automatically open the front door of the restroom. The doors are often awkward or heavy, and impossible to maneuver and hold open while trying to wheel myself inside.

Handicapped parking spaces are often farther away from the front door than necessary because a commercial enterprise only puts in one curb cut designed for a wheelchair. And that's just in this country.

Overseas, there are often no obvious laws to make disabled people's lives any easier. My book club once traveled to the modern, booming city of Toronto to celebrate our tenth anniversary together. The club members—ladies in their forties, fifties, and sixties, bless their souls—found themselves taking turns pushing me around and pulling "wheelies" to roll me onto the sidewalk so I could enjoy the city as much as they did. Canada—a country with a standard of living similar to the United States—had no accessible sidewalk curbs for my wheelchair in downtown Toronto or the ultra-chic neighborhoods of Montreal.

One afternoon in downtown Toronto, my friend Diane and I

wanted to visit a department store. You could only enter the store by walking up several steps. On the inside, it only had an escalator to transport customers from one floor to another. A saleswoman told us we had to go around to the back of the store and through a dark alley to enter. Then we had to find the loading dock and use a freight elevator to get to the store's upper floors, because there was no public access for people in wheelchairs. We had to return to the ground floor the same way and repeat the process when we wanted to leave.

It was most unsettling, particularly when Diane, who was patiently pushing me, suddenly noticed dark, angry clouds above us. Within seconds, we both got soaked to the skin from a horrific downpour as a thunderstorm swept through the alley. It so blinded us with sheets of water in the murky darkness that it was quite difficult to figure out how to exit the alley.

All of my book club members were horrified by our experience that afternoon. But they were most surprised that a country as progressive as Canada did so little to help disabled citizens.

In subsequent travel to other countries, my husband and I soon discovered an equal lack of thought for the wheelchair bound. In the poorest third world nations, for instance, those without limbs end up begging, pulling themselves along from one filthy street corner to the next, trying to survive on handouts from kind passersby.

Later, when I was planning a trip to South America, I was struck by the myriad ways the travel industry discriminates against the disabled—a rather strange practice, given the elderly comprise most of their passengers on high-end trips. For example, the prestigious small ship line we booked for the cruise discouraged my participation in 99 percent of their tours.

A cruise line employee angered me one day by saying the only way I could go on most of the onshore tours was to pay ten times what everybody else was paying for a similar trip. He said I would have to hire an expensive private car to take me to the same destinations the other passengers reached by bus. He made me so upset;

I refused to pay such exorbitant amounts for the simplest excursions. Instead, I immediately wrote an email to the president of the ship line's parent company. We happened to know him socially, so I was more frank than usual. I told him I found this practice discriminatory.

Naturally, he sent me a legal form letter, quoting an internal human resources policy that had little to do with the matter at hand. It was the usual corporate self-protection maneuver. The shipping company claimed it did not discriminate against the disabled. Why did the ship have only one handicap-accessible penthouse, then? Why did we have to contort ourselves to fit into a room where my wheelchair could not fit through any door of the suite? I gave the booking agent the exact dimensions of my wheelchair six months in advance. It did little good.

A customer service manager made all kinds of promises about building a ramp into our cabin's bathroom before we came aboard. It never happened. We could not even open the front door wide enough to enter without bumping into the bathroom door right behind it.

Incensed, I complained to the ship's concierge the first hour after we arrived. He offered us a smaller, cheaper "handicapped" room down a long hallway and around a corner from our suite. It was sparse and not as nicely appointed as our penthouse suite. It had no bathtub, and we only used the room when I needed to go to the toilet late at night after my prosthetic leg was removed and I used my wheelchair. Once seated, I could not fit through any of the doorways in our suite. It was a very stressful beginning to what should have been a dream trip.

I fight discrimination everywhere I see it in a Don Quixote fashion that does not always achieve my goal, but I can't seem to help myself any more than Don could.

CHAPTER 16

Swimming Again

NOT LONG AFTER MY ANKLE AMPUTATION, I STARTED SWIMMING again in the pool at Dreamcastle. It made me feel normal again, since my weightlessness in the pool offset the fact that my right leg was shorter than my left. Still, I wanted a state-of-the-art prosthetic that I could use in the pool, and it didn't take me long to start searching for one, despite what the prosthetist had told me after the surgery. Taking no for an answer when it meant swimming again was not an option. It took months of cajoling to get one.

My first prosthetist said he could not find one—or wouldn't find one, since he said my insurance company wouldn't pay for it. I went next to a young prosthetist who seemed eager to please, but she also claimed she could not find one suitable for me.

After listening to her do a lot of hemming and hawing, I looked at my husband. I had that "it's time to take matters into our own hands" expression on my face. Right in front of her, my husband pulled out his iPhone to surf the internet while we listened to her excuses. Within minutes, he found a place in France that was producing something called an Aqualeg.

Originally designed for amputees who wanted to re-enter water sports, Aqualeg was a rubber prosthetic that could go into salt or chlorine water. The water drained through holes in the bottom of the foot. A small gill in the middle of the calf let water in, acting as a ballast so the leg would not float on top of the water. It even had a flexible ankle so I could put my fins on and swim with my foot in a horizontal position.

It was perfect.

"What about this one?" my husband asked her, showing her his iPhone. She looked at the image of the prosthetic, thinking quickly.

"It may take some time to get through to them," she said. "It's in France, and they speak French, you know."

"*I* speak French," I replied, looking her in the eyes. "Let me know if you need me to get on the telephone for you."

"Well," she said, "your insurance company probably won't pay for it." That old line again.

"You let me handle the insurance company," I told her. "I have cost them millions of dollars over the years. This should not be a big deal. I can use it to shower too, so I won't fall down again. I'm sure they don't want me in the hospital again with an injury from falling down."

"Well, let my assistant see if your insurance will cover it first," she said.

"You do that," I said. "I'll work it from my side."

I called my insurance case manager to explain what I needed. Insurance companies give you case managers when you have as many high medical claims as I do. They believe if they intervene in your care regimen early enough, they might be able to better control costs. With an unpredictable illness like mine, that had not proven to work out very well for them. But over the years, I had gotten to know and like my case manager, and vice versa.

Apparently, my personality somehow oozes through the telephone, so she always told me she enjoyed talking to me. I asked her to get in touch with everyone appropriate to get my shower/swim prosthetic approved. Once my prosthetist's office received initial approval, they contacted the company in France to begin the process of ordering a swim leg for me.

Just a couple of months later, Frederic Rauch, the president of the Aqualeg company, flew to the United States to meet me personally and measure my stump for an Aqualeg. Frederic was himself an amputee. He lost most of his right leg as a child and desperately wanted to participate in water sports. So he started a company to invent a prosthetic leg cover suitable for use in water.

We finally met at my prosthetist's office in Bethesda, Maryland. Frederic was wildly excited to meet me. He told me I was his first American customer. We spoke in English for a while, then I switched to French, as I thought it might be easier to communicate that way. We spoke French so rapidly, we left everyone else in the room completely out of the conversation. My prosthetist's eyes kept switching back and forth between us like she was watching a tennis match, trying to decipher what we were saying.

She turned to Frederic's American representative and said, "There they go again."

Hearing that, Frederic and I resumed speaking English so they could understand what we were saying. He measured my stump and took photographs of my left leg so he could try to match its contours and color for my new swim leg. He pulled out color swatches with a wider variety of brown than the American company I had been dealing with.

I pointed this out to my American prosthetist. "Now see, your company should be ashamed that someone from France has more varied colors than you do. You only have two or three colors for darker people and a dozen for white people. Don't you know you have that backwards? Most of the world is composed of people of color. Half the United States is now people of color. You are not even keeping up with the times! How can that be good marketing?"

Frederic's American representative kept nodding, saying, "You're right, you're right."

But my American prosthetist just shrugged and blamed the prosthetic skin cover manufacturer. She said they only had a couple firms they did business with on a routine basis and their color selection for darker people was limited.

I was so enraged by that passive-resistant attitude, I wrote the president of the American prosthetic skin supplier to point out the error of his ways. He is just one of many executives in ivory tower offices across the country who has yet to acknowledge the changing demographics around him. I told him his company's persistent antiquated practice of offering so few darker skin tones was like "*Mad Men* living in a *Modern Family* world."

I have yet to receive a reply to my letter.

Around this time, I started having more difficulty breathing. I was diagnosed with pulmonary hypertension, a side effect of my sickle cell disease that deprives the lungs of oxygen and places a major strain on my enlarged heart. Armed with this news, yet another doctor thought she would stand in the way of my dreams.

"You cannot swim anymore," the doctor told me. She'd known me for only three minutes. "You can't breathe on land, how are you going to breathe underwater?" she added and left my room.

Tears sprang to my eyes against my will. Only fury can make me cry so suddenly.

"You don't know *me*!" I screamed back at her inside my head. "No one knows what I can do but *me*. Just watch me!"

The nerve of her, I thought.

"That's all right," I told myself, pushing down my anger. "People have underestimated me my entire life. Why should she be any different? So I can't breathe without oxygen. Fine," I thought. "I will just have to take up scuba diving." Nothing and no one would keep me out of the water. Every step of trying to return to some semblance of my pre-amputee, pre-pulmonary hypertensive existence seemed like walking a mile uphill.

It took a few months for the Aqualeg to arrive. In the meantime,

I drove to a Rockville, Maryland, dive shop to inquire about scuba lessons. Because of my pulmonary hypertension, I would require my portable oxygen concentrator at all times, so scuba diving was the perfect solution.

I decided to train for a variation of scuba diving called Zuba, or confined water diving. Zuba allows you to swim without the oxygen tank on your back. It was originally designed for diving in open water; the tank floats on the surface of the water and feeds divers air through a long tube. My course focused specifically on diving in swimming pools. I planned to set the oxygen tank on the side of the beach house's pool—the long oxygen tube would allow me to swim freely up and down the pool. Within a few months, I received my Zuba diving certification from United Team Diving. When the Aqualeg arrived—in a shade so close to my skin—I was ecstatic and ready to swim.

We arrived for the summer at Dreamcastle as usual. I had to wait a few days for our saltwater pool to heat up enough so I would not be unnecessarily chilled. I donned my new swim leg. It was one of the happiest moments I'd had in years.

Frederic and I have exchanged several emails and pictures since then. In one photo I sent him in July 2013, I am in my swimming pool at the beach house. My husband took a picture of me with my Zuba gear and my Aqualeg sticking out of the water with a fin on it. I am smiling broadly and waving. Frederic was so enchanted with the photo, he wrote me back immediately in French, calling me "Aqualeg's official mermaid."

When something matters so much to you, you simply cannot take no for an answer. Doctors are human, so they say what is easy or within their limited range of experience. But I try to push boundaries. I never accept no as the end of a conversation. I think it is part of the reason I am still here.

CHAPTER 17

A Husband's Terror

THERE IS A SAYING THAT GOES, "MAN PLANS AND GOD LAUGHS." In 2014, God must have been holding his sides he was laughing so hard. I spent almost a year planning our trip to South America. We were going to take a luxurious cruise from Argentina north up the coast of Brazil and into the Amazon for our thirty-third wedding anniversary. Even though I could not walk well and was reliant on oxygen, we thought we could do it as long as I spent most of the time on a cruise.

Planning that trip took the logistical sophistication of a military operation. I not only had to pack luggage, I had to bring along my oxygen concentrator, wheelchair with stump rest, walker, cane, and over a dozen medications, some of which need constant refrigeration.

Not one thing I imagined for our glamorous cruise happened. Instead, I almost met my maker in Rio de Janeiro. Three days into our dream cruise, my sickle cell disease decided to rear its ugly head with a vengeance.

I've asked my husband, Howard, to tell you the rest because I have amnesia. I cannot remember anything after those three days. He says that is a blessing, considering what happened next.

⌒

IT WAS A BEAUTIFUL, SUNNY MORNING IN LATE FEBRUARY AS we sailed into port in Rio de Janeiro, Brazil. The captain of the ship had permission to enter port through a scenic route that allowed passengers to take photos of famous sites like the Christ the Redeemer mountaintop statue.

I am sure many of our fellow passengers took the opportunity, cameras slung around their necks, peering around with wonder. But we saw none of it. We were down below in our penthouse cabin, dealing with our own personal hell.

After two days at sea, Gail had returned to our cabin from a massage complaining that her back hurt. Throughout the night, she battled what would ultimately become the first major sickle cell crisis she had experienced in over a decade.

As we pulled into port, I summoned the ship's doctor and nurse. The doctor took one look at Gail squirming on the bed in excruciating pain and gave her an injection of morphine to supplement her own pain pills. As we came closer to port, however, it became obvious that the severity of this crisis would mean we would have to disembark the ship and go to a local hospital in Rio.

Prior to our trip, I had obtained a State Department list of recommended hospitals for US citizens to use while abroad in certain countries. The list is filled with disclaimers and, in many ways, is just too broad. It doesn't say, for instance, "You better go here," or, even better, "No way in hell do you want to go there." Still, it serves as a guide.

I always use several sources for everything, and I had also received a recommendation from my friend Heidi Shoup, who at the time served as president of the World Affairs Council of Washington, DC. As fate would have it, the Brazilian ambassador to the United States was to be a guest of honor at the Council's major gala in Washington in March, so she had been in constant contact with him.

I began to feel uneasy when I saw the hospital the ship staff recommended, a suggestion from their port agent. The ship's crew viewed the port agent as an essential point person, but the hospital the agent selected for us was not one of the twenty on the State Department's list. It was also not the one suggested to Heidi by her Brazilian embassy contact.

The cruise ship's nurse accompanied our ambulance to a hospital in a gated middle-class community outside of downtown Rio. Having been in hospitals all over the United States and in foreign countries, I can usually quickly categorize the level of hospital Gail is entering. I sensed that it was not the top hospital in Rio, but we had to get treatment for her sickle cell crisis.

Even though I felt trepidation, it was too late to change course as the ambulance crew rushed Gail into the emergency room and I looked around for someone to help my ailing wife.

The cruise staff assured me we would go to an English-speaking hospital. In Buenos Aires, we had to check on a recurring eye problem Gail was having and we went to the British hospital, where they had English–Spanish interpreters. But this Rio hospital had very few English speakers.

Fortunately, there was a nurse on duty in the emergency room named Andre. Apparently, he was the "go-to" person when the hospital staff needed help communicating with English-speaking patients. Fearing a scenario just like this, I requested the ship's nurse accompany us. I thought she could bring her expertise to this unknown emergency room and, dressed in her official uniform, might help us get the attention we needed.

Usually when sickle cell patients go to the emergency room in the throes of a crisis, the staff puts them through the normal battery of inane tests, which delays treatment. Sickle cell patients are already in so much pain, they need high potency painkillers right away. Delays only make the crisis worse and last longer. We had experienced this many times, including when Gail had a crisis in New York City and the doctor made her wait for hours for any kind of pain relief.

To their credit, the hospital emergency team in Rio did not do this. An intensive care doctor I will call Dr. P took Gail's case. He started the standard treatments of painkilling narcotics, oxygen, and intravenous fluids. As her crisis intensified, Dr. P increased the dosage of morphine.

We learned the hard way that some of the narcotic painkillers used widely in the United States are not available in Brazil. As the third day of the crisis dawned, nothing seemed to be working for Gail. She was suffering terribly.

"We will have to use methadone," Dr. P said in his Portuguese-accented English.

My eyebrows rose in surprise. When I grew up in New York City during the 1970s, methadone was used to treat heroin addicts, so I was leery when he made this suggestion. It was such a strong narcotic, I often had a hard time telling the difference between a methadone patient and a heroin addict when they walked by me on the streets.

Since he was starting her on methadone, Dr. P wanted Gail in the intensive care unit so she would be under observation around the clock. The next thing I knew, they were wheeling Gail to the ICU. While I was relieved Dr. P was prescribing a stronger pain relief regimen for her, I felt constricted by the limited visitation allowed in the ICU.

While Gail stayed in the hospital, I checked into a nearby hotel the cruise line directed me to use. One evening, my mind raced as I tried to think of something that could improve our situation. I was trying not to panic. We were thousands of miles away from home in a country where we did not understand the native language. I had never felt so alone.

Unable to sleep, I fired off an email to the hospital's top doctor, Dr. M, an English-speaking Portuguese surgeon who was assisting in Gail's care. "I need better access to the ICU," I wrote. "Gail is 5,000 miles away from home and needs me with her, holding her hand and encouraging her. If she loses confidence in the process, and she stops fighting . . ."

I could not finish the sentence. It was too terrifying to think she might not make it.

Dr. M responded in person the next day. He granted me unrestricted access so I could stay by Gail's side. Dr. P had concerns about twenty-four-hour access, so we worked out a morning, afternoon, and evening visitation schedule that, while not perfect, gave me the time with Gail that I felt she needed.

Even when I wasn't in the ICU, I was at the hospital. The hospital staff kept encouraging me to return to my hotel and get some rest. But whenever I did go back to my hotel, I did everything but rest.

One night, after my interpreter and I had a discussion with a particularly disagreeable doctor, I returned to my hotel and wrote a group email to all the doctors treating my wife. I demanded assurances that everyone in the ICU was "doing everything to bring Mrs. Woolley back to good health."

"Mrs. Woolley is an institution in Washington and there are many people expecting her safe return to the US," I added. I had not lobbied the offices of Congress and the White House for over thirty years without learning how to bring a sense of urgency to a matter when necessary. Gail's life is a matter of great urgency to me!

I don't like to be over the top with people, particularly doctors, but when it comes to Gail's health, standing on ceremony is a luxury we cannot afford. I wanted to underscore that a bad outcome was unacceptable, and I did not want to end up standing outside of her hospital room while one of the doctors told me, "Sorry, Mr. Woolley."

Gail had been at the Rio hospital for about five days when her crisis nosedived.

This was the first major sickle cell crisis Gail had endured since her 2012 diagnosis of pulmonary hypertension, the latest in a series of awful side effects I had witnessed while holding Gail's hand through the hundreds of crises she's had since I met her in 1979.

When I returned to ICU one morning, a doctor told me, "We almost lost her last night."

"What?" I asked, too stunned to say more. Over many years and countless hospital visits, this was the first time that any doctor told me they almost lost my Gail. They told me Gail's blood pressure dropped dramatically the night before, and they had given her drugs to try to boost her pressure.

I stayed close to Gail while a few more days dragged by. She gradually became more alert. The effects of the methadone were subsiding, and she could manage light conversation. I was beginning to think the crisis was ending and we could return to the United States in a matter of days.

But that evening, Dr. P came out of the ICU looking dejected. I was glad my interpreter Eduardo was with me, but I did not need him at that moment. I could see in Dr. P's eyes that something was seriously wrong.

He told me an X-ray of Gail's lungs showed signs of pneumonia and acute chest syndrome. Gail's crisis had evolved into a potentially fatal condition. Acute chest syndrome occurs in some sickle cell patients. It is caused by inflammation, infection, and blocked blood vessels in the lungs. It was making it even harder for her to breathe. She now had a B-pap machine forcing 100 percent oxygen into her lungs as she lay semiconscious. The tight mask covered most of her face, and whenever she did stir she tried to pry it off, even as she gasped for breath.

Dr. P said he could not effectively treat the acute chest syndrome. He had no access to the latest drugs or treatments available back home in the United States.

"Is she going to make it through the night?" I said, my heart in my throat.

Dr. P just shook his head and shrugged his shoulders.

"So what is the plan?" I was beginning to get frantic.

He looked down and said in English, "I don't know."

"Look, doctor. We have got to have a new plan here," I said. "I will do anything for that woman in your ICU. I work for you now! I have resources. I am not poor. If there is something that you need and do not have, you must tell me so I can get it for you. I have means and I will use all of it for her!" I was almost shouting, not realizing my voice had been growing louder by the second.

I could tell he was thinking and trying to figure out what more he could do, but I could not just sit around and let my wife die. I called her doctor back home in Maryland. I had been keeping him in the loop via email and very expensive international cell phone calls. After my unnerving conversation with Dr. P, I put her home doctor on the telephone with my interpreter and had him consult with Dr. P.

After their conversation, the suburban Washington, DC, doctor and I spoke again. He said he had talked to Gail about the dangers of the trip for someone with her health issues. But Gail, the ever intrepid globe-trotter, said she would take his words "under advisement," and continued planning our anniversary adventure.

He and I agreed that Gail should live her life to its fullest. While it was important she knew the risks of foreign travel, he did not think she should be denied the opportunity. Throughout this nerve-racking period, I spent a lot of time on the telephone with Bill, my longtime friend from high school who is now a cardio-pulmonary specialist in Charlotte, North Carolina. I had Bill speak to Dr. P in Spanish, which helped bridge the language gap. Even though Brazilians speak Portuguese, many also speak Spanish since their neighboring countries do.

Bill assured me Dr. P had been following normal protocols for treating her condition. But now we were at a critical point where the best medical skill available mattered. I took that to mean the difference between her life and death.

At one point late in the evening I asked Dr. P, "What am I supposed to say to Gail about her condition?"

"Talk to her about the life you had together," he said quietly.

I did not like his use of the past tense—as if I should talk to my wife about our past, but not the future. In his own quiet way, Dr. P was telling me to say goodbye to Gail. How could I possibly say goodbye? At that moment I realized our tremendous life journey together could end suddenly in a small community hospital, thousands of miles away from home.

"No," I thought. "As long as I have a breath left in my body, it will not end this way."

Determined to think of something, I swallowed my fear and went into her room. Gail was not fully conscious, so I bent down next to her ear and whispered, "You need to get healthy to finish your bucket list. You need to finish your book. You need to get your next level of scuba certification, and we need to finish seeing the world together."

I downloaded our wedding song, "With You I'm Born Again," onto my phone and put the headphones into her ears. I hoped the music would reach her somehow, and I encouraged her to keep fighting for her life.

Gail did not react. I could not tell if she heard me or not. It was close to midnight, and I knew they would not let me back into her room in ICU again tonight. I didn't want to leave her alone. I was terrified that if I did, I would receive a call from a doctor telling me she had passed away without me there to hold her hand. I always held her hand, offering her whatever strength I could to keep her tethered to this world.

Reluctantly, I prepared to leave. But this was too important and I wanted to remember this moment somehow, in case it became our last one together. With nothing else on hand in the ICU, I wrote her an email on my iPhone.

From: HOWARD WOOLLEY
Date: February 25, 2014 at 12:34:24 AM EST
To: Gail Woolley
Subject: I kissed Gail's forehead. Told her I loved her.

On the evening of Feb 24th, when Dr. P told me I should talk to you about our life together. This is what I said and did.

I kissed Gail's forehead. Told her I loved her. I urged her to keep fighting. I reminded her that she is alive because of her own will and nothing else.

Sent from my iPhone

When I put my phone away, I pulled myself away from Gail and went back to my hotel. But I could not sleep. Instead, I made an urgent posting on Facebook to a subgroup made up of our friends and family.

"Gail is fighting for her life in Brazil. Please pray for her," I posted.

Dr. P's pessimism spurred me to action. I texted anybody important I could recall from my thirty years as a lobbyist in Washington. For days, I exchanged texts with doctors at Johns Hopkins Hospital in Baltimore, the top Brazilian pulmonologist, and our travel insurance contacts to plan our exit from this dire situation. I had three friends on standby, ready to fly to Rio de Janeiro to help me if necessary. Two of them were lawyers. The third was Bill. But all three encountered red tape when they discovered they needed a visa, and it would take at least ten days to get one.

Time was of the essence. Gail could die any minute. I could not afford to wait for reinforcements to arrive. So I called her main pulmonologist at Johns Hopkins Hospital.

The pulmonologist was a Lebanese gentleman who spoke Arabic, French, and English. I know about the French because he and Gail conversed in it whenever she visited him. He was delighted by her zest for life and the video we gave him of her scuba diving.

"She's one of his favorite patients," a nurse told me once when he came out of the office smiling. "I never see him smile with anyone else."

I am sure the pulmonologist was not smiling as I recounted the dire straits Gail was in. He immediately agreed to receive her at Johns Hopkins if I could find a way to get her there.

So I found a way. I contacted the travel insurance company, and they helped me hire a private ambulance jet to fly Gail from Brazil to Baltimore's closest airport. Thank goodness Gail always purchased good travel insurance for our foreign trips.

But setting everything up for that transfer was not so simple. Once the jet landed in Rio and the crew went to their hotel for a mandatory rest break, everything began to go wrong.

The morning we planned to depart, the air ambulance physician called to ask me how much luggage I planned to bring on the six-seat jet. I was flabbergasted because I had been told by my insurance company that I would be flying home on a commercial flight. I assumed I would take our luggage with me.

We had a ton of it because our cruise was supposed to be three weeks long. We had two large suitcases each for all the outfit changing required on a luxury ship. We had Gail's main oxygen concentrator, her portable oxygen concentrator, walker, customized wheelchair, and three carry-on bags. None of that was going to fit on a tiny private jet.

So, with the help of my interpreter, the hotel staff, and the iPhone, we tried to locate a FedEx office in Rio de Janeiro so we could mail the luggage home. We found a local printer and electronics store that also sent FedEx packages. I hired two taxicabs to carry all our luggage to the FedEx location. The printshop owner asked me to fill out several forms, including US customs documents. I had to show him my US passport.

I was particularly concerned about how he planned to pack my wife's delicate medical equipment. My interpreter jumped in to help the printshop owner carefully pack it. The FedEx employee suggested shipping her oxygen concentrator separately in case customs officials did not understand what it was and held up the entire shipment. He charged me $3,200 US dollars and promised to ship our belongings in a few days.

Later that evening, the jet's crew arrived at the Rio hospital's ICU to discharge Gail. They marched into the ICU like Marines. They wore gray and black uniforms. Using my interpreter and a Portuguese-speaking crew member, they were able to discuss Gail's condition with Dr. P.

Then the crew's nurse and its respiratory therapist began to disconnect Gail from the hospital's life-support machines and connect her to portable ones. Each time they disconnected a tube to reconnect it to the portable equipment, they said, "check." They were so official looking and precise, the hospital workers gathered to watch, wide-eyed. At one point, as they were moving Gail's unconscious body from her bed to a stretcher, one of the Portuguese doctors looked at me with concern.

"Are you okay, Mr. Woolley?"

I nodded to her as if I were fine, but it was upsetting to watch my wife's almost lifeless body moved around, side to side. She seemed so helpless, with a tube down her throat and her eyes shut because of heavy sedation. She is usually so in charge of her life and every decision about it. But she had no say in what was going on, and I knew she would hate it. As for me, I had none of her iron will to depend on.

They moved her into the hospital ambulance and I jumped in with the jet crew. We took her to the jet; she was carried aboard on a stretcher. Her doctors thought it best that she remain intubated and unconscious for such a long journey. A respirator was breathing oxygen into her lungs, trying to keep her alive until we could reach Johns Hopkins Hospital.

I felt the faintest glimmer of relief as we began to taxi down the runway at Rio's main international airport, then—BOOM!

A very loud noise came from somewhere below the plane.

"I think the tire blew!" one crew member shouted.

The pilot stopped taxiing and brought the airplane to a sudden halt. Then he jumped out of the jet to determine what had happened.

"Somebody left debris on the runway!" he exclaimed, dismayed. "Who does that?" He bent to examine the punctured tire as his other crew members joined him, discussing what to do next.

"Can you send another plane down from the United States?" I asked.

"No. Why don't we just get another tire here in Brazil?" the pilot said.

Since it was 1:00 a.m. by now, the pilot told me he would try to find a new tire the next day, asking his contacts for assistance. Meanwhile, the crew had to call an ambulance to return Gail to the hospital's ICU. I really wanted to get out of Brazil as soon as possible, so I went up to the pilot, who also owned the jet.

"I am willing to pay the additional cost of getting a new jet here," I told him, "even if the insurance company won't pay for it." At that time I actually had no idea what the cost would be, but this was for Gail.

But he did not respond and we all left the airport. I gathered my carry-on luggage, including Gail's prosthetic leg and medications, then took a taxi to the hotel, where my old room was still available. The crew stayed at the airport hotel.

The next day, there was little progress in finding a new tire for the jet. I called and emailed the travel insurance company multiple times to insist they send a new jet down to Brazil.

"They are more focused on fixing the jet than on my wife's health," I complained. The insurance company just gave me platitudes.

By that afternoon, there was still no new tire. I called the insurance company back and told them to hire a different jet company and send it to Brazil immediately. I was getting angrier by the minute. "I am willing to pay personally for another jet from a different company," I told them. "But if I have to find a new jet company on my own, then I am sending the bill to you!"

After I hung up, I called our longtime friend Agnes, an attorney in Boston. I told her all the trouble I was having. She called the travel insurance company on my behalf and reminded them in strong terms that further delay could cause Gail's death.

When I later talked to an insurance company supervisor, she told me they had ordered the jet crew to get their mechanic on an airplane from Miami to Rio with a new tire if they did not find one in-country by 8:00 p.m. that evening.

Later that evening, the crew found a source for a new tire, but obtaining it became a bureaucratic nightmare with Brazilian airport authorities. They insisted on sending the tire from São Paulo to Rio de Janeiro using a courier on a motorbike, a journey that could take twelve hours. The air ambulance crew offered to have one of its pilots lease a local plane and fly to São Paulo to retrieve the tire sooner, but Brazilian authorities said no.

While we waited for the tire, the jet crew asked me to relocate to their hotel. We had already endured a dehumanizing airport security process that completely disregarded the life-and-death nature of our mission when we tried to take off the first time.

The morning we tried to depart the second time, I had an early breakfast with the flight crew while the medical team headed to the hospital in Rio to discharge Gail again.

Over breakfast, the pilot apologized for the delay. He emphasized that blown tires because of runway debris "never, ever happen." I also apologized to him about being so hard on him and his crew. I was just so worried that my wife might die, I lost my normal cool reserve. He understood.

"I have extracted people from third world countries and they were a lot easier than this," he told me. "I never expected this much trouble with the Brazilian bureaucracy." The Brazilian officials would not even let him refuel his jet in the same hangar where the tire was being repaired.

Gail's ambulance arrived, and she was transferred to the jet for the second time in three days. As I strapped on my seat belt, I thought we might be nearing the end of our Brazilian saga. I even had a moment of levity watching the ambulance employees take selfies with their cell phones standing next to the Learjet. But then I noticed activity up in the cockpit. Suddenly, the owner jumped out of the jet, extremely furious. He was talking to airport officials and representatives from Bombardier, the plane company. I asked one of the crew members what was going on.

"Someone decided our flight plan needed to be refiled the old-fashioned paper way, rather than the modern electronic way," he said. "That means we will have to lose our place in line and get behind a lot of other nonemergency planes before we can take off."

Worried about yet another delay, I again called my friend Heidi at the World Affairs Council. She had done a lot of work with the Brazilian embassy in Washington. I asked her to contact the highest-ranking embassy official she could find to talk to the airport official in Rio. "Please stress we have someone in a life-threatening situation and we need to get out of here now!" I told her.

The local Bombardier officials got in touch with someone of influence, and we were allowed to take off after another thirty minutes.

This time, the takeoff was smooth. I sighed in relief; I could finally put the awful experience behind me. I vowed that I would never set foot in Brazil again as long as I lived. When we were in the air, and I could see Rio far below me, I started clapping.

We had to stop in Trinidad to refuel, but otherwise the ten-hour flight to Baltimore was uneventful.

Throughout my tense, sleepless ten days in Rio, I had been emailing family, friends, and doctors with progress reports on Gail. So when we landed that night around 9:30 p.m., some friends were there to meet us on the tarmac.

Elaine was there with her husband, Timothy, along with Bob and his wife, Diann, and Gail's former work colleagues and close friends.

There were an ambulance and a limousine sent by Johns Hopkins Hospital to help with my luggage. Bob brought me a jacket and a sweater to put on since it was about 30°F and I was dressed for warm, tropical weather.

Elaine walked over to the stretcher Gail was lying on, unconscious, and pulled the sheet over her bare shoulders before the crew placed her in the ambulance. She didn't like seeing her so vulnerable to the cold.

I thanked the Hopkins limousine driver but told him I wanted to ride in the ambulance with my wife, because we could get there faster with its lights and sirens blaring.

Our friends jumped in their cars and followed us to the hospital.

Timothy gathered my few bags and drove them to his house for safekeeping.

At Johns Hopkins Hospital, Gail was rushed directly to the ICU, where a team of doctors began working on her, putting her on a concentrated dose of antibiotics for the acute chest syndrome.

The doctors asked me to sign a permission form to give her a transfer transfusion, which involved removing 70 percent of her blood and giving her the equivalent amount of various donors' blood. I signed it, worried about why it was needed. The doctors sprang into action, hooking her up to a bewildering number of tubes and machines. They also shaved a spot on her scalp to inject a probe to detect whether she still had brain activity.

She did not regain consciousness for days.

The medical team convinced me to leave Gail in their capable hands and go get some rest, so I left with Elaine and spent the night at her home. But I was back the next day and booked a room at a hotel near the hospital so I could be on hand as much as possible.

When Gail did briefly regain consciousness, she was not coherent. The methadone in Brazil had really disoriented her, and she was hallucinating. Elaine spent much of one night with her, holding her hand. She said Gail kept trying to get out of bed and begged Elaine to get her out of there. But Elaine would always dissuade her and go find a nurse. Usually, Gail lapsed back into unconsciousness, forgetting whatever she had said.

On the third day in Johns Hopkins's ICU, Gail finally regained consciousness for good.

෴

WHEN I WOKE UP IN THE CRITICAL CARE UNIT OF JOHNS HOPKINS Hospital, I was bewildered. My mind was foggy. I was attached to several monitors and beeping machines. I could not move much, but I could move my eyes. I saw a beautiful Indian woman standing over me.

"Hi. I'm Dr. S . . . ," she said. "You almost died!"

I did not respond but merely stared at her, uncomprehending. I felt like my whole head was behind glass. My vision was blurred and my hearing was muffled. I had spent three days hallucinating. I could hardly tell whether what I was seeing was fantasy or real. She could have been a figment of my imagination; I had not been able to recognize people I had known for years when they came to visit.

"Do you understand me?" she asked. "I've spoken with your husband. We have kept him informed about your progress."

"Okay," I managed to respond.

I could not seem to form any other words. My mind was fuzzy and I could not remember how I had gotten to Johns Hopkins Hospital. But what was really at the forefront of my mind was how stunningly beautiful this woman was. She was the most beautiful woman I had ever seen in my life, anywhere in the world. She had arresting green eyes that shined brightly out of a face haloed by long, curly dark hair. Her creamy, olive skin was luminous. Even her drab white doctor's coat could not suppress her astonishing good looks.

"She could be a movie star," I thought to myself. "Why in the world is this stunning woman a doctor? She seems so out of place here among blood and guts."

Thank goodness I did not say that out loud. She would've thought I was crazier than I already appeared.

"I'll talk to you again later," she said when I still could find no words. Then she turned and left the room. I found out later she was the head resident on the team that saved my life. She was my pulmonologist's protégée and took her healing role quite seriously.

"I am glad to see you are doing better," the pulmonologist said later. "You had us very worried when you arrived. Your legs were swollen to three times their normal size, you were holding so much fluid."

He did not allow me to eat anything for five or six days after I woke up. Instead, I was fed via an intravenous tube. I could feel my weight dropping steadily day after day. My days and nights in intensive care blurred as one nursing shift supplanted another. I slept during the day and lay awake at night, listening to the rhythmic sounds of a hospital that never sleeps.

The nurses kept asking me questions: "Do you know what year it is?" "Do you know who the president is?" "Do you know where you are?"

From their questions, I deduced I had been pretty incoherent at first. And in truth, I had to answer, "I'm not sure" to some of their questions during those three days of hallucinations. I had no idea I had been dosed with methadone and other strange drugs during my ordeal in Brazil. My body was not used to these substances, and my mind took a holiday until they dissipated from my system.

Finally, Howard wandered in one morning, wearing the Australian jackaroo hat we bought for him in Sydney, Australia, at a jaunty angle. I find it so endearing.

He kissed me and I asked him, "How did I get here? The last thing I remember is being carried off the ship on a stretcher."

"I hired a private jet," he said.

"Oh," I replied, my voice scratchy and hoarse after days with an intubation tube down my throat.

"That must have been really expensive," I thought to myself. "He must have thought it was necessary or he would not have done it. I hope we can afford it. I guess you afford what you have to when it is a life-and-death situation."

I never said any of this out loud, though. Instead, over the next few days, I listened as if he were talking about someone else. He told me bits and pieces of what had occurred in Brazil. I had no memory of anything beyond our few days on the cruise ship. I did not remember anything from the ten days I was hospitalized in Brazil. I still have amnesia about it, except for one flashback.

It was weeks after I was released from Johns Hopkins. I woke with my heart pounding one night. I dreamed of a scene of me struggling with two or three foreign-looking men. They were trying to push a glass mask over my entire face and I was fighting them, afraid they were going to smother me.

I could hear the echoes of their voices calling, "Mrs. Woolley! Mrs. Woolley!" as they wrestled me flat onto the bed and forced the mask over my entire face.

I told Howard about my nightmare, and he suspected I was remembering when the medical team tried to put a B-pap mask on me to force 100 percent oxygen into my air-starved lungs.

"Gail, you did not like them putting that mask on your face," he said. "I told them to let you do it because you like to keep control of things. They let you try, but then they did not like the way you did it, and they started forcing it onto your face again while you struggled against them. I think that is what you are remembering."

I still bear the dark marks on my temple and jaw where they pressed the mask too tightly into my skin.

"At one point, you grabbed the mask yourself and put it on your face because you were gasping for breath," he said. "That was hard to watch. It really scared me when you couldn't breathe."

The forlorn look in Howard's eyes made me touch his face. I was sorry he had been so frightened for me. It underlined how sick and close to death I must have been. He must have been terrified, trying to navigate through a foreign hospital system to get us and all our stuff out of that country and back home where we could get more expert medical care.

His expression told me it had been dire, indeed. Other Hopkins doctors who wandered into my room during the next few days kept repeating the same mantra: that I had almost died. I must have really shaken some people up when I arrived late at night, unconscious and unresponsive.

I even found a bald spot on the right side of my scalp where someone had shaved off my hair. I found out later it was to insert a probe to see if I had any brain activity. I must have looked like I was practically dead on arrival for a doctor to order that test.

Now that I was awake, things improved gradually. One day blended into another as I lay there in the ICU, listening to the beeps of a handful of machines measuring my every vital statistic. I was so weak, I could barely lift my right arm. My left arm stayed mostly still by my side. It had so many tubes attached to it, it was cumbersome. Some of the tubes led to my chest. One wound into my nose. Nurses kept slapping my hand away when I tried to adjust it because it was so irritating, and I was already having a difficult time breathing through my oxygen tube.

There were several machines to my left, beeping or humming, lights blinking, delivering information to the nurses about my bodily functions. In some places on my body, I was tightly bound like a mummy. In others, like my back, my rear end jutted out, totally nude.

All in all, my body felt like it had been beaten up and ravaged. Nothing seemed to work quite right. I was heavily medicated and slept a lot at first. But after a few days, I was awake more often. I would glance around my room, trying to make sense of where I was. It was like I was under a bell jar, in my own world. Sounds seemed muffled and far away. I could look at people talking to me, but not make sense of their words.

One day, that mental glass shattered and I could hear again; it was almost as if my ears popped and sound rushed in. I was able to answer the nurse's questions about where I was and what year it was. I even proudly reminded them that Barack Obama was the president, which earned me a smile and a "Very good" from the nurse on that shift.

After days of clouds and rain, the sun came out one morning. I yearned to see that sunlight better, so I used my right arm to pull my-self over on my side. I shifted my left arm and its retinue of tubes out from under me, so the various machines didn't start beeping madly.

It was a struggle to turn over on my side. Gasping, I gripped the railing of the bed with my right hand and looked out the window at the sunshine. It was so simple, yet it made me so happy. The sunbeams streamed through a window painted with patches in various shades of blue. I idly wondered why this hospital wanted that type of glass in its patient rooms; the glass obscured a true view of the outdoors that bedridden patients crave.

As I lay there, random thoughts from our South American trip popped into my head. I could just remember snippets of our brief time in Buenos Aires. We stayed at a fancy international chain hotel, toured the sights, and watched people dance the tango. I also remembered the private tour I arranged for Howard and me in Montevideo, Uruguay. It was a Sunday and many buildings were closed, but the guide made the town come alive for us through her vivid descriptions of local life and culture. I befriended our guide and invited her and the driver to lunch. She was surprised and delighted. Her reaction told me most tourists coming from the cruise lines weren't usually as friendly. Truthfully, I had a lot of Uruguayan currency I could not spend anywhere else on our cruise, and I wanted to spend as much of it as possible.

I remember we sat at an outdoor café where we could watch the people spending Sunday afternoon with family or friends, whiling away their leisure time. "I used to be a tour guide, too," I told our guide.

"Really? Where?" she asked in her lightly accented English.

"I used to give French and English tours around Washington, DC," I said. "I did it while I was a university student. It was a fun job during the summer for a young person."

"Oh, how interesting," she said enthusiastically.

I remembered that her driver, who spoke little English, sat at our table, nursing a coffee and staring at the beach tourists, but as I lay there weak and barely able to move, I could not remember the sights we saw. Until Howard showed me the photos he took with his phone in Montevideo, my memory refused to return.

Amnesia is a strange, disconcerting condition. I spend so much of my life trying to create breathtaking memories, yet a drastic and sudden illness came along and snatched some of them away. Amnesia emptied out a part of my brain as thoroughly as wiping a hard drive. It is as if I never went to Brazil at all.

CHAPTER 18

A Meaningless Sign

"PUT YOUR FINGERS TOGETHER LIKE THIS," THE DOCTOR SAID. He demonstrated with his own hands, putting his two index fingers together, his nails facing down so the fingers appeared to be the heads of two swans held together in a loving posture. Although it was an odd, out-of-the-blue request, I did as he demonstrated. Holding my index fingers together, the tips pointed downward, the nails touching each other.

"See how the ends of your nails do not touch," he said. I noticed a triangle space between the ends of my nails. "Now look at mine," the doctor said. His nails were aligned together from top to bottom. "You see that little space under the ends of your nails? I see that space in every sickle cell patient I see," he said. "None of them are able to meet the nails together from top to bottom."

"What does that mean?" I asked him, concerned.

"Oh, nothing," he said, smiling slightly. "It's just something I have noticed with every patient I see." As the head of the Sickle Cell Branch at the National Institutes of Health, he saw a lot of patients who trickled in for the various experiments researchers conducted at the National Heart, Lung, and Blood Institute.

I participated in several studies there as my health worsened and

211

my symptoms became more severe. I was hoping to find the latest breakthroughs and treatments for my illness. But I got tired of being a guinea pig with so little return. The doctors always wanted so much blood for research purposes and my veins were tiny, deep, and hard to draw. The process caused me so much pain over the years as inept phlebotomists gouged my tiny veins, missed them, broke them, and bruised my arms in the process, often drawing little blood as a result.

Why the doctor took this little detour, I don't know. I took it as just another factor to further separate "sicklers" from "normal people."

It made me fondly recall my favorite primary care doctor, who has since retired. During one of our numerous visits, which were often punctuated by humor and laughter, I said, "Compared to normal people," when he was explaining the irregularities in my blood test results.

He responded by saying something that has endeared him to me forever: "It is normal *for you.*"

I just beamed, flushed with the unexpected show of support. It is so rare for me to have someone look at me as a regular human being, and not just some sick patient they have to deal with.

I held that comment in my heart for years. It was an enormous esteem builder. The results of all the hundreds of routine blood tests I have endured over the years are "normal for *me.*"

"See everybody! I am not just a disease! I am somebody too!" I wanted to shout out loud.

CHAPTER 19

Going Blind and Bald

I HAVE ALWAYS WONDERED HOW MY DISEASE WOULD, OVER time, begin its steady march through my body, the sickled cells acting as tiny wrecking balls. What parts of me would fail first? Would I wake up one morning and no longer be able to walk, or see, or hear, or breathe? I couldn't know—and the not knowing drove me crazy. Sometimes I lay in bed and stared at the ceiling, wondering what nasty surprises my cells were planning for me. All I did know was that the destruction would eventually come.

As I stepped through my fifties, I began to get my answers—and the knowing actually wasn't much better.

Losing half of my right leg left me profoundly depressed. I was certain it was the worst thing that had ever happened to me. But I was wrong; going blind was infinitely worse.

As I write this, I can barely see the page through a blurry right eye so distorted by floaters, it looks like dozens of gnats are flying erratically in front of my face. My left eye only has half vision, and I am peering out over a gas bubble placed inside my eye during a surgery to reattach my left retina.

My vision ordeal began as I was driving one day in July 2013 and a jellylike ectoplasm exploded inside my right eye, releasing dozens of black spots in my field of vision. I could barely see well enough to drive back to our beach house.

I found an ophthalmologist in the Outer Banks and made an appointment. He had retired to the beach and was clearly only working whenever he pleased. He did little but give me a cursory examination and shrug his shoulders helplessly, saying there was nothing to be done about floaters at my age. Most middle-aged people get them sooner or later, he added.

When I got back home to Maryland, my primary ophthalmologist immediately found the tear in the bottom right corner of my retina. It had torn while I was driving, flooding my field of vision with ectoplasm, spots, and webby blobs.

"You need retina surgery this afternoon," he said.

His solemn demeanor did not bode well. Who knew a spontaneous tear like that could lead to a detached retina and permanent vision loss? He said it is not uncommon in sickle cell patients, and he sent me to a retina specialist a few minutes later.

I sat through uncomfortable laser eye surgery that same afternoon. The retina specialist repaired the rupture after several uncomfortable minutes of shining a bright laser into the back of my eye to cauterize the wound. He claimed it would be painless, but it wasn't. Every time the laser seared a nerve, I jumped. After it was over, even that specialist said the usual "There is nothing I can do," about the floaters in my eye.

A few weeks later, my right retina tore again. This time I chose a different retina specialist to do the laser repair. She was much gentler manipulating my eye with her fingertips. But that wasn't the end.

In March of the next year, shortly after I was airlifted to Johns Hopkins Hospital after that nightmarish trip to Brazil, I went blind in both eyes. Just as I thought I was recovering from the acute chest syndrome, I woke up one morning and could not see the doctors talking to me. Their faces were silhouettes. Everything else around them was cloudy or dark.

"Why can't I see?" I asked.

"What do you mean you can't see?" one doctor asked me, puzzled. "I can hear you, but when I look directly at you, I cannot see your face," I said. "I am blind."

Going blind has always been one of my worst fears. My eyes have always been my tether to this Earth. Everything that mattered to me was visual—seeing the world, reading books, watching movies, examining people's expressions, admiring artwork, seeing underwater wonders and fish life when I dived.

I did not know how in the world I would finish writing this book when I could not see the text I had already painfully crafted. How could I drive? It had taken me weeks to learn to drive again using hand controls after my amputation. Then I had to wait months for the Maryland Department of Motor Vehicles to schedule a driving test forty years after I passed my first one, just to prove I was competent with the new controls. Driving gave me my only independence. Now I would have to rely on someone to drive me.

Without the ability to see, I felt like I was disembodied. I could hear things all around me, but not see them. I could not even see my own face when I washed it—my husband often wiped leftover soap or toothpaste from my skin. It was terrifying to be in the dark.

On my fifty-seventh birthday, while I was still recovering after the trip to Brazil, doctors from the Johns Hopkins Wilmer Eye Institute were called in to examine me. While some friends waited nearby with cupcakes and gifts for a small hospital room celebration, two doctors shined bright lights into my eyes, looking around but saying little.

"Why can't I see?" I pressed the older of the two doctors.

"We believe you hemorrhaged in both eyes," he said carefully. "There is a wall of blood in your left eye so thick we cannot see through it to your retina. Your right eye also has a lot of blood, but there are several floaters in the way as well. It's likely due to your sickle cell crisis. Both eyes filled with blood from dozens of ruptured vessels in the backs of your eyes."

Of course, they blamed my disease. But this had never happened before. I believe the intense pressure of having a BPAP machine forced over my face while I was unconscious caused the weak vessels in my eyes to rupture.

Since I was still hospitalized recovering from my trauma, the doctors said there was little they could do at the time. But they advised me to make an appointment at Wilmer once I recovered so they could address my eye issues. They also recommended I see their expert on sickle cell retinopathy.

A few weeks later, I followed up and made an appointment with the retinopathy expert. It turned out she was a young African American woman who shared much in common with me. First, she grew up in the same Washington suburb that I had. Second, she was dynamic yet soft-spoken, and was clearly in charge of dozens of doctors in her department who respected her expertise.

After she ordered an eye sonogram, we discovered my left retina had detached behind that thick wall of blood. I was totally blind in the left eye and mostly blind in the right eye. The doctor decided to repair the left eye first.

"This is very serious," she said. "Even after I reattach your retina, it will be weeks before you can see. And I may have to do a second surgery to remove the bubble I put into your eye to hold the retina in place. You will have to hold your head down as much as possible to keep the bubble in place. And your eye will be red and bloodshot for quite a while. You have to keep the dressing over your eye for much of the time."

Although she gave me the illusion of choice, I knew without the surgery, I would go blind forever. She also warned me the retinal surgery would accelerate the growth of a cataract in that eye, which would also hamper my vision.

"Okay," I agreed. "You do what you have to do."

We set a surgery date and left the minicity that is Johns Hopkins Hospital.

With everything else that has happened to me because of this disease, I hated blindness the most. It made finishing this book extremely difficult. I bought voice-over software, but the software made so many mistakes. I tried typing slowly while peering at my blurry screen through a magnifying glass, using only the partial vision in my right eye. It took many long, tedious hours to complete a page or two. But I persevered.

A couple of weeks later, I underwent the retinal surgery, not in the outpatient center the retinopathy specialist preferred, but in the main hospital. Some of the doctors who saved my life in March intervened when they learned of the specialist's outpatient plans. "We just saved her life," one said. "You are not operating on this patient unless you are in the main hospital where our teams can back you up in case something happens."

They also insisted I undergo my second blood transfer transfusion in three months to prepare me for surgery. The hematologists told me they believed this transfer transfusion would prevent another sickle cell crisis during my surgery when I was under general anesthesia. I thought it was an awful lot of trouble to go through when I had had dozens of surgeries before without such dramatic preparation.

The process was awful. I had to lie in their transfusion center bed with needles in the tiny veins of both arms—which were only found after a sonogram and several pokes. I had to lie still for several hours, while 70 percent of my blood drained into a gallon bag. In the other arm, eight or ten units of donated blood drained slowly into my vein. If I moved, it could affect the flow or dislodge the needles, so I remained still. Staying in the same position for so long made my arms cramp, then ache.

It is quite bizarre to see your life's blood draining into a bag over your right shoulder.

"I could be dead right now if they were not replacing what they are taking," I thought idly, listening to some music on my iPod while I tried to relax. Some of the songs that I liked to listen to most were "Reasons" by Earth, Wind & Fire, "With You I'm Born Again" by

Billy Preston and Syreeta, "Someone to Watch Over Me" by Ella Fitzgerald, "A Thousand Years" by Christina Perri, "Somewhere Out There" by James Ingram and Linda Ronstadt, and "Happy" by Pharrell Williams, which was also the ringtone on my cell phone.

"What are you going to do with my blood?" I asked the nurse supervising the transfusion.

"We throw it away as waste," she said, walking away.

Waste? I thought. *That's* what my blood is considered? So useless to me and others, disposable. I am just one more flawed thing to throw away in this society. I wonder if she even realized how hurtful that sounded.

The surgery followed two days later.

I regained some of my vision after my left eye surgery, but it caused a cataract that grows worse each month, making my vision almost permanently blurry. My right eye surgery was delayed indefinitely. Although I was thankful to see again out of my left eye, my vision was five times worse than it was before the retina detached. I was not confident I could see well enough to drive, but I was eventually able to after the cataract that formed was removed. I coped, thinking I was finally making progress in recovering from the trauma in Brazil.

A few months later, the other shoe dropped.

My hair started falling out by the handful. Apparently, my near-death experience in Brazil still had some surprises in store for me. A dermatologist told me it was the result of the trauma I had been through. "It's the same thing that happens to pregnant women," the dermatologist explained. "Your hair's growth cycle is interrupted by trauma. The older hairs fall out faster than you can replace them with new growth."

He also told me the dark marks on my temple and jaw were not the bruises I believed them to be. "Feel this," he said, putting my finger on my temple. "You lost several layers of skin here. This is another sort of trauma. It caused hyperpigmentation. It happens sometimes with darker skin."

He sent me home with a skin-bleaching prescription and told me to buy an off-the-shelf product that helps people regrow hair. I tried both products, hoping to get back to normal sooner or later.

I never imagined a single traumatic event could have so many lingering side effects. Six months after the Brazil drama, I was still having problems. Almost dying does a lot of strange things to a person's equilibrium. My body was still fighting its way back in so many ways, I just could not see below the surface.

I lived with bald spots and thin hair for several months before my own hair follicles kicked in, growing an inch or so every month. My hairdresser kept cutting the longer hairs to hide the bald spots until the shorter hair could fill in. She said it would take at least a year for it to get back to normal.

I had never had thin hair before. It was enlightening. I had no idea how to style it and just let it look wild and untamed during our summer at the beach house. Now I understood what my mother and friends had been telling me all my life. I had taken my long, thick hair for granted, and I missed it when it was gone.

At least the dermatologist didn't say, "I'm afraid there's not much we can do." I have heard that so many times, I want to scream, "Why not? Why can't you do anything? Is it lack of knowledge or lack of will?" Of course, I never do that. Yelling at doctors is counterproductive—most of the time, especially because I usually don't go back to any doctors who prove unhelpful.

As I said before, I do believe lying helpless and in agony in dozens of hospitals for so many years affected my personality. It has given me a calloused outer shell lined with bravado.

As I grew older and my disease worsened, I realized I do not have a lot of fear. My imminent death has hung over my head like some perverse sword of Damocles for so long, it has desensitized me to fear. More importantly, it emboldens me to move through life tackling whatever I please.

My husband is one of the few people who understands me. He

sees through my tough exterior to the tender underbelly where I hide my true self. If I cry, it is usually because I am frustrated or angry, rather than sad or depressed. I hate when people feel sorry for me, and I almost never feel sorry for myself. Don't they see I am living the very best life I can despite all my obstacles?

But even my husband is sometimes shocked by my daredevil spirit. When we return from a trip, he tells our friends how I try to pack in as many activities as I can that have the potential to kill us. Sometimes he bows out, preferring the safety of the golf course. But I always forge ahead.

I am quite different from the rest of my family. My frankness and fearlessness are rare among my kin. When I told my mother about how thrilling it was to swim with the reef sharks when I was in Tahiti, she was appalled.

"How could you do something like that?" she squealed. "You could have been killed!"

"Mom, I swim with sharks every day at work," I said, rolling my eyes. "At least I could see these coming."

She had no idea what an adrenaline rush it was to have sharks swimming just below my fins and all around me in forty-five feet of the clearest sea I have ever seen.

PART 5

Finding Peace

CHAPTER 20

Survivor in the Mirror

POTOMAC, MARYLAND, 2014

IN MY DREAMS I CAN RUN. ARMS AND LEGS PUMPING, I RUN UP and down hills, laughing with joy as the wind blows my long hair into my eyes. My arms are spread wide to embrace a beautiful day full of possibilities. It must be summer because I am barefoot. Yet the prickly shrub clinging to the dunes doesn't scratch my legs as I race up the hill, then slide down the other side, cool, smooth sand slipping between my toes.

As is the way of dreams, the scene shifts and the next thing I know, I am plunging into a warm, salty sea. When my head breaks the surface, I gulp in air, looking around for my marine friends. Spying them, I begin swimming through a gentle current toward a pod of dolphins that are jumping and frolicking as I draw near.

Once in their midst, I tread water until I can grab the back fins of two of them, and then my friends take off, pulling me through the water far quicker than I can swim. The thrill of their muscles contracting and releasing beneath their slippery, tough skin makes me giggle as we speed through the water.

I can still hear a faint echo of my laughter when I wake up. Still smiling, I snuggle back under the covers, hoping to recapture that magical dream about swimming with wild dolphins. In my dreams, the ocean water is never cold. My limbs never fatigue. Nothing in my body hurts. Sleep is my safe place. It is the only world where I am normal and healthy just like everyone else. It must be why I like to sleep so much.

But it is too late. I will never recapture that same dream, so I pry open my eyes. The morning chill in my bedroom chases the dreamy wisps away. As my mind regains full consciousness, I stretch my arms and legs. Suddenly, dread stiffens my whole body.

In the chill morning light, reality insinuates itself into my mind. I cannot run. I cannot even walk very well. I can no longer swim the way I used to, or go to the bathroom without a wheelchair and a lot of aggravating acrobatics. Driving a car is trickier now, using hand controls. And I have a whole closet full of right shoes that do not fit my plastic foot very well.

My vision has not been very good since my eyes hemorrhaged. My hair is still growing back. Trauma, I'm told, can do that to a body. Maybe trauma can, but sickle cell can do so much more. I do not know what my disease will do to me next.

So much unpredictability can be unsettling. Last summer, while we were relaxing at Dreamcastle, our beach house, my heartbeat became erratic. While I was resting in bed, it sped up to 160 beats per minute, a tachycardia episode I could not control. I ended up in the tiny Outer Banks Hospital, where a cardiologist prescribed some heavy-duty drugs to try to keep my heart from racing so fast. I might as well have been running wind sprints.

Although the heart episode was unnerving, I did not panic. Panic serves no purpose because you cease to think. I must keep thinking if I want to survive the obstacle course that has been my life these last five decades. Though I never know what is coming next, I try to deal with each new pitfall with as much grace as possible.

In bed, I inhale deeply, remembering that scare. The only way I can better control my congestive heart issue is to refrain from salt, my doctors warn. I am trying, but that is easier said than done. At our ocean-side house, salt is in the very air we breathe. So I take a dozen different medications that do weird things to my body. It is like walking a tightrope; I cannot let my body veer into any extreme that will suddenly collapse the whole house of cards.

The real bane of my existence is the nasal cannula that I use to breathe highly concentrated oxygen every hour of the day. It is attached to a hollow plastic tube that dangles from my face, down across the mattress and off the side of my bed, before running fifty feet along creaky wooden floors and under the double doors at the entrance to my bedroom. At the other end of the tube, a mechanical whirring signals the oxygen concentrator is working as designed, forcing oxygen into my body and helping my heart and lungs work better in the face of the pulmonary hypertension that has weakened the arteries in my lungs and strained my enlarged heart.

After decades of sickle cell anemia ravaging every vein and capillary in my body, it is difficult for my heart to pump oxygenated blood through me. A simple walk up a few stairs leaves me breathless. Pulmonary hypertension is an incurable condition that occurs in about one-tenth of adults with sickle cell disease and will, one day, cause my heart to completely fail. It will likely be the thing that kills me.

Oh, joy. Now I am a minority of yet another minority—the story of my life. I should be used to it by now.

I push that dispiriting thought out of my mind, throw off the sheet, and sit up on the side of the bed. Then I forget—again—and glance down.

Even after a few years, I am still startled by what I see. My right leg ends abruptly in a shriveled stump just below my right knee. I wiggle the toes on my left foot to remind myself they remain intact. In the dim morning light, I glance at myself in the mirrored doors of my husband's closet, which faces our bed.

Looking back at me is a drawn, aged stranger with one and a half legs peeking out of her nightgown. Her shoulder-length hair is still dark, with just a few grays peeking out near a face that is puffy; her jowls and neck are beginning to droop in that basset-hound look of middle age. There are permanent frown lines between her eyebrows from decades of squeezing her eyes shut to withstand bouts of agonizing pain. Around her mouth are permanent smile lines, a symbol of the never-ending dichotomy that is her life. There's some swelling around her middle, but her hips are narrow and boyish. Every other bump under her nightgown just seems to droop.

"That cannot possibly be me!" my mind screams at the reflection in that hostile mirror.

Where is the outgoing, slim young girl with the long flowing hair and smooth caramel complexion whose quick mind and infectious laugh made everyone around her grin whenever they heard it? Where is the girl who made everyone guffaw at her incisive wit? Where in the world did *she* disappear to?

But the mirror, that utterly ruthless teller of truth, reminds me the stranger I'm viewing is, in fact, me. This is the battle-scarred me, after decades of fighting an epic crusade inside my own body that I am gradually losing.

I swear I can hear the mirror laughing under its breath. It takes pleasure in mocking me with a reflection of an almost-old woman who is physically stooped and world-weary. I move slowly in the mirror because her—no, *my*—back aches as usual when I stand and brace my left foot on the floor to swing myself into the wheelchair sitting beside my bed. I prop my right stump on a pad specially designed to hold it horizontally, and my left foot on a normal footrest, then release the brakes on my wheelchair and roll myself toward the double doors of our master bathroom so I can relieve myself.

It's funny, I spent the first fifty years of my life living with sickle cell disease as best I could and never *once* thought of myself as disabled. Losing half of my right leg changed my mind. Having my body suddenly break down in unexpected ways convinced me even more. Dragging oxygen around everywhere and no longer being able to read street signs cemented the idea. Yep, I am old and decrepit—especially for someone with sickle cell disease, the medical establishment insists. Most of my fellow sufferers died a long time ago. I am just lucky to still be alive.

My husband and I spent a small fortune remodeling this master bathroom to make it more accessible for me now that I am a permanently disabled amputee.

Getting from my bed to the toilet takes much longer than it used to when I had two legs. I transfer from my bed to the wheelchair so I can travel into the newly widened doorway of the toilet room. I grab a stylish crescent-shaped metal bar we had installed to accommodate my new reality, and I balance on my left leg just long enough not to fall before I can safely sit on the raised toilet. This maneuver is an acrobatic accomplishment I never dreamed I would have to master back in the days when a middle-of-the-night pee run was a mindless, sleepwalking endeavor.

Now, every movement I make matters, and I must take great care not to fall, my physical therapists tell me. Not because I am afraid of falling, but because getting back up is a real challenge when you only have half a leg on one side, and a wobbly left leg weakened by a fractured pelvis that refuses to heal on the other.

I am lucky, they assure me, because I still have both my knees, even if they are artificial. I use them to help myself climb back up from the floor whenever I do fall. I use my upper-body strength to help swing myself back into my wheelchair or onto the closest solid surface.

Once I get my breath back, I swing myself back into my wheelchair. The pulmonary hypertension makes me perennially breathless. I will breathe concentrated oxygen through a plastic tube for the rest of my life—however long *that* may be. It is a tether I would rather not have, but one I cannot live without.

I am resigned as I drag its long tubing behind me everywhere I go around my house. I often trip over it, like when the plastic tube gets tangled around my prosthetic. I cannot feel the tubing snaking around my false ankle until it is almost too late. I sometimes bump my artificial foot into strangers waiting in line in front of me or under a table at a restaurant because I cannot feel anything below my right knee.

Not at the moment, anyway. For months after my right foot, ankle, and shin were amputated, I felt millions of phantom pains. I still feel thousands of tiny needles, burning into a heated numbness at the end of my stump, usually after a day of being savaged by my ill-fitting prosthetic leg.

I can lie in bed at night and tell you when the big toe of my right foot wiggles. Or waken to my foot on fire or feel a nagging ache or itch on the left side of my right ankle, even when it is no longer there. I rub my stump to remind my brain there is nothing below my knee anymore. But my brain is stubborn. It sent and received signals from my foot for over fifty-five years. Why should today be any different?

It is a confusing state of mind.

"I am queen of your central nervous system!" my brain insists. "Do not believe your eyes. Eyes can lie. Only nerves tell the truth."

Who am I to believe—my eyes or my brain?

Today, my eyes win and I don one of the two prosthetic legs I own. I have to wear a rubberized sleeve against my skin to protect it. The sleeve has a long screw protruding from the end of it. I must insert the screw into a hole inside the prosthetic. Once the screw correctly fits into the hole, the prosthetic is firmly attached to my stump. Then I must don yet another rubberized sleeve over both the prosthetic and my leg to secure the thing in case of hazardous conditions. Pulling all that rubber paraphernalia over my stump takes me at least fifteen minutes. It is hot and makes my stump perspire during the summer. Underneath all that rubber, I must wear stockings made with silver thread because my sensitive skin broke out in blisters several times until I got used to wearing an artificial limb. Silver provides an inhospitable environment for infections. I also must wear some clear, soft rubber discs around the fibula bone protruding at the end of my stump. Otherwise, the prosthetic rubs against it, causing sharp pain and eventually a callous.

I have no idea how I will quickly exit my house in case of fire, but that is a problem for another day.

I do not like the color of my prosthetic leg very much. The color is much darker than my own skin. The prosthetic people claim the rubbery plastic covers that hide the metal parts of the prosthetic do not come in enough colors to capture the olive undertone of my skin, so it is a dull chocolate brown created by some dull, unimaginative manufacturer.

I believe the people who make and market such products don't look like me and don't care if the color matches mine or not. It is the same war women of color had to fight for decades to get main-stream makeup manufacturers to produce colors that flattered our many shades of nonpink skin. I wish the American prosthetic manu-facturers would follow suit.

Despite my distaste for my prosthetic and its perennial dis-comfort, I struggle into it most days. I have no choice if I want to walk. I have ruined all my fingernails dragging two rubbery sleeves onto my stump to hold it in place every day.

Even with one rubbery liner on my skin and the other on the prosthetic to help secure it to my thigh, sometimes I still have to wear several socks so the prosthetic cup properly fits my stump. It shrank to half its size over the first year after the amputation. By the second year, it shrank again, and my prosthetist was slow to make another leg that fit me better. Each new leg is still as ugly and oddly colored as the first one.

My mother was adamantly opposed to the idea of my leg being amputated.

"Don't let them cut off your leg!" she said, crying over the telephone from a thousand miles away. "Isn't there anything else they can do?"

For over a year, she had been pushing me to fight hard to save my leg. But the MRSA kept winning and spreading its malicious poison up my leg.

"Mom, you don't understand," I said. My mother, ill herself and confined to bed for months with various frailties, had not seen my struggle. She had not been there for the depressing visits to the prestigious treatment hospital or seen the fatalistic look in my ankle surgeon's eyes. "Would you rather visit me here in the hospital or at the cemetery? Because those are the only choices I have right now."

"I don't want you to die," she conceded quietly, sniffling.

"Neither do I."

It was a very sad exchange—one of many difficult conversations I have had with her over the years. She has trouble accepting the gravity of my health. I don't always understand why we cannot agree. Since I am not a mother, I can only imagine the anguish she must feel watching her children sicken and die before her eyes. She watched my brother Tim die at thirty-five. She has watched me go through almost twenty surgeries and numerous sickle cell crises. Now she has to see me hobble around on a false leg with oxygen tubes on my face all the time. I guess that is a lot for any mother to internalize. I will never know.

Once, and only once, when I was middle aged, and she was ill and confined to a rehabilitation center for months, she confessed, "Maybe I should never have had children."

"No, Mom, maybe you shouldn't have," I said sadly. "I would never have known the difference." And I would not have had to suffer such a painful life, I thought to myself.

But that is an alternate universe. *This* is my life.

My husband and friends all tell me I am strong. A tough life of suffering can make you strong. But underneath, I am just a tender-hearted girl lucky enough to have lived a life that could include moments of pure joy.

Dr. Z, a doctor friend of mine at Johns Hopkins Hospital, once told my very concerned husband after I nearly died, "Gail is alive because of Gail. It's not because of anything *we're* doing."

I keep living through sheer will—not for myself, but to keep a promise I made to the earnest young man I agreed to marry when we were journalism students at Syracuse University. I swore to Howard that no matter how much my body hurt, I would never leave him if I could possibly help it. No matter how tempted I might be to end the pain once and for all, I will not swallow a bottle full of the narcotics that have helped me cope with my life. I will not succumb to that temptation. I will stay with him as long as I can—no matter what. I have kept this promise well into my fifties.

In return, he has kept his promise to love me with everything he has in him. He has tempted fate numerous times, has jeopardized his own career every time he abruptly left a job because I needed him. He never leaves my side, no matter how bad things get. He has held my hand while I endured the agony of seven hip replacements, two knee replacements, a failed ankle fusion, a partial leg amputation, two life-threatening infections, numerous surgeries to remove diseased organs, and a catastrophic lung episode that nearly smothered me to death halfway around the world.

He was there for me when my bowels obstructed and my stomach bloated with toxic bile. He slept curled in a chair by my hospital bed for weeks, afraid to leave in case I did not make it through the night. Two surgeries and thirty days later, he supported my weight, holding me up as I hobbled out of the hospital, thirty-five pounds thinner, pale as a ghost and unsteady as a newborn.

For thirty-five years, I have seen the tears in his eyes as I screamed in pain through sickle cell crisis after crisis until a doctor mercifully ordered a nurse to give me an injection of narcotics strong enough to knock me out for a short while.

Thankfully, love and contentment help take my mind off the pain. We have had a wonderful marriage. I love my husband more than I love myself. How else could I endure so much for so long?

Last summer while we were staying at Dreamcastle, Howard and I stopped at a local joint called Hurricane Mo's for a late lunch. It attracts a good happy hour crowd of mostly locals who like to swap tall tales over beers and hot wings.

As I slowly made my way through the tables, Howard hovered

nearby, ready to help me any way he could until we sat down at a table. Once seated, a cheerful waitress asked us a few casual questions. One of them was how long we had been married.

"Thirty-three years!" she exclaimed. "Did you discover the fountain of youth?"

I preened. She saw our smiling, contented faces and thought we were more youthful than we appeared. Then she asked me about the oxygen tubing in my nose. "Do you always have to wear that?"

"Only for the rest of my life," I said serenely.

"But you look too vibrant to have to wear that!" she said.

"Dear, I have to wear this for my lungs, which don't work as well as they should. And I have an artificial leg, too," I said. "But I do not let either of those things stop me from doing anything I want to do. I am even learning to scuba dive."

"Good for you!" she said. "That's great. You should live your life."

"Oh, I do. And I intend to keep living it, doing just what I want until the last second of the last minute of my last day," I told her.

"You have a great attitude," she said.

I agree. Yes, I do. But it took a great deal of pain to get me there.

Any beauty I once had is long gone, beaten down by the ravages of my disease. I am nobody's idea of a femme fatale these days. My body has more scars than a heavyweight prizefighter's. The scars are a map of my misery from multiple surgeries—all to live just a little bit better.

I am sometimes ashamed of my scar-riddled body when I put on my well-worn one-piece bathing suit to swim laps with my scuba tank in the pool at our beach house. Someday, in the not-too-distant future, I want to be cremated and have my ashes spread in the ocean at the Outer Banks because it is a place I have always found peace. I hope a few of my ashes will float and wander the Earth the same way I did in life.

My husband never notices my scars. Nor does he think they are ugly.

"They are not ugly because they are part of *you*," he tells me, kissing my right leg stump, my scar-crossed abdomen, and lastly, my mouth. He is so dear to me. I reach out and caress his whiskered cheek. He, too, has aged. There is more hair on his chest than on his head these days, most of it gray. Slightly wrinkled, his face is still more kind than handsome.

But it doesn't matter to me. I married who he was inside, not outside.

Nothing I could say drove him away—not even when I told him it was better for him to find someone else if he planned to have children one day. I told him I could not take the chance that any child of mine would carry my disease into the next generation.

He looked at me a second, knowing he was one of the last males in his family that could ensure their name survived in the future. But then he squared his shoulders and cleared his throat.

"But I love you too much to let you go," he said softly. And he never has.

Even after all these years together, he still tells me I am beautiful. I just smile sadly and tell him he must be blind. I am nowhere near beautiful. I am so much *more* than something as fleeting as "beautiful."

I am a survivor.

CHAPTER 21

Fate, Forgiveness, and Acceptance

MY BROTHER KENNETH AND I FEEL LIKE WAR REFUGEES sometimes. Having witnessed the battle between our parents rage on for decades, we are shell-shocked and weary middle-aged children.

Now that we are all getting older, we see my father less as a man to fear than one to pity. Decades of drinking ravaged his brain. His severe dementia makes him shuffle when he walks behind a full-time caregiver my mother fears they cannot afford much longer. After successfully battling the tongue cancer caused by his chronic alcoholism, his voice is now a raspy whisper. The cancer ravaged his throat; the radiation finished it off. Now, he is just a shrunken and thin shell of his former self. It's as if he is disappearing before our eyes. His mind is that of a small child, and he can remember nothing for more than a few moments. My mother is the only one he recognizes instantly. He seems to harbor a constant fear of her abandonment.

It has been a constant battle of wills between me and my mother about moving them out of their house and into assisted living. She clings to their house like it is made of gold bricks. I can understand her fear of losing control—of her possessions, independence, even her life.

She has fallen several times on the steps leading up to their living room and broken bones in her ankle. Their house is too difficult for her now that she spends more time in a wheelchair than shuffling awkwardly behind a walker. But she is stubborn, her mind still sharp at eighty, and she refuses to listen to reason. I do not understand why she wants to remain trapped in that house with a man losing his mind. They have no social interaction for months on end. But I suspect she fears change.

My brother has joined me in searching for an assisted-living spot for the two of them where they will get twenty-four-hour care and be able to socialize with others their age. But my mother is horrified she will have to leave a lifetime of possessions behind. My brother is part of the sandwich generation—stuck between the needs of his growing kids and his aging parents.

I am the sensible one because I have had to be. I am the only one who finished college and planned for the future, so of course they look to me whenever their finances are tight. The reward for doing right is to always be saddled with your extended family's problems. Sometimes I wish I had been the badass child instead; then no one would expect anything from me.

I am too tired from my own problems to have others endlessly pulling at me. Especially since every visit to my doctors these days yields nothing but bad news. My kidney function is worse. My hemoglobin count is low despite everything the doctors are doing.

At the hematologist's office, my poor husband, clearly shaken, asks if we should try something drastic, like a stem cell transplant—if I can find an appropriate donor. I can see the fear in his eyes.

"A fourth of those patients die," the hematologist replies. "I don't think she's a good candidate for that."

I can feel the end coming.

It's September 2014. When we go to our college reunion at Syracuse University, my husband wheels me around campus in a wheelchair. It is a far cry from the carefree walks we used to take around campus when we first fell in love over three decades ago.

"I think this is the last time I will ever see this place," I say to Howard, glancing at the fancy new part of the Newhouse complex, part of the communications school from which we both graduated. After we donated a small fortune, the college named a broadcast journalism laboratory after us in the Newhouse II building. Without children of our own, we feel it is important to leave our legacy behind somehow. We hope it helps future generations of journalism students remember that average people can make a difference if they put their minds to it. We also endowed a scholarship for minority students that should last for generations.

"What do you mean?" Howard asks me as we prepare to make the long drive home. I can tell he is bothered by my statement.

"I mean it feels like the last time I will ever be here," I say, hedging it a bit for his sake. I gaze at the mountains surrounding the scenic campus. He looks at me without comment, clearly worried that I am being pessimistic. It is not like me. I am usually an optimist. But too much harsh realism can take its toll on even those who wear rose-colored glasses.

We try to carry on with our lives.

Every day, I find it harder to catch my breath after the simplest things, like walking to my kitchen. Howard has to help me more and more. He makes most of our meals. He drives me everywhere because I cannot see well, despite the eye surgeries.

Howard tries to keep both of our spirits up by setting up fancy evenings like we used to have—at the Kennedy Center, Ford's Theatre, and numerous black-tie dinners like the ones he used to attend when he was a lobbyist in Washington.

One day, I stop him with the truth.

"I am not the same person I was five years ago," I tell him, gently taking his hand. "If we went to the Kennedy Center Honors now, we could not sit in our usual seats." We always sat in the balcony overlooking the Presidential Box. "Now I have oxygen to drag around," I add. "I would need a wheelchair to get most of the way to my seat, and then I would have to lean on you just to make it down the stairs. With my luck, I would probably trip over my evening gown and fall off the balcony."

"I don't think I want to go anymore," I finally say. He looks so sad. "I am not giving up," I add quickly. "I am just trying to be realistic. Do you know how hard it is for me to go into a room full of people who used to know us, before all this happened to me? Now I have an oxygen tube over my face. That and a wheelchair can really ruin a girl's entrance." Nobody would see my pretty gown or the trouble I took with my hair and makeup. "They just see somebody pitiful," I say. "Do you have any idea how *hard* that is to me?"

I tell him that I don't like people seeing me like this. That I don't feel very beautiful in a wheelchair with an oxygen tube over my face. That I don't like the limp my prosthetic leg gives me. "I know what you are going to say," I say when he starts to jump in. "It is what it is."

"Yes, but I don't want you to completely withdraw from the kind of life we have shared for years," Howard says. "Everyone knows you've been ill. They are just happy to see you out and about."

"I know who my real friends are," I say quietly. "And they are rarely at some glitzy affair rubbing elbows with strangers, networking just for their own gain. That is *your* world, not mine. I only went to those black-tie dinners for you."

"We can't withdraw from everything." I can tell by his facial expression that the conversation is a difficult one for him.

"Yeah, well. I will have to pick and choose what events I venture out for," I say. "You know how much trouble it is to travel anywhere with me now. You are the one that ends up carrying all the equipment, packing it in the car, and setting it up for me. It must get irritating."

"I don't mind," he says softly.

"I know, and I love you for helping me so much. I know it cannot be much fun for you," I say. "That's why I encourage you to spend time with your friends now that you're retired. Being my caregiver is a lot of work and I understand when you need a break sometimes."

"I will do anything for you, honey," he says.

I believe him.

It's November 2014, and my labored breathing is so obvious, my primary care physician sends me to a cardiologist he knows from their days at the Temple University School of Medicine.

They put their heads together and run several diagnostic tests. My doctor calls with a serious, deadpan voice. The news is not good.

"Your heart is failing," he says. He knew the pulmonary hypertension was affecting the right side of my heart, but now I have fluid backing up in the left side, too. "I think you need to be hospitalized," he says, "so we can monitor you while we change some of your drugs."

He brings my pulmonologist into it, and they put me on a blood thinner right away, out of fear I might otherwise have a sudden embolism or a stroke.

Thankfully, my pulmonologist is a calm fellow. He sees drastic cases every day and does not get excited about much. He issues instructions to wean me gradually from some of my blood pressure medicines and increase my diuretics to eliminate the extra fluids that are so overworking my heart.

"Can you live with heart failure?" I ask him, knowing he is the man who helped save my life after Brazil.

"You are like a cat with nine lives," he says. "You have only used a few of them so far."

I chuckle at the truth of *that* and try to internalize his calmness. I feel myself relaxing in his Zen-like presence. Over the next few weeks, I follow his commonsense instructions, including sticking to a low-salt diet that should help reduce the fluid in my body. None of his directions mention being hospitalized. I have already had enough of that for a lifetime.

The water flows out of my system as I try to stick to the low-salt regimen. My meals are mostly tasteless, but I shed the extra water weight that hampers my heart, and I start breathing better. It is a temporary respite. I am, above all other traits, a realist. I know my time is limited.

I have been waiting to die for so long that I've spent most of our marriage preparing my husband for my imminent demise. That's what you do when people keep telling you to expect an early death and when your brother, suffering from the same disease, succumbs to it at thirty-five. I have never been sure how long I have left.

Still true to my Goody Two-Shoes ways, I have never smoked, I rarely drink, and I have never touched illegal drugs. Who has time? I can barely keep up with the dozen prescriptions I take daily just to stay on an even keel. On my fifty-fifth birthday, Howard reminded me that I was beating the odds. "You see?" he said. "Doctors don't know everything." It was a nice gift to be reminded that my longevity has been helped a little by medical science and a whole lot by *me*.

Tonight, my husband and I talk once again about how I am constantly preparing him for life on his own. I have taught him how to pay bills online and prepare simple, nutritious meals so he will not be helpless and overwhelmed by "the casserole brigade"—the widows and divorcées anxious to remarry who aggressively pursue widowers.

My husband is a fairly healthy man who exercises regularly, but like most of us in middle age, he could afford to lose a few pounds. He has no chronic illnesses and only feels pain when, for instance, he sprains an ankle running. He is fond of martinis straight up and salty snack foods, but he only indulges occasionally.

He is in our master bathroom shaving one morning when I feel a certain urgency to say something important. Now, to be fair, he would say I talk all the time, and he needs to filter most of it because it is impossible to absorb every word. But this time, I want him to listen.

"Howard, look in the mirror and hug yourself," I say. "Thank whatever higher being you believe in that you have a body that works the way it should. It does not hurt you without reason. You have legs that walk or run when you mentally command them, and arms that can reach whatever you try to grasp. Your body works right. It does not betray you at every turn the way mine does."

He doesn't stop shaving, but asks from his position in front of his bathroom mirror, "Why are you telling me this?"

"Because you are normal and healthy and should always remember how very lucky you are," I say. That makes him come around the bathroom door, shaving cream covering half his face, to look at me. Who knows—maybe he thinks I'm going crazy.

"I have not felt healthy and normal since I was seven years old," I say. "That's most of my life." I look him in the eyes as tears fill my own. "Do you have any idea how much I would pay to have been born healthy? There is no amount too high."

Howard, always empathetic, comes out of the bathroom to kiss me, trying to bring back my good spirits. "I am serious," I say between kisses. "Don't take your good health for granted."

"I won't."

"You know better than anyone how not knowing what will hit me next has kept me from fully succeeding in the work world," I say. "Employers just do not understand when you suddenly call in sick and cannot work for a week or more. The only reason they ever believed I was really sick was because I was usually in a hospital, and all they had to do was call me there to prove it."

"Don't worry about it so much. That's all in the past," he says, trying to calm me down.

"Please," I say, "do whatever you have to do to stay healthy. Exercise, eat right, you know the drill. Appreciate good health for the precious gift it is, and don't squander it with bad habits. Bad habits kill more people than disease does."

"Yeah, I know," he says, relieved my fretting appears to be over. Then he returns to the bathroom to finish his morning shave.

I think my message was delivered. I hope he heard it.

My biggest fear is not my own death. My greatest fear is my husband not surviving *me*.

That night, we hold each other tightly. "If you die before me," I whisper softly in his ear, "I will be catatonic. Someone will have to feed me, make me drink fluids and take my medicines, insist that I sleep. Without you, I will do whatever it takes to die as quickly as possible so I can find you again—somehow."

My friends often tell me that they don't know how I do it. That my attitude is so good. That I am a role model. "Kiddo," I tell them, "every day I am alive is a good day."

Without knowing my full history, they marvel at my reply, shake their heads in wonder. They have only heard terrible things about the severity of my illness. Most know very few details about its stark reality.

I can see them mentally trying to put themselves in my shoes. Every single one says that they, in the face of a dire illness, could not react with the same positivity I do. But they don't have my long-term perspective. I have had a death sentence hanging over my head since childhood, and I appreciate every year I live beyond my pediatrician's doomsday prediction.

I forgave him decades ago for terrifying my family. I am sure he meant well. Doctors are human. They make mistakes, just like everybody else. He was relaying what little he knew about our illness at the time. "He was practicing medicine until he got it right," I quip when I tell people the story.

His prediction empowered me to know my sickle cell disease *will* kill me one day. It made me realize I could not afford to waste any time. I needed to do whatever I wanted to do with my life as soon as possible.

I know everybody will die someday. But few of us have our lives narrowed down so precisely by a medical profession still stumbling in the dark. Even so, they might be right, and so I do not waste precious time on things that do not matter. And I do not let anyone else define who I am or what I am capable of doing.

That includes listening to doctors who cannot hide their surprise when they see I am still alive in my mid-fifties. Some even double-check my medical chart to see if I have misspoken when I say I have the disease instead of the sickle cell trait. They cannot believe I am still standing, albeit with poor vision, a prosthetic leg, and oxygen blowing through my nose trying to reach my failing heart and lungs.

I am looking forward to my next great adventure.

It is easy to kill yourself. It is infinitely harder to survive decades of agony with a smile on your face. Love is an essential ingredient for happiness.

I am thankful to have had the love of a good man for most of my life. We have had great adventures in remote locales and have laughed ourselves silly with good friends. Laughter has been my very best medicine of all.

To jog my memory for this book, I leaf through the hundreds of photographs we have taken in magical places over the last thirty years. Each one depicts some of the happiest moments of my life.

In one photograph, a favorite, I am in Egypt, smiling widely in a khaki outfit. We had trekked through part of the Sahara, and I had thought the photo would not show so much of the sand coating us. I am holding a giant ankh, an Egyptian symbol for life, in my hand. Behind me is the magnificence of Abu Simbel, a gigantic stone temple complex dedicated to Pharaoh Ramesses II and his most cherished wife, Nefertari. She was a Nubian woman, as brown as I am, who was revered for her beauty. Her massive image equals Ramesses II's in size, which historians say indicates his reverence for her.

As an African American woman, it gives me great pleasure to know our beauty was prized so many centuries ago.

I saw many of the world's wonders with my own eyes and met people whose lives were vastly different from my own. I have had the honor of dressing in lovely gowns, diamonds twinkling at my ears, throat, and hand while I danced at the inaugural balls of four US presidents. I have had my picture taken with three of them at the White House, smiling as widely as any tourist would. I have traipsed through jungles and bush to see some of the Earth's disappearing wildlife. I have photographed stupendous animals—hippos yawning in an African river at dawn, a lioness on a night hunt—that may no longer exist one day. These photos still make me smile.

It has been an interesting life.

Today, I cannot travel as I once did. I can no longer do all the adventurous things I used to do. But I try to fill every day with simpler pleasures.

I remind myself that life is a gift. It is meant to be enjoyed. I focus on taking pleasure in the sunlight glistening off the pristine snow outside my bedroom windows or birds fluttering about on the roof of the gazebo that graces one end of the deck of our home in Maryland. My bed is surrounded by windows so I can feel the sun on my face in the morning. With a turn of my head on the pillow, I can glimpse the rosebuds and leaves sprouting on thorny bushes outside.

When I am at our beach house, I giggle like a child, clapping my hands in joy at the dolphins frolicking in the waves. I watch the relentless ebb and flow of the tide, envisioning myself joining that tide one day when my ashes are scattered in the sea to wander the world I so love to explore.

I am glad to wake up every morning, and if I find the aches and pains bearable and the oxygen tube in my nose not too irritating, I concentrate on consciously being happy to have one more day. I indulge my love of reading books, and when the floaters in my eyes permit it, I read late into the night.

I still think in terms of the future, though more prudent minds question my judgment and sanity. But optimism is what helped me fight so ferociously to survive this long.

Now I have congestive heart failure. I cannot walk a block without huffing and puffing as if I had just climbed a mountain. I try to stick to my low-salt diet. Doctors think it will help me live a little bit longer, but I think it will just seem longer with nothing to look forward to at mealtimes.

I have known all along that this disease and its endless complications would end me one day. But it saddens me to be so aware that my end is near. I do not want to know. Nobody does. I want death to be a surprise. That gift was taken from me when I was seven, and I have had over fifty years to get used to the idea. It does not mean I am ready. I cannot help feeling that there is something I have not yet done or something I have not said. We always believe that, whether or not it is true.

Almost everyone I know believes their souls will go to heaven when they die, that they will rejoin loved ones for eternity. I want to believe in that future, but my inherent skepticism makes it hard to imagine.

I am torn.

I want to believe that when the sun dims for me the last time, my spirit—if I have one—will break free of my scar-riddled shell. It will soar high, fast, and free of all pain, flying wherever whim takes it. My spirit self will be able to walk on the beach again and swim in the waves with my dolphin friends. It will dance and laugh and run. One day, I hope Howard's spirit will join mine on that beach, so we can walk holding hands along an infinite shore.

That's the end I want. Just not today.

AFTERWORD

*G*AIL CAMPBELL WOOLLEY DIED ON MARCH 16, 2015. She took her last breath at Johns Hopkins Hospital in Baltimore at about 11:00 a.m. on a chilly morning. Even though Gail had been preparing for this day since she was seven years old, and she had been preparing me since we started dating at Syracuse University almost forty years ago, I somehow wasn't ready for the shock. It had happened. *She was gone.*

In the end, it was the pulmonary hypertension that brought about her demise. Her body just couldn't rid itself of the fluid buildup. She had warned me back in 2012, when she was first diagnosed with the pulmonary hypertension, that this was the one to watch. She had beaten back many ailments over the previous five decades, but she sensed that she might not be able to beat this one. It was a real surprise to us after accepting the challenge of her recent amputation to have this new life-threatening disease, pulmonary hypertension, become part of our daily life.

When I heard the doctor's words telling me my wife was gone, my first thought was that I *had* to get in the room to see her. I felt like we had a bond that transcended life and death; our connection was so strong that somehow we would still be able to communicate our love for each other.

I stepped into the room and was stunned by the sight of her lifeless body. For nearly four decades we had been each other's protectors; I had a hard time accepting that role was now over for me. I walked over to the bed and felt the overwhelming need to touch her. I reached out and rubbed her forehead, stroked her face. I had a few last words I needed to get out.

"Gail, honey, we had a great life together, didn't we?" I said softly. "I will love you forever. Our love will be eternal. You had a great run, babe. You did everything you wanted to do. We went around the world, just like you wanted. You were able to have the career you wanted. We always knew it would come to this, but boy, did we have great times together. Goodbye, my love."

I leaned forward and kissed her forehead, kissed her lips around the tube that was sticking out of her mouth. From the moment part of her leg was amputated in May of 2012, I always treated it the same as her other leg. So I rubbed her normal leg and I reached down and rubbed her "stump," which was what the medical people called it—I never embraced that term.

The room felt very still and lonely. Over the years I had thought a lot about what it might be like when she was gone, about how I would feel. The previous summer, as she wrote intensely to finish this book, I had to take her to the hospital several times in the Outer Banks. At one point she looked at me and said, "Howard, it must be hard on you, watching me die."

The night before she died, when she was still at our local hospital in Potomac, Maryland, before being transferred to Johns Hopkins, I think Gail in her own way let me know the end was coming. I was telling her that I had to go home and pack an overnight bag so I could stay at a hotel near Hopkins, which was about an hour away. I said I would meet her in Baltimore. But before I could leave the room, Gail called out to me.

"Howard! Howard!"

I assumed she was going to tell me to bring her big water container, which she always had at her side so she could stay hydrated. It's important for people with sickle cell to drink a lot of water—although things had gotten complicated for her because people with pulmonary hypertension should try to stay dehydrated to get rid of fluid.

"Yeah?" I said, turning around. She motioned for me to come back to her. I walked over to the bed and leaned down to see what she wanted. She surprised me by pulling me down and planting a kiss flush on my lips. There were no words exchanged, but after the kiss we stared into each other's eyes. When I look back on it, I realize that kiss was her way of saying goodbye to me. I think she knew that our magnificent journey together was coming to an end.

Gail wrote in her advance directive that she wanted to be cremated and have her ashes scattered off the coast of the Outer Banks. Weeks after her passing, I woke at about 5:00 a.m. in the beach house the Saturday before Memorial Day, and I realized it was time. We had already held a celebration of her life in Washington—a beautiful ceremony where friends and family got to share stories and remembrances. I was in the Outer Banks to do a smaller ceremony for our beach community friends and those who couldn't make it up to Washington. Some family and friends from Washington, DC, were staying in the house with me, but they were still asleep.

I pushed myself out of bed and went to get the urn containing her ashes. Before I walked out to the beach, I knocked on the door of the bedroom where Gail's brother, Kenneth, was sleeping. He came to the door, still groggy.

"Kenneth, I'm going to do this," I said.

Kenneth instantly knew what I was talking about.

"Don't stop," he said.

I nodded. I walked outside and trekked the sixty yards or so down to the beach. I had a spot in mind, but there were people already standing around in that location. I needed to be alone when I did this, so I kept walking. I went to Sea Hawk, one neighborhood over from us. I found a spot that I liked because there was a sign at the beach access that could serve as a marker for me in the future. I walked to the edge of the surf. I collected my thoughts. I opened my mouth and the words flowed out.

"Gail, this is it, honey," I said. "You said you hoped your ashes would travel the world, just like you did. So, you're about to start your journey. I love you, honey."

I scattered the ashes into the water. I watched the rough tide quickly pull them out to sea. There was sadness, but I also felt some joy in my heart. I was happy that I was able to fulfill her wish. Gail was in the place she loved most of all: the ocean.

It's been more than a year since she left me, but I'm still hit with very powerful memories when I move around our houses in Potomac and in the Outer Banks. Gail put such a strong stamp on these places—the woman not only designed the Outer Banks house, but she hand-sewed our window treatments!—that I see her everywhere I turn. One day when I opened up a cabinet in the master bathroom, I was smacked by a wave of her fragrance, like she was standing right next to me.

When you live with someone for thirty-four years, you become accustomed to thinking of yourself as part of a unit. It was strange for me now to make decisions for myself and by myself without taking Gail's needs and wants into consideration. I miss the balance that her presence provided me.

During the first year without her, there were times when I had to pick up the phone and call one of my friends or a family member because I was in so much pain, crying my eyes out. But I'm starting to have fewer of those intense moments. I think I'm slowly becoming better adjusted to my new life. I've even recently decided to start dating. I'm not looking to replace Gail, of course, but I don't want to be alone anymore. Before I went out on my first date, I called up a few of Gail's friends to make sure they approved. They gave me their blessing.

My friends, the friends Gail and I shared, have been so incredibly supportive to me. They have helped me immensely just by their presence, which is all you really want when you're grieving. I told one of them that if they were ever in a similar situation, I'd want to be there for them in the same way they were there for me.

"You already have been," the friend responded. "That's why you're getting it all back now."

When I went to the mailbox a few weeks ago, I opened it to find a letter from one of the many doctors who treated Gail over the years. He told me how fond he was of Gail and how much he admired her. It was a powerful letter and it warmed my insides.

Hopefully I will have many more years here on Earth before I join my sweet Gail. When she was alive and talked about her desire to be cremated, I would always counter that I was still an advocate of burial for my remains. But I've changed my mind. The thought of that raging fire still scares the hell out of me, but I now want to be cremated just like Gail was. And as for my ashes? I want them to be scattered in the ocean, right there on the beach at Sea Hawk. I just know my ashes will set out to sea and find Gail, so that we can be together again. Into eternity.

—Howard Woolley

ACKNOWLEDGMENTS

GAIL'S FAMILY WOULD LIKE TO THANK ALL THE RELATIVES, friends, colleagues, medical professionals (including the doctors, nurses, and physical therapists), and everyone else who helped Gail along her magnificent journey through life.

FURTHER READING

$\mathcal{A}$LTHOUGH ADVANCES HAVE BEEN MADE IN THE STUDY and treatment of sickle cell disease, it remains an often overlooked and misunderstood disorder. For more information related to sickle cell, consider the following resources:

Centers for Disease Control and Prevention (CDC) Sickle Cell Disease landing page
https://www.cdc.gov/ncbddd/sicklecell/index.html

Centers for Disease Control and Prevention (CDC) Sickle Cell Disease National Resource Directory
https://www.cdc.gov/ncbddd/sicklecell/map
/map-nationalresourcedirectory.html

Johns Hopkins Sickle Cell Infusion Center
http://www.hopkinsmedicine.org/hematology/sicklecell/contacts.html

National Institutes of Health Sickle Cell Program
https://www.nhlbi.nih.gov/research/intramural/researchers/programs
/sickle-cell-program

Sickle Cell Disease Association of America
https://www.sicklecelldisease.org/

ABOUT THE AUTHOR

$\mathcal{G}$AIL CAMPBELL WOOLLEY (1957–2015) GREW UP IN
Washington, DC, and was diagnosed with sickle cell anemia at age
seven. She studied journalism and international relations at Syracuse
University and worked as a reporter for the *Washington Star*, the *Baltimore Sun*, and the *Washington Times* before beginning a career in
corporate public relations. She and her husband, Howard, split their
time between Maryland and the Outer Banks of North Carolina. She
died at age fifty-eight, exceeding the life expectancy her childhood
doctor predicted by more than twenty years.